THE COMPETITIVE ADVANTAGE OF GREECE

To my parents

The Competitive Advantage of Greece

An application of Porter's diamond

IOANNIS KONSOLAS
Regional Development Institute, Athens, Greece

Routledge
Taylor & Francis Group

LONDON AND NEW YORK

First published 2002 by Ashgate Publishing

Reissued 2018 by Routledge
2 Park Square, Milton Park, Abingdon, Oxon, OX14 4RN
711 Third Avenue, New York, NY 10017

Routledge is an imprint of the Taylor & Francis Group, an informa business

Publisher's Note
The publisher has gone to great lengths to ensure the quality of this reprint but points out that some imperfections in the original copies may be apparent.

Disclaimer
The publisher has made every effort to trace copyright holders and welcomes correspondence from those they have been unable to contact.

A Library of Congress record exists under LC control number: 2001095869

ISBN 13: 978-1-138-72319-1 (hbk)
ISBN 13: 978-1-138-72317-7 (pbk)
ISBN 13: 978-1-315-19317-5 (ebk)

Contents

List of Figures

List of Tables

Preface

International competitiveness has been at the forefront of academic research for a long time. The question of why certain firms or certain industries based in particular countries are highly successful in international competition has troubled researchers but, despite the recent major advances in trade theory, a comprehensive model has not yet been produced. In the 1990s, Michael Porter (1990) has made a contribution to this field of research, by following well-established theories and combining them with extensive empirical work, undertaken in ten industrialised nations. The resulting diamond framework captures a wide range of attributes that, according to Porter, explain the creation of competitive advantage. The aim of the diamond framework is to categorise the national influences on the competitiveness of industries, and industry segments, in its four sides and two outside forces. Thus a more comprehensive answer to the international competitiveness question can be provided, which includes the influence of factor conditions, domestic demand conditions, related and supporting industries, firms' strategies and structures and domestic rivalry. Government and chance are 'peripheral' influences to the competitive advantage of industries, based in a country, as they work through the other four determinants.

This ambitious undertaking by Porter has influenced the thinking of both business strategists and, especially, policy makers. The relative simplicity of the framework and the wide range of issues it addressed made it instantly appealing to government institutions all over the world. The prescriptions, however, suggested by Porter, are based on the premise that the diamond framework is, at least, an accurate taxonomy of the forces that shape competitive advantage and their creation processes. The framework has also received much criticism, from scholars from many different fields. Therefore, each part of the diamond needs to be examined and its implications assessed. Moreover, the entire framework requires further investigation, so that we can appraise the effect of the individual forces on each other.

The present study applies the diamond framework to the case of Greece. The purpose of this application is two-fold. Firstly, insights will be gained on the applicability of the framework in this particular case and the possible need for modifications. Secondly, the competitive industrial structure of Greece and certain sectors in particular will be studied in-depth, using Porter's methodology for identifying and studying competitive industries. The selection of Greece as a suitable candidate for an investigation of Porter's diamond framework was based on a variety of reasons.

Greece's level of development is slightly lower than that of most of the countries studied in Porter (1990). Nevertheless, Greece is a country where the framework must apply, since Porter does not claim that the framework only applies to highly developed nations, and includes countries like Korea and Singapore, the level of which is close to that of Greece. However, it is also a country where conditions are not ideal, at least compared with the nations forming the basis for the diamond, and where serious development deficiencies can provide certain interesting observations on the diamond framework and its applicability.

Greece also has some other features that make this application a worthwhile pursuit. The most important among them are the small size of the Greek market, the country's distance from many developed markets and the poor transportation links even with the closest ones. These peculiarities of the Greek case offer a great opportunity to explore the relevant issues, that have been the subject of much criticism directed at Porter's inadequate attention on the constraints they pose to the upgrading of competitive advantage. Another important characteristic of Greece is the fact that it is a member of the European Union. Although Porter studied several EU countries (Germany, the U.K., Italy, Sweden and Denmark) he did not place great emphasis on the effects of EU integration on the process of creating and sustaining competitive advantage. In this study, however, the role of the European Union and the closer links of Greece with the other members, will be further explored.

The objectives of the present study will be achieved by a presentation of Porter's framework, its applications and the relevant criticisms, followed by an analysis of the Greek economic environment and the Greek trade data. Then five in-depth case studies of particular industries will be analysed, which will offer the necessary basis for reaching certain conclusions regarding the applicability of the diamond framework in the Greek case.

The fact that the diamond framework has not yet been applied, to this extent, to the case of Greece is part of the original contribution of this study. Moreover, although many applications of the framework have been made since its initial presentation, very few have concentrated on its critical evaluation. Another area to which this study aims to contribute, is in providing a case study of a non-competitive industry and examining whether the diamond forces are equally effective in explaining its lack of competitiveness.

The present study is divided into eight chapters. Chapter 1 summarises Porter's diamond framework and the competitive development of national economies as they are presented in *The Competitive Advantage of Nations*. Those applications of the framework, by Porter himself and by other researchers, that are relevant to the Greek case are also briefly described. Then, a review of the major criticisms for the diamond framework and other related issues is combined with excerpts of Porter's views on these issues.

Chapter 2 focuses on the competitive advantage of Greek industries, within the context of the Greek economic environment. The evolution of Greece's economy is examined, using a historical perspective as well as a wealth of current data. The available literature on the competitiveness of Greek industries is then critically reviewed. In the final section of the chapter the structure of Greek industrial clusters is explored using Porter's methodology and Greek trade data for three particular points in time.

In chapters 3, 4, 5, 6 and 7 the five case studies are presented. The cement, rolled aluminium products, tourism, men's outerwear and dairy industries, that were selected for further research, provide a good understanding of the forces that shape competitive advantage. In all five chapters, the industry's products, processes and recent developments are presented, along with its current status in the European Union. Then the developments in Greece are given particular attention in order to achieve the main goal of each chapter, the identification of the sources of competitive advantage for the particular industry studied. In the summary of each individual chapter, an overview of the role of all the diamond determinants and their interactions is provided.

The final chapter, chapter 8, summarises the results for each diamond determinant as they are apparent from the case studies. Certain issues arise for the applicability of the diamond framework that are further investigated, along with the more general implications of the Greek case. In addition to the conclusions on the diamond framework and Porter's approach, the last section focuses on the possible implications of this study for company strategies and future government policy in Greece.

Acknowledgements

There are many people that have made it possible for me to bring the present work to a completion and to all of them I owe my sincere thanks. I am especially grateful to all my interviewees, academics, executives and industry experts for agreeing to discuss with me issues related to their industries or research interests. Particular mention should be made of certain individuals who offered me a large amount of their time and a wealth of valuable information, Z. Demathas for the evolution of the Greek economy, P. Kondylis and K. Simeonidis for the cement case, A. Meyir, A. Athanassakopoulos, M. Lidorikis, E. Ganakou, K. Kalogeridis, and K. Vassiliou for the aluminium case, R. Lalaitou, P. Dimitriadis, and especially D. Lagos for the tourism case, G. Psaropoulos and A. Lyberaki for the men's outerwear case, and I. Georganas, K. Nikolaidis and I. Kassiouras for the dairy case. I should acknowledge with gratitude the prompt help of M. Nikitaridis, T. Karaganis and P. Paraskevaidis in the data gathering phase of the project. I would also like to express my thanks to the staff in the libraries of the Centre of Planning and Economic Research (KEPE), the Foundation of Economic and Industrial Research (IOBE), the National Statistical Service of Greece, and the Regional Development Institute of the Panteion University of Social and Political Sciences who provided me with special access to data and documents.

Professor Peter Abell, Director of the Interdisciplinary Institute of Management at the London School of Economics and Political Science, has played a major role in shaping this study with his sound advice and constructive criticism. I owe him much gratitude.

I am particularly indebted to my parents, to whom this book is dedicated, for their continuous encouragement and assistance that were instrumental in its preparation. I would also like to thank Ozlem Oz, of the Middle East Technical University (Ankara, Turkey), for her insightful comments and observations that proved invaluable in the completion of this book. I also have to express my gratitude to Maria Tassopoulou for her constant support, understanding, and advice in every phase of this project.

List of Abbreviations

CEDEFOP	European Centre for the Development of Vocational Training
EC	European Community
EEC	European Economic Community
EMU	European Monetary Union
ERMCO	European Ready Mixed Concrete Association
ETVA	Hellenic Industrial Development Bank
EU	European Union
FDI	Foreign Direct Investment
GATT	General Agreement on Tariffs and Trade
GDP	Gross Domestic Product
GNTO	Greek National Tourism Organisation
IEA	International Energy Agency
ILO	International Labour Organisation
IMP	Integrated Mediterranean Programs
IOBE	Foundation of Economic and Industrial Research (Greece)
IT	Information Technology
KEPE	Centre of Planning and Economic Research (Greece)
NICs	Newly Industrialised Countries
NSSG	National Statistical Service of Greece
OECD	Organisation for Economic Co-operation and Development
OETH	Observatoire Européen du Textile et de l' Habillement
OTE	Hellenic Telecommunications Organisation
PASOK	Panhellenic Socialist Movement
R&D	Research and Development
RIT	Research Institute for Tourism (ITEP - Greece)
SA	Société Anonyme
SITC	Standard International Trade Classification
UN	United Nations
UNESCO	United Nations Educational, Scientific and Cultural Organisation
WTO	World Trade Organisation

1 The Competitive Advantage of Nations

This chapter introduces the concepts contained in *The Competitive Advantage of Nations*. In the first section, the two main contributions of Porter's (1990) book, the diamond framework and the model of economic development, are summarised. The next section contains a description of those applications of the diamond framework that are relevant to the Greek case. The third section encompasses the various views expressed on particular issues in Porter's (1990) work.

The Competitive Advantage of Nations: The Diamond Framework and The Competitive Development of National Economies

The Diamond Framework

The main goal of Porter's work was to determine the attributes of the national environment, which influence the competitive advantage of firms, in particular industries or segments. The result was the well-known 'diamond framework' (Porter, 1990: 71-130), where four groups of determinants - factor conditions, demand conditions, related and supporting industries, and firm strategy, structure and rivalry - individually and through their interactions promote or hinder the creation and sustainability of competitive advantage for industries within a nation. There are also two additional determinants - government and chance - shaping the national environment in an indirect way, that is, working through the other four determinants, as can be seen in Figure 1.1.

Factor conditions The first determinant consists of the production factors necessary for an industry. Porter favours a detailed classification, including human resources, physical resources, knowledge resources, capital resources and infrastructure. Competitive advantage stems from possessing low-cost or high-quality factors, efficiently and effectively deployed.

Factors can be categorised as basic and advanced. Basic factors, that include climate, location, unskilled and semiskilled labour, etc., are

1

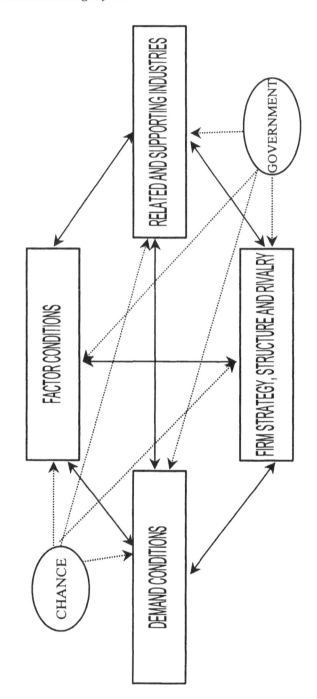

Figure 1.1 Porter's Diamond Framework
Source: Porter, 1990: 127.

essentially inherited or created through simple, unsophisticated investment. Advanced factors, such as a digital data communications infrastructure, university research institutes, etc., are much harder to create, demanding large and continuous investment and often the presence of appropriate institutional structures.

Another categorisation is between generalised factors that can be used by many industries (such as the highway system) and specialised factors that are specific to an industry or a limited group of industries (for example, narrowly skilled personnel). Specialised factors offer a more sustainable advantage for an industry than generalised factors. The presence, however, of these specialised factors usually requires an appropriate level of generalised factors.

Competitive advantage can also be gained by selective factor disadvantages. Faced with disadvantages in particular factors, industries are forced to innovate in order to improve their competitive position. In the process, new technologies and new ways to use or circumvent specific factors, emerge, which often provide the industry with a more sustainable advantage. Nevertheless, the condition of the other diamond determinants affects the ability of the industry to instigate the necessary processes.

Demand conditions The second determinant is demand conditions, and refers to the nature of home demand for the industry's products or services. Porter (1990) identifies three major attributes of home demand as essential. The first one is the home demand composition, that is, the segment structure relative to world demand and the *sophistication* of the home buyers. Segment structure is important because 'a nation's firms are likely to gain competitive advantage in global segments that represent a large or highly visible share of home demand but account for a less significant share in other nations' (Porter, 1990: 87). Customer sophistication is also essential, as demanding buyers pressure firms to meet the highest standards, and consumer needs that anticipate global trends stimulate innovation.

The second attribute is the home demand's size and pattern of growth. Absolute home market size is important only in some industries or segments, where, for instance, production economies of scale are present or R&D requirements are high. A rapid growth rate, especially in periods of technological change, the presence of a number of independent buyers or an anticipatory early demand, can positively affect a much wider range of industries. Early or abrupt saturation in the home market can also be a source of advantage as firms are forced to compete on low prices, improved product features, and innovative products, or expand to foreign markets.

Internationalisation of home demand is the third attribute. This refers to mobile or multinational buyers that use products from their home base, and demonstrate to other firms the benefits of entering a foreign market. Additionally, internationalisation of home demand can be a result of various influences on foreign needs and perceptions of a country's products that are acquired by foreign nationals when travelling, working or training in the home country or are transmitted through historical, political and cultural ties.

These three demand attributes reinforce each other and their importance differs according to the evolutionary stage of the home industry. Firms are always affected by the nature of their home demand as they pay greater attention, understand better and respond quicker to the needs of their domestic market.

Related and supporting industries   The presence in a nation of related and supporting industries, is the third determinant that shapes competitive advantage. These industries can be suppliers to the competitive downstream industries, offering efficient, early and, although less often, preferential access to certain inputs. They are also a source of early and accurate information sometimes through informal networks, which are facilitated by the cultural proximity. However, the suppliers must be internationally competitive, or 'strong by world standards' (Porter, 1990: 104) if they are not competing globally, for these exchanges to be beneficial.

Moreover, an industry can benefit from the presence, in its home base, of other competitive industries with which it is linked through, among others, common inputs, technologies or distribution channels. Again, the relative ease of information exchange, that sometimes even results in formal alliances, enables firms to share these activities and benefit from each other's innovations. Nevertheless, an industry can source its inputs from abroad, form alliances with foreign firms and achieve some of the benefits of having competitive domestic related and supporting industries.

Firm strategy, structure and rivalry   The fourth and broader determinant includes the strategy and structure of firms in the domestic industry, as well as the rivalry among them. The firms' strategies and structures, including aspects such as management practices, modes of organisation, willingness to compete globally, company goals, etc., must be appropriate for the industry in which the firms are competing. The way firms are organised and managed is affected by national conditions, such as the educational system, and historical trends. National firms succeed in industries where the required characteristics match the country's prevailing organisation structures as well as in those 'where there is unusual commitment and effort' (Porter, 1990: 110).

The pattern of home rivalry is also considered by Porter as one of the major attributes that shapes competitive advantage. Competing firms pressure each other to improve and innovate, and domestic competition is more visible than competition from foreign firms. Moreover, domestic rivalry can be emotional or personal, as pride drives managers to be more sensitive towards domestic competitors, leading to better products or exports, since there are no excuses and 'unfair advantages', that are often cited as the reasons behind the success of foreign companies. Sometimes, rivalry can also lead to the upgrading of competitive advantage, as simple advantages, like basic factors or local suppliers, are not sustainable against other domestic competitors.

The formation of new businesses is also an important part of this determinant because it increases the number of competitors. The intensity of domestic rivalry, however, does not depend only on the number of competitors. Their commitment to the industry and the lack of extensive co-operation among the competitors are much more important. Porter even concedes that 'a completely open market along with extremely global strategies can partially substitute for the lack of domestic rivals in a smaller nation' (Porter, 1990: 121).

The role of government   Government influences competitive advantage by an array of policies that affect all the other four determinants. Regulation, education, tax and monetary policy are examples of government's impact on the competitive environment of firms. The role of government, however, is partial, according to Porter (1990: 128), as government policy can confer an advantage only by reinforcing the other four determinants. Its role can be positive or negative, and policies are usually affected by the national attributes forming the diamond.

The role of chance   Chance events, i.e. occurrences usually outside the power of firms, also play an important role, usually by creating discontinuities that allow shifts in competitive position. These events, which include inventions, wars, natural disasters, sudden rises in input prices, surges of demand, and political decisions by foreign governments, among others, have a diverse impact on industries of different countries. The way national firms exploit the advantages, or circumvent the disadvantages, is determined by the condition of the diamond determinants.

The dynamic nature of the diamond   The determinants of national advantage reinforce each other, creating a dynamic system where the cause and effect of individual determinants become blurred and competitive advantage depends on the entire 'diamond' system. Porter, however, states that not all the determinants are necessary to succeed in international competition, as a disadvantage in one determinant can be overcome by 'unusual advantage in others' (Porter, 1990: 145). His only emphatic assertion is that competitive advantage in more sophisticated industries rarely results from a single determinant.

Porter (1990: 143) also considers domestic rivalry as having a very direct role in helping firms 'reap the benefits of the other determinants'. He also connects domestic rivalry with another very important feature of competitive industries, geographic concentration. A large number of industries studied by Porter (1990, 1998b, see also Enright, 1990) were based in small regions or even in individual cities within countries, and, in a few European cases, in adjacent regions of different countries. Proximity increases the concentration of information and the speed of its flow, raises the visibility of competitor behaviour and attracts the necessary factors and resources.

Another finding of Porter's (1990) study is the presence of groups of successful industries in every nation. This finding led him to develop his 'cluster charts' which are described in detail in Chapter 2. Clusters of related industries, with constant interchanges among them, work in ways similar to the geographic concentration (in fact, those two phenomena often coincide). Accelerated factor creation, increased information flows, spreading rivalry and a tendency for resources to move away from isolated industries, and into the clustered ones, are all observations made by Porter (1990) in several cases.

The Competitive Development of National Economies

Porter (1990), in the 'Nations' part of his book, describes the pattern and evolution of industrial success in eight of the ten nations he studied. Using the data gathered during his project, he attempts to extend the framework, in order to assess 'how entire national economies progress in competitive terms' (Porter, 1990: 543). Linking the upgrading of an economy with the position of firms exposed in international competition, Porter (1990: 545-573) identifies four stages of economic development for a country: factor-driven, investment-driven, innovation-driven and wealth-driven.

Countries, in particular points in time, belong to the stage of development that corresponds to the predominant pattern in the nature of competitive advantage of their firms. Although these stages do not fully explain a nation's development process, they can highlight the attributes of a nation's industries that are most closely related to economic prosperity.

In the factor-driven stage, advantage for virtually all internationally competitive industries results from basic factors, usually natural resources, climate, land conditions and semiskilled labour. Indigenous firms compete essentially on price, in industries where technology is not required, or is widely available. Domestic demand for exported goods is modest and the economy is sensitive to world economic cycles and exchange rates. The range of industries may widen over time, with the creation of domestically-oriented industries through import substitution. However, these industries usually lack international competitiveness.

The investment-driven stage is characterised by the willingness and ability of the private and public sectors to invest aggressively. Firms construct modern facilities and acquire product technology from abroad. They are able to absorb the foreign technology and improve on it, refining the production processes to suit their particular needs. Firms, citizens and the government also invest in modern infrastructures, education and other mechanisms, which create advanced factors. Firms' strategy and structure, as well as the increasing number of home rivals are additional sources of advantage for domestic industries. Demand is growing, even for exported goods, but sophistication is still low, while related and supporting industries are largely underdeveloped. The government's role can be substantial at this stage with, for example, capital aids and temporary protection measures.

The innovation-driven stage is where all the diamond determinants are at work. The nation is competitive in a wide array of industries, with deeper clusters and even the establishment of entirely new groups of industries. Sophisticated service industries also develop because of knowledgeable and demanding customers and the presence of skilled human resources and infrastructure. Firms create technology, production methods and innovative products, and compete in more differentiated segments, on the basis of their high productivity. Global strategies emerge, as firms develop their own international marketing and distribution networks, usually depending on their established brand names. Foreign direct investment also increases with the relocation of certain activities to nations with more favourable endowments in particular factors. Industries are less vulnerable to price shocks and exchange rate movements in the world markets. Also, the national economy is less dependant on a few sectors. Government's role becomes more indirect, with emphasis on improving advanced factors and the quality of home demand and preserving domestic rivalry.

The wealth-driven stage is where firms in a nation start to lose competitive advantage in many industries with intense international competition. Rivalry decreases as firms are interested in preserving their established positions, there is less motivation to invest and constant calls to the government to protect the status quo. Rising wages with slower productivity increases, mergers and acquisitions that seek to preserve stability, and reduced willingness to take risks, especially in starting new businesses or transforming existing industries, diminish the international competitiveness of many of the nation's industries. This causes a de-clustering process, where the loss of position of one industry affects all the others in its cluster. The range of industries, where a nation can still compete, narrows to those that are related to personal wealth, basic factors and those where no technological changes occur or where the nation still has strong brand names.

Returning to the ten nations from which his main observations are drawn, Porter (1990: 565-573) categorises them according to their stage of development. Singapore is still considered to be in the factor-driven stage, while Korea has moved to the investment-driven stage. Denmark in the 1960s, Japan in the 1970s, Italy in the 1980s and Sweden soon after the war, reached the innovation-driven stage where they now are. Germany, Switzerland and the USA had reached this stage even before the Second World War. Porter (1990: 570-572) sees elements of the wealth-driven stage developing in the last three countries, while the UK is viewed as having been in that stage for decades now. Nevertheless, recent productivity gains and other developments in the UK are considered by Porter (1990: 573) as signs of an impending reversal, which is still not certain.

Applications of the Diamond Framework

The first applications of the diamond framework are essentially presented in *The Competitive Advantage of Nations*. Porter (1990: 277-541) devotes three chapters to study, in more detail, eight of the ten nations included in his original research. Although these applications can by no means be considered a test of the theory, as these are the countries providing the empirical observations for its inception, a brief summary can provide interesting insights on the way the framework can be applied. Particular emphasis will be placed on the European nations studied by Porter (1990) and especially Switzerland and Sweden, two countries with small home markets, Italy, that exhibits an industrial structure, in terms of clusters, very similar to the Greek one, and Germany, that represents a major supplier and market for many Greek industries. The other four nations analysed by Porter (1990), Japan, Korea, the UK and the USA, will be briefly examined.

Subsequently, Porter has applied his framework to a number of other countries. Particular mention will be made of the two most widely disseminated applications, the reports for Canada and New Zealand. These studies are again not critical of the framework, they are, however, interesting given the small size of the New Zealand market and the heated debate surrounding the Canadian case. Three attempts to test parts or all of the diamond framework will also be presented. These attempts are based on observations from New Zealand (as a complement to Porter's analysis), Ireland (a small EU nation) and Turkey (a neighbouring country with a similar industrial structure to Greece).

The first European nation mentioned by Porter (1990: 307-331), as a post-World War II winner, is *Switzerland*. Switzerland was competitive in a wide array of manufacturing and service industries. Natural resources were little related to Switzerland's success, as Porter (1990: 318) considers only the available hydropower and the pleasant landscape as advantages. Location and political neutrality had been much more important as was a highly educated and skilled pool of human resources. Low interest rates and easily available capital, along with a world-class transportation infrastructure, complete the picture for basic factors. These factors were upgraded through the educational system and the well-developed apprenticeship system, as well as the extensive in-house training of employees. University research, especially in chemistry and physics has also helped all related industries, while close relations with foreign research centres guaranteed the successful assimilation of foreign technologies.

Demand conditions have been central to the success of many Swiss industries. Geography and climate have created a sophisticated demand for industries such as heating controls and railway equipment. Swiss affluence has also resulted in sophisticated demand for premium consumer goods. The presence of multiple cultures (French, German, Italian) has also been important, as it can account for the wide range of competitive industries. Firms from related and supporting industries have often initiated the creation of competitive industries. Also, interchanges among industries were frequent and open.

The strategy of firms in the most successful Swiss industries has been to concentrate on small industries or highly differentiated, high-quality segments. Pharmaceuticals is the only major exception, since Swiss companies already had the scale to compete with foreign rivals. Swiss firms have generally done well in industries where contact with the buyer is required. Rivalry is a characteristic of many competitive Swiss industries, although mergers and cartelisation have reduced the number of competitors. The Swiss federal government has intervened to a very modest extent in most industries, and primarily in a positive way, while Switzerland's neutrality in the two Wars has been a major source of benefits.

Sweden is the second European post-World War II winner examined by Porter (1990). The Swedish economy has also been the subject of a separate book (Solvell, Zander and Porter, 1992), where the role of the Swedish 'home-base', for Sweden's trade-dominating multinationals, is examined in more detail.

Sweden had a narrower competitive base of industries but the competitive clusters were very deep, especially the materials/metals, forest products and transportation ones. Natural resource advantages, such as extensive forests, large deposits of iron ore and inexpensive hydroelectric power, were originally important for many of the most competitive Swedish industries. Later, these advantages played a less crucial role for these industries' success. A universally high level of education, a number of excellent technical universities and research institutes, and the early licensing of foreign technologies, constituted the essential factor advantages for Swedish industries. High wages in all skill levels led to the restructuring and the automation of Swedish manufacturing industries, while the long winters caused an emphasis on energy conservation, and the long distances a sophistication in logistics.

Demand for reliable transportation equipment and services, also stemming from Sweden's long distances, was one from a variety of demand conditions that affected competitive advantage. Similar roles were played by the high levels of automation in Swedish firms and Sweden's climate, geography and geology, which placed extraordinary demands on, for example, mining and power-related industries. The resource-related industries were also very sophisticated industrial buyers, especially given certain factor disadvantages they faced. Disadvantages in demand conditions were evident because of the large state sector which was sometimes an unsophisticated buyer and the high tax level that reduced demand for consumer goods, and especially luxury items. Clusters of competitive industries were prevalent in Sweden. Collaboration among vertically and horizontally related industries was very high, partly due to the high level of cross-ownership among related companies and the Swedish culture of co-operation.

The structure of Swedish firms and the characteristics of their employees (like open communication, and trust) were favourable for competing in technologically-complex industries that require extensive international networks. Internationalisation strategies were also beneficial for those industries, in addition to capital markets with a long-term view. Rivalry was intense in some competitive industries but not present at all in others. While Porter (1990: 350-351) considers this a disadvantage, he concedes that Sweden's small open market and the high levels of Swedish presence in foreign markets can partly compensate.

The government played a substantial role, which was at times positive, for example in the enforcement of strict safety and environmental regulations, or negative, with its focusing only on large companies. Chance events have occurred in many industries. The Second World War, however, and Sweden's neutrality were uniformly important.

Demand strengths, supplier-buyer relationships and human resources were among the traditional advantages of Swedish industries. Domestic rivalry, dependence on basic factors for some industries and individual motivation were problematic areas in the diamond framework. A loss of position in many industries, especially in sophisticated ones was, according to Porter, a worrying sign.

Italy is considered by Porter (1990: 421) 'particularly interesting' as a success story, given its limited resource endowment and its image of chaotic government. Italy had a very high number of exporting industries, which were, however, highly clustered. The country enjoyed high shares in textiles and apparel, household products, food and beverages, personal products and metal goods and associated machinery. Competitive industries in Italy were also geographically concentrated, with small regions or cities being the home base for sometimes hundreds of firms in many industries.

Factor conditions were not entirely favourable for Italian industries. Inherited and socially-created factors were absent from Italy. Natural resources were few, wages, especially in the 1980s, were close to those of other Western European nations and real interest rates were high. Part of the educational system, both high-school and university, was of excellent quality and its links with local industry became a major source of advantage. Demand conditions were a major strength of most competitive Italian industries. Italian consumers were discerning buyers for many types of goods, such as clothing, furniture or tiles. Consumer goods firms were also demanding buyers of machinery and other inputs. Internationalisation of Italian style and taste, caused mainly by the increased world-wide exposition of Italian design and the millions of tourists visiting Italy every year, exerted a positive influence.

Clusters in Italy were very deep and vertical relationships among firms in related industries were very strong. Co-operation among firms with common distribution channels and family links, in many geographically concentrated industries, were also common. High specialisation and constant model changes were characteristic of firms in successful Italian industries. Small and medium sized enterprises with little organisational structure and increased autonomy for employees had been at the forefront of the aggressive internationalisation of Italian firms. Extraordinary rivalry, often at a personal or family level, was present in almost all the competitive Italian industries.

Italy, according to Porter (1990: 447), is the case that proves that government is not central for competitive advantage. Many of the disadvantages for the Italian industries were created by the national government. Local governments had been much more supportive of industries, with appropriate investments and limited interference. The relatively late post-World War II boom that enabled Italian firms to invest in modern production technologies, without commitments to older generations of process technology, had been the only major chance event.

Geographic concentration, demand conditions, domestic rivalry and extensive clustering created and broadened the competitive advantage of most Italian industries. Better functioning capital markets, a more effective national government and properly organised and managed large firms could have contributed to a widening in the range of industries where Italy competed successfully.

The *German* case, noted as 'important' by Porter (1990: 356), is central to the development of the European Union. Germany had 345 competitive industries in 1985, including both consumer and industrial products, with especially strong positions in production machinery. Natural resources (mainly iron and coal reserves) contributed to the initial formation of some competitive industries. Their role gradually became smaller, while the presence of highly educated, skilled and motivated workers, a scientific and technical knowledge base and a well-developed infrastructure, were very important. Universities, high-quality technical colleges, a distinctive apprenticeship system and a host of research institutes led to the continuous upgrading of human capital and the knowledge base. The large size of the market and its early saturation in many products had been advantageous for many German industries. However, the most important demand attribute was the presence of sophisticated, extremely demanding and quality-conscious consumers and industrial customers. Clustering was high in Germany and suppliers and buyers collaborated extensively in technical issues.

The hierarchical structure and the emphasis on precision engineering exhibited by most competitive German firms has led to international success in high-performance segments. The technical orientation of firms has also resulted in increased competitiveness in industries requiring complex production processes. Rivalry has been strong in the internationally competitive industries and competition has focused on technology and performance.

Government has been less protective of industry than in most other nations, while its role has been substantial in factor creation. The two World Wars were at the same time a source of many losses for Germany and a challenge to overcome them and recreate a strong industrial base.

The first of the Asian nations mentioned by Porter (1990: 384-421) is *Japan*. Japan's achievement of becoming a major economic power and the rapid rise of many of its industries is examined using the diamond framework. Japan was another country with few natural resources (except natural ports and available hydroelectric power) whose industries took advantage of a disciplined, educated work-force, good labour-management relationships and a, more or less, constructive government. These initial advantages were later supplemented by a large pool of engineers, low cost of capital, a tendency of related diversification for large firms, which promoted clustering, particular home demand conditions and an emphasis on product quality and automation. Fierce, emotional domestic rivalry was another characteristic of competitive Japanese industries.

The only other Asian nation analysed in detail by Porter (1990: 453-479) is *Korea*. There, competitive advantage has primarily depended on human resources, investment-oriented company and managerial goals, as well as domestic rivalry. A major weakness for most Korean industries has been demand conditions, with the exception of the shipbuilding, construction and defence industries.

The last European nation examined by Porter (1990: 482-507) is the *United Kingdom*. Competitive British industries were found to possess advantages in all diamond determinants, while the declining ones were experiencing low or less sophisticated home demand, a shrinking number of related and supporting industries, low commitment by employees and investors, and eroding rivalry.

The same observations are made by Porter (1990: 507-535) about the *United States* in 1985. Again, inadequate factor creation, eroding demand quality, weaknesses of supplier and related industries, and low levels of rivalry characterised many American industries that declined during the 1970s and 1980s. America's home market size, natural resources and wide range of competitive industries remained a sound base for upgrading competitive advantage. There were, of course, still many competitive industries across most clusters with highly skilled employees, sophisticated home demand, strong domestic suppliers and intense rivalry.

Porter, after his original work, studied other nations and regions using his framework. These approaches were not an attempt to test or 'evaluate' his theory, as pointed out by Cartwright (1993: 56) for the New Zealand study. The framework was used as the 'ideal condition' and industries were examined against this benchmark. Two of these studies were published and widely disseminated. Both will be mentioned here, the first one, regarding New Zealand (Crocombe et al., 1991), in more detail, since New Zealand, like Greece, is a small nation with a limited base of competitive industries. The second study, concerning Canada (Porter and Monitor Company, 1991), a nation with few common characteristics with Greece, will nevertheless be briefly presented, as it has sparked a great deal of criticism, especially by Canadian scholars.

New Zealand was strong in very few clusters, notably food/beverages, textiles/apparel (primarily the wool-related industries), materials/metals, forest products and, to some extent, housing/household (Crocombe et al., 1991: 209-212). The research team studied twenty export industries of three categories: traditional, developed in the 1970s and 1980s and emerging. Factor conditions were found to be universally important, while the uniqueness of New Zealand's demand needs provided some advantage, especially to the agriculture and sport-related industries. Related and supplier industries had played a positive role, although they were absent in some cases and most clusters were not geographically concentrated. Cost-based strategies and lack of international orientation had affected the ability of industries to compete in differentiated segments. Rivalry was considered by the team as a weakness for New Zealand, although the data presented show a substantial number of competitors in many of the competitive industries, especially given the country's size. Government had played a prominent role, considerably aiding certain industries, while impeding others from upgrading. Favourable chance events affected almost every competitive New Zealand industry.

Almost all of the industries studied in New Zealand drew their advantage from basic factors and chance events. Created factors, demand conditions, related and supporting industries and firms' strategy, structure and rivalry also exerted some influence on most industries. However, only one of those four groups of determinants exerted 'strong' or 'moderate' influence (as characterised by the researchers, see Crocombe et al., 1991: 96) in each case, with the exception of the electric fences and yacht-manufacturing industries. Government was also affecting most of the industries, while about one-fourth of them relied extensively on its role.

An attempt to test Porter's framework using cases from *New Zealand*, was made by Cartwright (1993). Interval scales were used for all diamond determinants, with the exception of chance, and different maximum values were assigned 'to reflect Porter's apparent views about the relative impact of strongly developed determinants' (Cartwright, 1993: 61). Ten industries were placed in two groups using both profitability and export share to determine whether an industry was placed in the more competitive or the less competitive group. The results of the test showed a divergence between the characteristics of the industries in the competitive group and those in Porter's 'ideal' model, as, moreover, these 'ideal' characteristics were found to be more closely associated with the less competitive industries of the second group. The many restrictions of the testing method, also acknowledged by the author himself (Cartwright, 1993: 65), limit the usefulness of this test. Its results, however, do put a question mark on the framework's applicability.

Porter's study of *Canada* (Porter and Monitor Company, 1991) exhibits similarities to that of New Zealand. Twenty-five industries were studied, with export shares being the primary selection criterion. Four cases were picked based primarily on the high level of foreign control, which was also present in five others. Factor conditions were found to be of 'high' or 'medium' importance in almost all cases, while each of the other determinants was important in 11 to 13 cases. Chance was instrumental in two cases and positive in five more, while the government affected positively sixteen industries and negatively two.

Porter's classification of Canada as a country belonging to the factor-driven stage of economic development, and his view that competitive advantage based on natural resources and dependency on a highly developed neighbour is not sustainable, angered many Canadian scholars. Rugman (1991: 61), who otherwise found the diamond concept 'brilliant', claims that the classification of Canada as a 'factor-driven' nation is 'inaccurate and dangerously misleading'. Rugman and Verbeke (1993) refer to Porter's work in Canada as flawed and Rugman and D'Cruz (1993: 17) say that the framework needs to be adapted to explain Canada's resource-based multinationals and other features of the Canadian economy. An opposing view is expressed by Nicholson (1993: 290), as he considers Porter's views on Canada's problems as correct and helpful, but already 'well documented by others'.

Two more attempts to test Porter's model will be mentioned here, besides the one for New Zealand already analysed, as they are both relevant to this study. The first was made using data from Ireland, another small EU nation. The second was more extensive and concerned Turkey, a close neighbour of Greece with a very similar industrial structure (for the striking similarities in cluster export shares see Konsolas and Oz, 1996).

In the *Irish* case, O' Donnellan (1994) investigates the extent of sectoral clustering and geographic concentration and their relation to industrial performance. Vertical links were found to exist among some, but not all, of the industries in the same cluster, although part of the problem was the misplacement of certain industries. Sectoral geographic concentration was also present in Ireland, further than would be expected given the general concentration of employment and manufacturing firms around Dublin and Cork. Vertical linkages, however, among the concentrated industries were evident in only two groups of sectors, food, and wood transformation and printing. Moreover, little association was found between clustering or geographic concentration and enhanced industrial performance, in terms of exports, productivity and innovation. Although some of the results did support Porter's hypotheses, O' Donnellan (1994) wonders whether the lack of many groups of industries both geographically concentrated and vertically linked may have been responsible for the low correlation with industrial performance. He seems more in favour of promoting vertical linkages and sectoral clustering than geographic concentration, for which he considers there is a very limited potential, given Ireland's size (O' Donnellan, 1994: 230).

In the *Turkish* case, Oz (1997: 75-94; 1999: 38-55) identified competitive industries according to Porter's methodology. Turkey was very competitive in the textiles/apparel, food/beverages, materials/metals and housing/household clusters. Turkey's strong positions were mostly in final products, while the machinery industries were relatively weak. Five industries, four competitive (glass, construction, leather clothes and flat steel) along with one uncompetitive (automobiles) were studied by Oz (1997: 98-339; 1999: 59-159). After a thorough investigation and analysis, the competitive advantage (or disadvantage in the automobile case) of these industries was found to be closely related to the determinants in the diamond framework, and their interactions. Certain issues, however, concerning the role of basic factors, domestic rivalry and government intervention did arise from the case studies. Specifically, two of the industries (leather clothes and flat steel) drew little advantage from basic factors, in the glass and flat steel industries there was no domestic rivalry and the role of government in three cases was much more direct that what Porter envisages. Oz (1997: 356; 1999: 170-171) concludes that although some of the aberrations can still be explained within the diamond framework, others require further applications of Porter's framework to conclude whether the observations made are 'generalisable'.

Evaluation of The Competitive Advantage of Nations

Porter's (1990) *The Competitive Advantage of Nations* has sparked a debate regarding many of the subjects of the book, such as the determinants of trade patterns, the process of economic development and the identification of competitive industries. This section presents a review of these debates, in an effort to summarise the views of other scholars on Porter's work. Where appropriate, excerpts from *The Competitive Advantage of Nations* are also used in order to clarify Porter's positions and contrast them with those of his critics. An attempt has been made to group the various comments on Porter's work, starting from general criticisms, proceeding to specific points about the study, followed by comments on the diamond framework, his model of economic development and the methodology. Nevertheless, certain issues appear in more than one category, with a different focus each time. Also, certain aspects of Porter's work are part of a wider issue (for example, stage theories of development) and a broader perspective was deemed necessary.

General Assessment

Porter's diamond framework has influenced both the strategy of firms and, especially, the policy choices of national, regional and local governments throughout the world (De Man, Van den Bosch and Elfring, 1997: 53; Malecki, 1997: 9). It has also attracted the attention of scholars from a variety of disciplines, including management, economics, international relations and others.

The approach that Porter (1990) uses in presenting his theory does not comply with the traditional forms of analytical models. The absence of a typical structure and the overuse of cases and examples, created an opportunity for criticism. The strongest point to this effect was expressed by Greenaway (1993: 146) who stresses that Porter is constantly referring 'to a "theory" of competitive advantage which is never formally presented, nor formally tested'. Additionally, Gray (1991) makes two valuable arguments. First, certain phenomena mentioned by Porter are 'not identified as integral parts of the diamond' and, second, 'the treatment of some phenomena becomes an obiter dictum rather than a closely reasoned deduction' (Gray, 1991: 510).

Stopford and Strange (1991: 8) attack the characterisation of Porter's contribution as a theory, terming it instead 'an explanatory framework' because, among others, it does not resolve 'the causality between policies to create growth and those aimed at structural reform'. The weakness of the framework 'in generating clear predictions' that has been pointed out by Grant (1991: 542-543), who is perhaps the most careful reader of Porter's study, is an additional argument in favour of avoiding the term 'theory' for Porter's work. Other writers, who have used extensively Porter's approach, also prefer the term 'framework' (De Man, Van den Bosch and Elfring, 1997) or 'taxonomy' (Singleton, 1997).

It is common practice to look for the degree of originality in any new scientific contribution. This is why an extensive discussion has been conducted regarding the originality of Porter's framework. De Man, Van den Bosch and Elfring (1997: 53-54) point out that Porter's view is not completely new. The core of his innovativeness is the 'combination of theory, practice and tools' and 'the integration of various research approaches'. This view is challenged by many researchers (for example, Rugman, 1991: 61; Dunning, 1992: 139) who argue that almost all the determinants of Porter's framework are analysed and/or incorporated in previous studies of prominent scholars. Others stress that there is nothing particularly new in Porter's study (Thurow, 1990); that it is a 'rehash' of the theory of comparative advantage (Côté, 1993: 312), a partial repetition of models of trading economies (Bruce, 1993: 80) or a repeat of facts that are part of the theory of intra-industry trade (Gray, 1991: 506). A different approach is adopted by Magaziner (1990: 189) who argues that Porter's contribution is new to policy makers, although not to business strategists. Indeed, Porter's approach has been used in practice by various governments (De Man, Van den Bosch and Elfring, 1997: 53) and has been characterised by policy makers as 'a valuable contribution to the policy debate' (Geelhoed, 1997: 66) that provides 'insights' (Smit, 1997: 67) into a region's economy.

In terms of the individual determinants, a brief summary of the criticisms regarding their originality is provided by Penttinen (1994: 9). He argues that the role of factor conditions is similar to the theory of comparative advantage, the importance of home demand has long been pointed out, for example, by Vernon (1966), while most of the attributes included in the 'strategy, structure and rivalry' determinant have been covered by industrial economics. The other components of Porter's theory can also be subject to criticisms similar to those mentioned above.

Malecki (1997: 152) considers Porter's identification of regional clusters as 'nothing new in the economic geography of industries' although he admits that Porter 'illuminated the phenomenon for many unaware of the concept'. Indeed, clusters and geographic concentration are concepts that can be found, for example, in the work of Weber (1929), Isard (1960) and other regional scientists in their writings concerning location theory. In fact, the importance of networks for innovation, as De Man, Van den Bosch, and Elfring (1997: 53) point out, had already been established long before Porter's work.

Smith (1993: 399) considers Porter's way of thinking about development policy original, and his work a 'serious attempt to develop a really original grand theory of national economic development'. His views are in contrast with most of the other writers, although they are not irreconcilable. Grant (1991) also devotes a substantial part of his extensive critique to analyse Porter's contributions. He finds that Porter integrates the theory of competitive strategy with the theory of international trade and comparative advantage and reformulates the strategy model in a dynamic context, with his emphasis on innovation and upgrading. Grant (1991: 548) also states that Porter's work will eventually lead to 'a redefinition of the boundaries of strategic management' and considers that Porter offers 'new insights into the development of industries and nations within their international context', thus influencing the direction of international trade theory.

De Man, Van den Bosch and Elfring (1997: 45-48) point to another aspect of Porter's work, the way he approaches international competitiveness. They define his contribution as an effort to integrate the three, up to now separate, schools of competitiveness, which emphasised the firm level and superior management, the industry level and industrial policy and the macro-economic environment of countries.

Although most parts of the diamond framework have been the subject of earlier works, it is true that Porter has combined these in an original way, in an effort to illustrate the multitude of influences on trade patterns. In this attempt, Porter has also made use of his own earlier work on competitive advantage and has emphasised the importance of the local environment, linking firm strategy to sectoral and spatial circumstances.

Porter has also brought attention to many of the issues mentioned in his work, inspiring other authors to develop original ideas. The improvements to Porter's framework, which have already been proposed, also contain some original concepts and more work is continuously being done on the framework by other scholars and Porter himself.

A lot of the shortcomings of the framework 'in theory, exposition and empirical analysis' are related to the fact that it is ambitious in its scope, as Grant (1991: 548) points out and Magaziner (1990: 189) confirms. Both writers, however, see many important insights present in the framework. Malecki (1997: 29) believes that Porter emphasises many substantial issues, such as the importance of services in the clustering process. Maucher (1990: 188) expects *The Competitive Advantage of Nations* to 'make history, setting a new framework for an old problem', while Smith (1993: 404) sees Porter's focus on the long-term success of the firm as something lacking from development theory. Grant (1991: 540) in addition to his observation that Porter encompasses 'many of the central themes of established theory', argues that 'Porter is able to broaden and integrate many recent contributions to the theory of international trade'.

Bellak and Weiss (1993: 112), on the contrary, believe that new trade theory, which takes account of economies of scale, imperfect competition and product differentiation (for a brief review see Krugman and Obstfield, 1997: 122-142), proves that there is no need for a 'new paradigm' as Porter claims. Porter (1990: 16), however, while acknowledging these recent contributions, points out that they fail to answer an important question, that is, which nation's firms will be able to gain competitive advantage in particular industries. Porter's work tries to provide an answer to this question and only extensive testing of Porter's assertions will prove whether they are indeed correct.

An additional general criticism is made by Grant (1991: 548) that considers Porter's definitions as 'adjusted to suit the needs of different parts of the analysis'. This is especially true in the economic development part of the book, as well as in many cases where the industry-level concepts are adapted to the national level.

Moreover, concepts are not always well-defined, according to Thurow (1990: 95), who mentions that 'sentences and paragraphs have to be read several times to decipher their meaning'. Thurow (1990: 95) also considers the book far too long, a view shared by Dobson and Starkey (1992: 254). Grant (1991: 548) believes that Porter uses repetition to reinforce his ideas. Despite these criticisms, Jelinek (1992: 509) considers the book a 'careful, structured discussion' with a 'wealth of detailed examples' and 'well-developed case-studies', that 'gathers power in the course of the roughly 750 pages of text', 750 pages that are required to present this 'highly detailed and complex explanation'. Although it is true that the book is quite long by any standards, it certainly fits Porter's usual style of presenting his views.

Criticisms of Particular Issues

Geographical aspect Given the high level of development of the countries studied by Porter and their concentration in Western Europe, North America and East Asia, a lot of writers have questioned the applicability of the diamond in other countries. Narula (1993: 85) thinks that Porter's framework is not applicable to developing countries. A similar point is brought forward by Hodgetts (1993: 44) who considers it 'unlikely' that the framework can be applied to countries with less economic strength than those studied by Porter. Rugman and D'Cruz (1993: 26) believe that Porter's analysis is not relevant for Canada and that '90% of the world's nations potentially cannot be modelled by the Porter diamond' due to the insufficient attention paid to the role of multinationals.

Bellak and Weiss (1993: 117) also consider Porter's emphasis on the home market and indigenous firms as relevant only to large countries. The only point that should be made here is that Porter (1990) in his 'stages of economic development' classifies most countries of the world in the factor-driven and investment-driven stages, where not all of the diamond determinants are present and even those that are present are less than perfectly developed.

Another issue concerning the geographic scope of Porter's work is the relevant level of analysis. Jacobs and De Jong (1992), in their study of clusters in the Netherlands, find industries whose advantage is closely related to a specific region and others where the nation is the relevant unit of analysis. They also mention the presence of cross-border clusters, a fact already noted by Porter (1990: 158-159). Their conclusion is that the geographic unit of analysis should change according to the cluster or industry examined. This is seen by De Man, Van den Bosch and Elfring (1997: 56) as a clarification and extension of Porter's analysis. There is no doubt that the framework can be easily applied to regions or even large cities, as Porter himself (1990: 158) states. Porter (1990: 154) also observes that industries are 'often' concentrated in particular regions or cities. Nevertheless, he argues that there are more similarities between regions in the same nation than across nations; and that central government policies, social and political values and other characteristics are more nation-specific. Another justification for Porter's selection of countries as the unit of analysis in his original work is the availability of reliable data. In most countries export and other data are often not available for particular regions, and certainly not for cities, and when they are, their accuracy is much higher at the national level.

Many writers have argued for the opposite, i.e. the importance of other nations or of supra-national entities for competitive advantage. Several scholars (for example, Rugman and D'Cruz, 1993; Rugman and Verbeke, 1993; Hodgetts, 1993) have proposed a double diamond approach, where the diamond of one country is linked to that of a larger or more developed nation. Jacobs and De Jong (1992) also point out that in certain industries competition is at a global scale, and production is carried out by international networks. Dunning (1993: 12) refers to a 'supranational' diamond replacing the national diamonds in the EU countries. Porter (1990: 159) sees such a development as unlikely in the near future, as he considers national differences among EU nations in demand conditions, factor creation and other determinants as persisting. This is a rather bold assertion and, despite the fact that national differences in important determinants are showing little change, other attributes of production and demand are heavily influenced by developments at the EU level as the integration process moves on.

The impact of national culture Porter (1990: 129) examines the role of cultural factors in shaping the firms' environment. He considers that they work through the other determinants and that they cannot be separated from economic outcomes. In fact, economic circumstances often shape the social norms and values, which are an important part of the 'national culture'. Nevertheless, Porter (1990) occasionally mentions cultural influences as important and essential attributes of the national environment, which cannot be easily emulated.

Van den Bosch and Van Prooijen (1992: 173), on the other hand, consider that national culture is given too little attention, especially since, as they claim, 'the national diamond rests on the base of national culture, and the latter is exogenous to the firm'. The two authors object to the fact that although Porter (1990) recognises the importance of culture, he does not include it in the diamond (Van den Bosch and Van Prooijen, 1992: 175). Their analysis is not in contrast to Porter's, in fact, the authors admit that culture works through the other determinants; they only advocate a more explicit treatment of culture and further research on its role in determining competitive advantage. Porter's reply (1992: 178) to their article summarises the points already made in *The Competitive Advantage of Nations*. Its main addition to those arguments is the emphasis on the fact that culture is not necessarily exogenous to firms but 'changes over time and can be changed', presumably by firms. He also stresses that culture might have different effects on different industries. While it is true that culture is mentioned and analysed by Porter, it is also true that it is not explicitly incorporated in the diamond.

Macro-economic policy and exchange rates Exchange rates and macro-economic policies that affect production costs are considered by Daly (1993: 130) and Jasinowski (1990: 196) as being downplayed in Porter's analysis. Gray (1991: 154) also agrees that exchange rates affect price competitiveness and that Porter does not take this fact into account.

Porter (1990) believes that an undervalued currency can only confer an advantage in the short-run, and only in price-sensitive segments. In the long-run, domestic industries are prevented from upgrading their competitive advantage, and remain trapped in price competition through exchange rates that cannot ensure their success, once conditions change. Porter (1990), nevertheless, emphasises the importance of other macro-economic factors (such as interest rates) for competitiveness. However, he emphatically points out that his theory is 'aggressively industry (and cluster) specific' (Porter, 1990: 283). Therefore, factors that affect all industries in a nation are much less important than factors that are specific to an industry or a group of industries.

Criticisms About the Diamond Framework

Factor conditions are, according to Jelinek (1992: 508), an elaboration of the traditional factors of production, with increased emphasis on upgraded and industry-specific factors. Grant (1991: 537) considers that Porter's contribution, through his treatment of factor conditions, is 'to analyse in much greater detail' their characteristics, while also exploring their creation mechanisms.

The first point criticised by many in Porter's factor conditions, is the 'hierarchy' of factors and his preference for advanced factors, as they are seen to provide a more sustainable advantage. Cooper (1992) states that minimum retraining and better marketing can offer a comfortable living for New Zealanders, exploiting the country's scenery and open spaces for tourism purposes. A similar view is expressed by Grant (1991: 541) that sees Saudi Arabia's competitive advantage in the supply of crude oil as sustainable, although it is related to a natural resource endowment. Other writers (such as Cartwright, 1993; Rugman and D'Cruz, 1993; and Hodgetts, 1993) see basic factors as a sustainable source of advantage, usually complemented by other attributes, such as export policies or managerial and marketing skills.

A second point, that has been criticised, is the presence of selective factor disadvantages. These disadvantages, according to Porter (1990: 81-85) can foster innovations, which often eliminate the disadvantage and create new sources of advantage. Grant (1991: 542) correctly points out that 'Porter fails to clearly define the conditions under which advantages in the supply of basic factors are an advantage, and the conditions under which they are a disadvantage'. The only clarifications made by Porter (1990: 83) is that disadvantages 'must be *selective*' and should '*send the proper signals* about circumstances that will ultimately confront firms elsewhere' (emphasis in the original text).

In his second determinant, Porter analyses a variety of demand conditions that affect international competitiveness. His critics have paid particular attention to the question of demand size and the related issue of whether a small market can have buyers with the characteristics envisioned by Porter (sophistication, anticipatory needs, etc.). Rugman and Verbeke (1993: 76) believe that 'demand conditions in the United States are just as relevant as Canadian demand conditions' for most Canadian Multi-National Enterprises (MNEs). Rugman and D'Cruz (1993: 30) view the Canadian home market as too small to support the required economies of scale. Cartwright (1993), examining the case of New Zealand, finds that for many export-dependent industries, sophisticated demand is present only in foreign markets. Porter (1990: 86), nevertheless, emphasises that the quality of home demand is more important than the quantity and that the home market has a disproportionate effect on 'a firm's ability to perceive and interpret buyer needs', thus highlighting the pivotal role of domestic demand, regardless of its size.

The emphasis on related and supporting industries, as a major influence on the international competitiveness of an industry, has been the subject of much praise, as one of Porter's main contributions. Jacobs and De Jong (1992: 246) describe Porter's method for analysing clusters as 'a valuable tool for strategic policy making'. Rugman (1991: 61) finds that the identification of clusters is accurate and relevant to managers.

Grant (1991: 542) points out a serious overlap in the related and supporting industries determinant. He claims that the role of related and supporting industries is to affect factor conditions and demand conditions. Specifically, successful supplier industries are providing resources, 'horizontally-related industries contribute to factor creation' and competitive downstream industries are important buyers. Although it seems that many of the effects of this determinant are captured by factor and demand conditions, Porter (1990: 103) argues that 'mere access or availability of inputs' is not the primary benefit from internationally competitive domestic suppliers. Their role is more important in the various interchanges, of technology, ideas, etc., which promote innovation and upgrading. The same role is envisaged for related industries, where sharing of activities and extensive co-ordination are the driving forces for a successful, internationally competitive cluster.

Porter has also been praised for his emphasis on the firm, as the major actor in international trade. Rugman (1991: 61) considers that Porter's model 'has exactly the correct perspective by its focus on the strategies of firms'. However, Harris and Watson (1993: 246) point out that although the firm's role is acknowledged by Porter, very little is said about it. Grant (1991: 542) offers another general criticism on this determinant by pointing out that the variables included 'do not form a coherent group'. For example, domestic rivalry is an industry-level variable clearly defined, while management training and practices are national characteristics, possibly related to factor conditions.

Dobson and Starkey (1992: 255) direct much of their criticism towards this determinant. They consider the book 'weak on how firms should structure their internal organisations to foster competitive advantage'. They point out that the book emphasises an inter-organisational perspective and inter-firm rivalry rather than an intra-organisational one. It is true that Porter makes few suggestions for the firm's organisation. His main purpose is to examine the national characteristics that shape certain aspects of the way firms are organised and managed, and thus affect their competitive advantage. Nevertheless, actions of individual firms are analysed and suggestions are made regarding the benefits and costs of internationalisation, diversification and other issues related to a firm's strategy and structure.

In terms of domestic rivalry, Dobson and Starkey (1992: 254) again question the fact that 'unregulated competition is the way forward'. Porter (1990) offers an array of examples where rivalry has been central to the creation and sustainability of competitive advantage, especially in the more developed countries. He emphasises what Smith (1993: 401) calls the 'dynamic economic benefits of intense domestic competition' and its effect on reducing reliance on government subsidisation and protection policies, which affect equally all producers in an industry. On the rivalry issue, Dunning (1992: 155) also stresses that 'the optimum structure of the market for competitive and innovatory stimuli has always been a matter of debate'. On that point, Porter (1990: 121) argues that the number of competitors required for effective rivalry varies among industries. Dunning (1992: 155) also points out that 'it would be erroneous to argue that a greater population of firms necessarily means more effective competition'.

The indirect role attributed to government by Porter (1990) has been the subject of extensive discussion. A very comprehensive analysis is provided by Van den Bosch and De Man (1994) that criticise Porter on three major points.

The first one is the limited attention Porter pays to regional and local governments. Although it is true that Porter's suggestions usually refer to the national government, explicit mention is made of regional and local governments as well. The second point, that the two writers consider important, is the apparent shift from macro-policies to meso- and micro-policies, which makes governments much more involved in shaping the proximate environment of firms. The conclusion that they reach is that government should be included in the framework as a fifth determinant. Porter (1990: 128), however, considers that 'by viewing government as an *influencer* of the national "diamond" [a] far broader array of public policy options and outcomes' can be explored, including various micro-policies. Dunning (1992: 141) also considers Porter's classification of the government's role, as an influence on the structure and efficiency of the system and not an attribute of the diamond, as probably correct.

The third and final point made by Van den Bosch and De Man (1994) is that the appropriate role for government can vary according to the particular point in its life-cycle where an industry finds itself, regardless of the country's level of development. This is a valid point, especially in regard to Porter's advice to governments, which is based on his 'stages of economic development'. In fact, a similar point is made by Hodgetts (1993: 44) in his critique of Porter's model of economic development, where he mentions that there might be industries or companies, within the same country, belonging to different 'stages of development'.

The issue of introducing government as a fifth determinant is also raised by Stopford and Strange (1991: 8-9). Dobson and Starkey (1992: 254) envisage a far more active role for government in factor creation. Harris and Watson (1993: 250), however, are sceptical of the ability of government to act, even in an 'influencing' role, according to Porter's prescriptions, since 'governments are called upon to be consistent, thoughtful, sophisticated, and original', while 'there is ample evidence that real-world governments simply do not behave this way'.

Narula (1993: 88) considers the role Porter (1990) attributes to chance as disproportionate. Indeed, it seems that Porter includes a large number of unrelated phenomena in the chance category, some of which could have been treated separately, as Bellak and Weiss (1993: 112) point out. Nevertheless, the question that Porter (1990: 125) tries to address is not what events will take place or when they will take place but 'what nation exploits them', i.e. where is the most favourable diamond, given the changes brought about by these unpredictable and often uncontrollable events.

Criticisms About the Stages of Competitive Development

As was mentioned before, Porter (1990) uses his extensive industry-level research to propose four stages of competitive development for a country: factor-driven, investment-driven, innovation-driven and wealth-driven. The transition to each successive stage is not inevitable, nor is it a pre-condition for a country to pass through all the previous stages to reach one of the two final ones. Countries can also move backwards, even as far as the first, factor-driven stage.

In a critique of this model of economic development, Grant (1991: 547-548) has concerns about the ability of Porter to use the micro-foundations of his theory to arrive at an explanation of national economic development. He considers this part of Porter's analysis as the 'least successful' one and doubts whether his prescriptions should be used to guide governments, a point also made by Rugman (1991: 64) regarding the Canadian case. Bellak and Weiss (1993: 115) and Thurow (1990: 96) find the model of economic development inadequate and vague, since the criteria for classifying countries in every stage and the transition mechanisms among stages are not analysed in detail. Jasinowski (1990: 196) considers Porter's model problematic because it is based, as Jasinowski perceives it, on the fact that 'the principles governing the company are equally applicable to nations'.

Côté (1993: 311) follows another line of criticism pointing out that Porter emphasises only the traded sector of an economy and assumes that economic expansion is contingent upon the expansion of the traded sector. Harris and Watson (1993: 247-249) also believe that Porter relies on trade data and case studies of industries exposed to international competition 'to construct a grand generalisation'.

In an article devoted to Porter's model of economic development, Narula (1993: 85) finds that its most critical shortcomings are that it is 'static' and 'based on a subjective analysis of a few industrialised countries'. The attempt to extend the model to countries 'with entirely different economic structures should be founded on a larger data base' (Narula, 1993: 89). Moreover, gradual evolution is ignored as all developing countries are essentially classified in the factor-driven stage (Narula, 1993: 89).

Government intervention is another area of concern, as it is deemed unfeasible for industrialised countries according to Porter (1990). Narula (1993: 89), however, points to the regional integration attempts as an example of government 'collusion between countries to consolidate their mutual or complementary competitive advantages'. Moreover, the main criticism is that the model 'does not address the mechanisms of growth' and is thus 'essentially a static model' (Narula, 1993: 88).

Narula (1993: 88) concludes that 'the "diamond" as it is presently configured cannot be justifiably used to examine the dynamic process of development'. An extension of the diamond is deemed necessary that would include multinational activity as a third exogenous variable, as Dunning (1992) proposed, and accumulated technology as an endogenous variable affecting and being affected by the other four endogenous variables and, indirectly by government, chance and 'international business activity' (Dunning's additional variable).

The extended 'diamond' is then used by Narula (1993: 97-104) to suggest five stages of development, where the growth mechanisms that enable a country to progress from one stage to the next, are related to the rate of technological accumulation and the use of technology in the international trade and investment activities of indigenous firms and foreign multinationals investing in the country.

Kottis (1981: 257), in his extensive critique of the stage theories developed until the 1970's, asks three fundamental questions:

a) How can a development policy be formulated by the government if the transition mechanisms among stages are not clearly defined?
b) Can we be sure that all countries will follow the same path?
c) Can we exclude the possibility of a nation reverting to a previous stage than the one where it currently is?

Porter's (1990) stages of economic development address the last two questions by accepting the possibility of nations reverting, even as far as the first stage, and moving from the factor-driven to the innovation-driven stage directly, skipping the transition to the investment-driven one. Regarding the first question, Porter (1990: 560-562) offers a list of forces that enable transitions between the stages. However, the exact mechanisms by which these forces will be activated are not clear.

Porter's model of economic development exhibits a lot of the weaknesses of similar models that categorise many diverse countries in a few groups. Moreover, the data used by Porter to produce this model are limited, mainly industry-specific, and focused on the traded sector. The questionable link between the competitive advantage of industries and the development of national economies is another problem with the theory of economic development. Therefore, this part of Porter's (1990) study is of limited value for the analysis of the case of Greece.

Criticisms About the Methodology

The methodology used by Porter (1990) is analysed in Chapter 2 along with specific points of critique relevant to the application of this methodology to Greece. However, the broad lines of criticism for the methodology will be mentioned here, as they are related to other points previously made in the present chapter.

The identification of competitive industries is the first part of the methodology that has been criticised. Rugman and D'Cruz (1993: 22), and Bellak and Weiss (1993) disagree with Porter's reliance on export shares as the primary indicator of competitiveness. They prefer foreign direct investment data that are, however, already used to some extent by Porter. Cartwright (1993: 58) also criticises Porter for his bias towards selection of exporting industries against those that produce abroad or make use of foreign value-adding subsidiaries. Again an internationally comparable, widely available measure of competitiveness, other than export shares that is, is not proposed. Cartwright (1993: 62) uses profitability in his definition of competitive New Zealand industries, along with export shares. Porter (1990: 739), however, considers profitability 'unreliable' as an internationally comparable measure of competitiveness, because of protectionist policies, differences in reporting requirements and accounting standards, the availability of data, and company diversification, which makes comparisons among industries very difficult.

Porter's criteria for excluding industries from the competitive lists were also the subject of much discussion. Porter (1990: 740) excludes industries whose trade 'was almost exclusively with neighbouring nations'. In his study of Canada, though, Porter (Porter and Monitor Company, 1991) slightly modifies his views. He makes a distinction between industries that are successful mainly in the USA market and those that are also exporting to many other markets, without, however, excluding those in the first category from the competitive lists. In general, this is a rather vague criterion that appears relevant only where one country is the main recipient of another country's exports. Therefore, it was not applied in the Greek case.

Another exclusion criterion has caused a much wider debate. Porter (1990: 740) excluded from the competitive lists industries whose exports are 'dominated by foreign companies who produced in the nation as part of a global manufacturing strategy'. This has attracted a lot of criticism from Canadian scholars (Rugman, 1991; Rugman and D'Cruz, 1993) who consider Porter's views on inward Foreign Direct Investment (FDI) as a serious flaw in his diamond framework and one that makes it impossible for the diamond to be applied in the Canadian case.

Hodgetts (1993) and Bellak and Weiss (1993) also believe that Porter should have paid more attention to inward FDI, that is equally or more important than outward FDI for certain countries. Porter's treatment of inward FDI implies that only when a subsidiary is strategically autonomous, is it able to reap all the advantages of a nation's diamond. Otherwise, it is established to selectively tap into certain advantages, and thus, its presence is only an indication that these few advantages exist in the nation, rather than the full diamond. In this case, the multitude of advantages are located in the multinational's home-base, and a global strategy is used to add to these or to offset home-base disadvantages.

Porter (1990: 679), however, does not dismiss the role of multinationals' investment, especially in developing countries, stating that 'multinationals can seed a cluster', but only in industries where the nation's firms might eventually gain competitive advantage. This assertion makes the exclusion of industries dominated by exports of foreign subsidiaries more contentious for countries less developed than those studied by Porter (1990), as is the case with Greece.

On a related point, Porter (1990: 606) is adamant in his assertion that 'a firm can only have one true home base for each distinct business or segment'. According to De Man, Van den Bosch and Elfring (1997: 57) this view, supported by recent empirical evidence, contradicts the views of Ohmae (1990), that globalisation reduces the role of the place where a firm is established. Rugman and Verbeke (1993: 72) also challenge Porter's position that the core competencies and the innovation processes of multinationals depend upon the characteristics of their home base. Grant (1991: 537) agrees with Porter when he states that 'while multinationality permits access to global scale economies and the resource advantages available in different countries, this is quite consistent with Porter's basic proposition that national environments exercise a powerful influence on the competitive advantage of companies'. Doremus et al. (1998: 8-9), using a multitude of empirical evidence, conclude that nationality continues to affect the strategic behaviour of multinationals, especially those based in the USA, Japan and Germany. Malecki (1997: 203) also considers that 'global firms continue to rely on their domestic base'.

The next step in Porter's methodology is the preparation of the cluster charts. Jacobs and De Jong (1992) applied the same methodology to the Netherlands and came up with some interesting critical observations.

They first point out that the classification of industries in clusters takes primarily into account the consumption side, while a more balanced approach should also incorporate the production side. Then they discuss the classification of machinery industries that are sometimes put in the 'primary goods' category instead of the 'machinery' one, as the emphasis, in these cases, is on the machinery being exported rather than integrated in the domestic cluster. The lack of extensive service trade statistics and the maximum number of industries in each cluster (that, indeed, can vary widely) are two more points of concern. These points, however, are more related to the UN trade statistics, Porter's (1990) main source of trade data, and the Standard International Trade Classification (SITC) than Porter's use of them.

The final step in Porter's methodology is the preparation of detailed case-studies. The use of case-studies by Porter has also been a contentious issue. Greenaway (1993: 146), while accepting that this approach can yield 'insights that escape more formal methods', points out that 'many of the insights which are yielded are inevitably case-specific'. Narula (1993: 86) and Cartwright (1993: 65) point to the subjectivity in the analysis of the information available that affects the validity of the conclusions. Bellak and Weiss (1993: 116) question whether the conclusions from case studies are generalisable and comparable among countries. Yin (1994), in a general analysis of case studies, considers analytic generalisations possible if cases are not considered as a 'sample' but as a series of replications.

A more specific point for Porter's use of cases is his preference for studying more competitive industries. Harris and Watson (1993: 248) believe that a study of failing industries, 'the same way' as the successful ones 'would be a very useful lesson'. This issue is further discussed at the end of Chapter 2, where the criteria for selecting the Greek case-studies are analysed.

2   The Greek Economy: Evolution and Competitive Advantage

In this chapter, the emphasis shifts to the particular attributes of the Greek case. The first section deals with the Greek economic environment, through a historical overview and the presentation of the relevant data from the most recent periods. Then, the literature that addresses the issue of Greek industrial competitiveness is reviewed. In the final section, the structure of Greek industrial clusters is explored, with the help of Porter's methodology for identifying and grouping competitive industries. This is also where the rationale for selecting the particular case-studies is explained.

The Greek Economic Environment: Past and Present

The history of the Greeks is, of course, a very long one. However, the history of the modern Greek State is much shorter, spanning only about 170 years. The major developments throughout this time are going to be presented below, with the purpose of revealing the influences that led to the current Greek industrial profile. The presentation is arranged in chronological periods and special emphasis is placed on the rapid development period of the 1950s and 1960s and the current period (after the 1974 restoration of democracy).

From Independence to the Second World War

The modern Greek State was created in 1830 after a fierce War of Independence from the Ottoman Empire that started in 1821. Since then and up to the end of the Second World War (1945), the Greek economy was affected by many important events, three of which were of major significance. The first was the continual expansion of Greek territory with the addition of new provinces, starting with the Ionian islands in 1864 and ending with the Dodecanese islands in 1947. The second was Greece's active participation in the two World Wars and in regional wars as well as in a series of conflicts with the Ottoman Empire (up until 1923) for the liberation of territories where Greeks lived. The third was the enormous effort for the development of the country and its productive sectors, an effort that was seriously hampered by various external and internal factors.

After the liberation struggle of the 1820s, the main objectives of the new State were to restore production to the level it was before the 1821 Revolution, to create the necessary infrastructure, which was, for the most part, destroyed during the war operations, and to mobilise the financially powerful Greek communities, outside the then Greek territory, mainly in Constantinople, Smyrna and Thessaloniki, for revitalising trade. At the same time, the state was interested in using the commercial fleet of certain islands and coastal cities to recapture the trade routes, especially with Western Europe (Petropoulos and Koumarianou, 1977: 16-18, 94-95).

Emphasis was initially given to promoting small-scale agricultural production, developing commerce and establishing small units in the shipbuilding, construction materials and textile industries. For many decades there was also continuous construction of port facilities, roads and public buildings. The wide range of irrigation and drainage works increased agricultural production and, consequently, the first major food producing firms were established and with them, exports of some agricultural products, mainly tobacco and raisins, increased. The agricultural reform of 1871 further revitalised agriculture as peasant farmers became land-owners. The first efforts to exploit the country's natural resources, the development of merchant shipping and commercial banking, the creation of the rail networks and the establishment of the first steam-operated industrial units in Athens, Piraeus, Patras and the island of Syros shaped the new structure of the Greek economy near the end of the 19th century (Kofos, 1977: 310-312).

In the first decade of the 20th century, economic development continued, without substantial external borrowing, despite some lingering public finance and agricultural problems. This development gave Greece the financial means to wage a series of wars, which ended with the annexation of the Northern Greece provinces (Oikonomou, 1977: 196-197).

Three important periods for the country's economy followed. From 1914 to 1922, increases in demand for industrial products and the war effort strengthened traditional industries and favoured the creation of companies in new industries, such as chemicals, electrical goods and some textile products.

After 1922, the country's population was greatly increased because of the influx of Greek refugees from Asia Minor (1.3 million approximately) and at the same time the quality of the workforce improved, since among the refugees were many skilled craftsmen and semiskilled industrial workers. From 1925 to 1930 part of the current electricity network was constructed, without however fully satisfying the constantly increasing demand.

In the decade before the Second World War, there were no major changes in the Greek economy, as the repercussions of the world economic crisis were felt in Greece, too. A decrease in agricultural exports was another negative development of this period.

During the Second World War, Greece was part of the allied forces. After the German invasion, the country's economy suffered from mounting inflation and the financial burden imposed by the occupying forces. The total economical loss for the occupation years is estimated to be around $549 million (Oikonomikos Tachydromos, 1996: 60). The ensuing Civil War increased the problems and constrained even further the country's development.

Concerning the economic policies of the Greek State from its establishment to 1939 the following characteristics can be discerned (Stefanidis, 1952): In the first period (1827-1893) state intervention was indirect and fiscal policies ineffective. From 1893 (when the state declared bankruptcy) until 1909, the state's role in the economy was increased, and monetary and fiscal policies became more robust. The third period (1909-1923) was characterised by attempts to promote development mainly by assisting industrial activity and seeking foreign investment. In the fourth period (1923-1939) the state's direct intervention was very high, leading to the creation of public enterprises, the protection of local industries, the passing of labour laws and the institutionalisation of agricultural credits.

The Reconstruction (1945-1952)

Like all the other countries that took part in the Second World War, Greece should have started its reconstruction efforts from 1945. However, the Civil War that took place from 1945 to 1949, further eroded the country's infrastructure and created lasting social problems. The development process started effectively at the end of 1949, when priority was given to rebuilding what the two wars had destroyed (Agapitos, 1993: 47).

When the occupying forces left Greece in October 1944 the Greek economy was in a 'chaotic' state (Drakatos, 1997: 11). All sectors of the economy, and especially manufacturing, were not functioning. Food supplies were limited, infrastructure networks were seriously damaged, the banking system was almost non-existent, health and education services were inadequate and the drachma - the national currency - had effectively been replaced by gold and 'barter' transactions.

In November 1944 the 'new drachma' was introduced and, in 1946, the Monetary Committee was created, with wide-ranging powers in monetary and credit policies. The British and USA aid of the first post-war years was also very important for industrial reconstruction and for financing the increasing trade and budget deficits. In 1948 the 'Reconstruction Council' was established and the first 'Long-Term Plan for the Economic Reconstruction of Greece 1948-1952' was proposed. This plan, though, was not implemented due to the lack of domestic and foreign funds (Drakatos, 1997: 31).

The Civil War caused problems in Greece's balance of payments. Commercial transactions were subject to various controls. Imports increased, mainly depending on foreign aid funds, but could not cover demand. Exports were also growing, although industrial production was still at low levels. Exports were 27.1% of imports in 1947 and that ratio went down to 23.6% in 1951 (Drakatos, 1997: 24). In 1949, the drachma was devalued to strengthen exports and encourage capital inflows. In order to tackle the increasing current account deficit (1951: $284.7 mil.) the government also took other measures to promote exports and restrict imports. An immediate result was the reduction of the trade deficit from $329.7 million in 1951 to $160.4 million in 1952 (Bank of Greece, 1978).

Since 1945 already, some factories were operating, although faced with considerable difficulties because of the lack of raw materials, fuel and capital. In 1945 industrial production was at 33% of its pre-war level. The reconstruction policies, however, had such an effect that in 1951 industrial production was up 30% from its 1938 level, while agricultural output was at 93% of the 1938 output (Wexler, 1983: 94-95). Investments in manufacturing increased from 21.5% of total 1948 investment to 26.1% in 1951. These developments affected GDP growth, which in 1949 was as high as 20.1%, although it fell subsequently. The composition of GDP at the end of the reconstruction period was: Primary sector: 27.4%, Secondary sector: 18.8% and Tertiary sector: 53.8% (Ministry of Co-ordination, 1976).

In this critical period, 1945-1952, organisational shortcomings of the state, the condition of the infrastructure networks, fiscal problems, increased military spending and the slow increases, mainly in agricultural but also, to a lesser extent, in industrial production, caused serious delays in Greece's development efforts, despite the substantial foreign economic aid. This was not the case for the next period, 1953-1974, when Greece's development accelerated.

The High Growth Period (1953-1974)

The period from 1953 to 1974 (when the 1967 dictatorship ended) is particularly important for Greece's economic history, because during that time economic development was promoted, after a short preparation process in the period's early years.

The period was characterised by noteworthy events, with both positive and negative consequences, such as the devaluation of the drachma by 50% against the dollar, the liberalisation of imports, the protection of foreign investment, the increase in private and public investments, the association with the European Community, the military dictatorship and the economic crisis of 1973-1974.

In the first three years of this period (1953-1956) the economy was still adjusting after the previous troubled periods to the new, more stable environment and a development strategy was formulated aiming at monetary balance, which would enable faster economic development, larger infrastructure projects and the establishment of modern industrial units. The stabilisation policy that followed, produced satisfactory results in decreasing inflation and budget deficits, but did not affect the narrow industrial base, the balance of payments problem, the rise in imports and the restricted capital inflows. What was becoming apparent was that the drachma was overvalued, a fact that did not correspond with the government's strategy. The devaluation of the drachma on the 9th of April 1953 (raising the dollar exchange rate from 15,000 to 30,000) and the associated measures that were taken proved to be the starting point of the country's post-war economic boom.

After the devaluation, a series of measures followed, such as a wide-ranging liberalisation of imports and the end of food rationing. The banking system augmented its financing of private investment while competition was intensified with the creation of new companies in many industries. Substantial incentives were also given for attracting and retaining foreign investment. Private investment was complemented by public investment in transportation, electricity generation, telecommunications, port and airport facilities, etc. During the same period, in 1955, a comprehensive system of income taxation was introduced, with mixed results (Drakatos, 1997: 34-42).

The liberalisation of imports and the small capacity of domestic units resulted in the reduction of exports to 45.1% of the level of imports in 1956. However, the increased remittances from Greek workers abroad and from those working in the Greek merchant fleet proved to be valuable sources of foreign exchange, and in 1956 the Bank of Greece's reserves had increased to $190 million (Bank of Greece, 1978).

Investment during the years from 1953 to 1956 was mainly directed to construction (42.4% of total investment) in order to deal with the increasing urbanisation, as population migrated from the rural areas to Athens and Thessaloniki. Despite the increases in the utilisation of productive capacity, there was a shortage of jobs, especially for those leaving the agricultural sector. The result was a strong migration wave towards Western European, especially West Germany, and North American countries. Nevertheless, the GDP in this sub-period continued to rise, with the secondary sector accounting for most of the increases. The next sub-period (1957-1972) was characterised by rapid economic development, the association agreement with the European Community and the military dictatorship, that changed the political circumstances.

In this sub-period, economic growth was aided by the increase in demand for consumer goods, the monetary stability and the positive circumstances in the world's economy. Despite this economic progress, the required changes in the administration, the educational system and other institutions were not made. Especially during the dictatorship period, consumer spending was given a big boost, without any structural adjustment measures.

Investment started growing at a high rate, aided by the incentive schemes, the organisation of the capital markets and the creation of specialised organisations for industrial and tourist development. In the 1960s, foreign investment also increased. Its characteristics were the establishment of big units, mainly in new industries for Greece (petroleum, chemicals, steel, aluminium, large-scale shipbuilding, pharmaceuticals, etc.), vertical integration, seeking of domestic market share, substantial exports and concentration in capital and intermediate goods industries (Giannitsis and Vaitsos, 1987: 64-65).

This was a time of prolonged high growth, among the highest in Europe. GDP grew at an annual average rate of 6.6% between 1957 and 1972. The rise in industrial production is reflected in the detailed changes in GDP, where the secondary sector's product increased by 9.6% annually (manufacturing: 9.3%), while the primary sector's product by 4.2%, and the tertiary sector's by 6.4% (Ministry of Co-ordination, 1976). Manufacturing production soared both as a result of domestic demand and of exports of manufactures, that rose five-fold between 1957 and 1972.

The current account balance, during the same years, was almost constant, with a deficit of around $200 million. In terms of the trade balance, what should be noted is that the years until 1960 were characterised by exports of agricultural products and raw materials, whereas from 1960 to 1972, growth in exports came from manufacturing goods mainly (Giannitsis and Vaitsos, 1987: 48).

Between 1961 and 1972 the total workforce decreased. Unemployment was also decreasing and this can be attributed to the great number of workers migrating to foreign countries. Domestic population experienced a great rise in living standards. Per capita domestic consumption increased by an average annual rate of 5.2% between 1961 and 1970, while for the same period per capita GDP grew by 10.3% annually, an impressive figure that was matched by very few countries with similar levels of development at the time, with the exception of Japan's 'miraculous' growth that corresponded to a 15.6% average annual GDP increase (Drakatos, 1997: 70-71).

In the rest of Europe an important development was taking place. In 1957, the treaty of Rome was signed, establishing the European Economic Community. The first country that submitted an application for association and subsequent membership to the Community, was Greece. The application was submitted in 1959 and the Athens association agreement was signed on the 9th of July, 1961, ratified by the law 4226/14-3-62, and went into force on November 1962. The association of Greece with the Community was an act of political choice, but also of economic significance. The goal of the agreement was for Greece to become a full member within 25 years. The agreement stipulated: a) a customs union, b) policies harmonisation and c) economic assistance (Ministry of Foreign Affairs, 1980: 13-16).

Tariff reduction or elimination, regarding both European Community tariffs for Greek industrial products and Greek tariffs for Community products, especially those not manufactured in Greece, was a result of the agreement. A more gradual adoption by Greece of Community external tariffs was also under way. In terms of policy co-ordination, especially agricultural policy that was considered an important obstacle for Greece's accession, the achievements were not very spectacular. Economic aid was given for the financing of investments, however, only a portion of the planned sum was provided to Greece. In the first years after the agreement the balance of trade situation remained unchanged. There were also some positive effects in the business climate since Greece was seen as economically stable and a good location for exporting to the EC countries (Drakatos, 1997: 73-74).

The main event that limited the agreement's potential was the 1967 military coup. During the dictatorship period (1967-1974), no funds were dispensed from the EC and, therefore, from the $125 million that were initially allocated, Greece only received 55%, that went mainly to road and irrigation and drainage works, while the remaining were frozen by the Community.

The short-term orientation of the dictatorship's economic policies, the misallocation of essential resources and the disproportionate emphasis on the construction industry, brought, in 1972, the first signs of a crisis that coincided with the oil crisis of 1973-1974.

This third sub-period (1972-1974) is characterised by inflationary pressures, as well as stagnation in industrial and agricultural production, which failed to keep pace with demand, especially for animal products. The major problem of inflationary pressures was exacerbated by imported inflation. The rises in oil prices caused Greece's current account deficit to triple, from $401.5 million in 1972 to $1191.5 million in 1973. The devaluation of the drachma against most European currencies also contributed to the rising cost of imports.

In order to deal with these problems a series of anti-inflationary measures were implemented, leading to a stifling of economic activity. The situation was not helped by the political uncertainty of this period that culminated in the overthrow of the military rule in July 1974.

The Current Period (1975-2001)

In the period starting with the restoration of democracy, in July 1974, the economic policies of Greece are related to European integration. It is, therefore, a period with specific targets, which the economic performance of Greece had to achieve, and also a period of structural changes in the world economy.

The goals of converging with the economies of the other EU states and of stabilisation and restructuring of the economy were pursued with considerable social cost and mixed results. During most of this period, stagflation and reduced investment, combined with alternating economic policies, prevented Greece from achieving the necessary economic stability.

Important events for Greece, after 1974, were the second oil crisis (1979), Greece's accession to the EC (1981), the victory of the socialist party (PASOK) in the 1981 elections, and the restrictive economic policies that were first implemented in 1985 and 1986. These policies were reversed in 1987 and, to make things worse, a period of 'short-term' governments followed. In April 1990, the conservative party of New Democracy won the elections and restored the restrictive policy that continued even after the return of PASOK to power (1993).

The detailed analysis of the economic indicators of this period will be presented in four phases that correspond to the analysis of export performance, using the Porter methodology, which is presented in the last part of this chapter, and also to the different phases of Greece's effort to converge with the other EU members. These phases are: a) 1975-1980, b) 1981-1987, c) 1988-1992, and d) 1993-2001.

The analysis and the data used in the remainder of this section come primarily from Tables 2.1, 2.2, 2.3 and 2.4 that present the main indicators for these four phases. An overview of the GDP and the Trade Balance is also given in Figures 2.1 and 2.2, for the 1960-1997 period. To illustrate the changes in the four phases mentioned above a trend line has been drawn, with the help of a regression analysis, using as explanatory variables the time trend and a set of dummy variables that correspond to the four phases (Pindyck and Rubinfeld, 1991: 104-108).

The 1975-1980 period Following the fall of the dictatorship the most important event of this period was the re-instatement of Greece's application for full membership to the EC. The association agreement was

Table 2.1 Basic Indicators 1975-1980

	1975	1976	1977	1978	1979	1980	Average
GDP (constant 1988 prices) - billion Drachmas	6512.4	6968.6	7137.3	7671.9	7895.3	8102.4	
GDP growth, %	4.6	7.0	2.4	7.5	2.9	2.6	4.5
Investment, % of GDP	29.4	29.4	32.2	33.7	34.5	28.5	31.3
Inflation, %	13.4	13.3	12.2	12.5	19.0	24.9	16.2
Interest Rates, 1-Year Treasury Bill, %	9.8	9.8	8.3	10.3	14.3	14.3	11.1
Public Debt, % of GDP	24.7	24.6	25.7	28.0	27.5	28.6	26.5
General Government Deficit, % of GDP	3.0	1.7	2.5	2.9	2.4	2.6	2.5
Trade Balance, % of GDP	-12.4	-12.5	-12.6	-11.5	-13.3	-14.0	-12.7
Current Account Balance, % of GDP	-3.9	-3.5	-3.5	-2.5	-4.0	-4.6	-3.7

Source: Ministry of National Economy, 1998.

Table 2.2 Basic Indicators 1981-1987

	1981	1982	1983	1984	1985	1986	1987	Average
GDP (constant 1988 prices) - billion Drachmas	8110.0	7893.3	7736.8	7838.0	8147.0	8105.3	7855.9	
GDP growth, %	0.1	-2.7	-2.0	1.3	3.9	-0.5	-3.1	-0.4
Investment, % of GDP	25.7	25.8	27.7	23.0	24.2	24.2	23.5	24.8
Unemployment, %	4.0	5.8	7.9	8.1	7.8	7.4	7.4	6.9
Inflation, %	24.5	21.1	20.2	18.5	19.3	23.0	16.4	20.4
Interest Rates, 1-Year Treasury Bill, %	14.3	15.3	15.3	18.0	18.5	18.5	19.5	17.0
Public Debt, % of GDP	34.5	41.3	41.9	48.0	54.7	55.9	62.2	48.4
General Government Deficit, % of GDP	9.1	6.8	7.6	8.4	11.7	9.5	9.2	8.9
Trade Balance, % of GDP	-15.0	-12.8	-12.8	-13.1	-15.4	-11.9	-12.5	-13.4
Current Account Balance, % of GDP	-5.4	-4.1	-4.5	-5.2	-8.1	-3.7	-2.2	-4.7

Source: Ministry of National Economy, 1998.

Table 2.3 Basic Indicators 1988-1992

	1988	1989	1990	1991	1992	Average
GDP (constant 1988 prices) - billion Drachmas	8318.3	8576.1	8499.0	8719.9	8789.7	
GDP growth, %	5.9	3.1	-0.9	2.6	0.8	2.3
Investment, % of GDP	23.6	24.6	26.0	26.6	25.5	25.3
Unemployment, %	7.7	7.5	7.0	7.7	8.7	7.7
Inflation, %	13.5	13.7	20.4	19.5	15.9	16.6
Interest Rates, 1-Year Treasury Bill, %	19.0	20.0	24.0	22.5	22.5	21.6
Public Debt, % of GDP	66.8	69.9	80.7	83.3	89.0	77.9
General Government Deficit, % of GDP	11.5	14.4	16.1	11.5	12.8	13.3
Trade Balance, % of GDP	-11.8	-13.6	-14.9	-13.8	-14.1	-13.6
Current Account Balance, % of GDP	-1.5	-3.8	-4.3	-1.7	-2.1	-2.7

Source: Ministry of National Economy, 1998.

Table 2.4 Basic Indicators 1993-1997

	1993	1994	1995	1996	1997	Average
GDP (constant 1988 prices) - billion Drachmas	8640.3	8882.2	9077.6	9250.1	9527.6	
GDP growth, %	-1.7	2.8	2.2	1.9	3.0	1.6
Investment, % of GDP	25.1	23.7	24.2	25.8	27.4	25.2
Unemployment, %	9.7	9.6	10.0	10.3	10.3	10.0
Inflation, %	14.4	10.9	8.9	8.2	5.5	9.6
Interest Rates, 1-Year Treasury Bill, %	20.3	17.5	14.2	11.2	11.4	14.9
Public Debt, % of GDP	111.6	109.3	110.1	112.2	109.5	110.5
General Government Deficit, % of GDP	13.8	10.0	10.6	7.5	4.0	9.2
Trade Balance, % of GDP	-13.6	-13.7	-14.8	-14.9	-15.2	-14.4
Current Account Balance, % of GDP	-0.8	-0.1	-2.5	-3.7	-4.0	-2.2

Source: Ministry of National Economy, 1998.

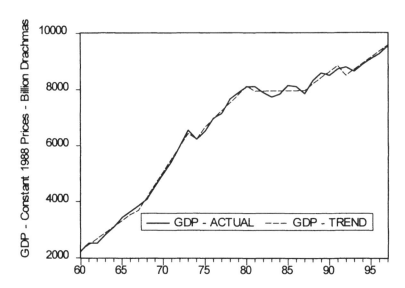

Figure 2.1 Greek GDP, 1960-1997
Source: Ministry of National Economy, 1998.

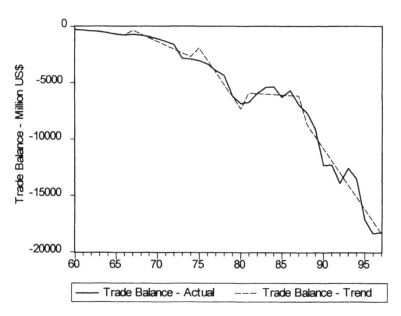

Figure 2.2 Greek Trade Balance, 1960-1997
Source: Ministry of National Economy, 1998.

again activated, at the end of 1974, especially the part related to the financial transfers from the EC. Although Greece had not reached the level of development of the other nine members (in 1975 the per capita GDP of Greece was 44% of the EC average), the Greek government pursued vigorously the goal of accession to the EC. The application was submitted in 1975, the agreement was signed in 1979 and in 1981 Greece became the tenth member state of the Community. There was, however, a five year transition period, during which Greece had to make the necessary changes to conform with EC policies and regulations.

Another characteristic of this period was the economic stagnation, that had already started in 1973. The annual rate of increase for investment was much lower than in previous decades, especially in the manufacturing industries, where there was an average annual decline of 1.5% in investment levels, compared to a 10.8% average annual increase between 1958 and 1973. Inflation was again on the rise, with the consumer price index growth doubling. From 13.4% in 1975, inflation reached 24.9% in 1980 (see Table 2.1), and the average for the period was 16.2%, while the OECD average was 9.9%. The main reasons behind this development, according to Drakatos (1997: 81-83), were the high prices of imported goods, the increased business profits and wages, the large subsidies and the excess liquidity.

A positive development was the continued rise of GDP at a 4.5% average annual rate. Although this rate was lower than the average for previous periods, it was still almost double the EC average. The composition of the GDP remained stable with a small extension of the services sector's share.

Public debt as a percentage of GDP, increased gradually during the previous period and was around 25% in 1970. In this period it remained almost constant (average: 26.5%) with small yearly variations. The same is true for the general government deficit, that remained at 2.5% of GDP, on average. However, government expenditure was on the rise and the budget deficits were mainly controlled by restraining public investment.

The trade deficit, as a percentage of GDP, increased by 1.6% between 1975 and 1980 and the current account deficit by 0.7%, both affected by the 1979 oil crisis. What restricted the expansion of the current account deficit was the change in tourist receipts, from $643 million in 1975 to $1733 million in 1980.

During the 1975-1980 period, the economic indicators continued to signal a depression. It was the preamble of a longer period of negative developments and macro-economic difficulties.

The 1981-1987 period In 1981, Greece became a full member of the EC. In 1982, the new socialist government requested a special status for Greece's relation to the EC. The government claimed that the impending accession of Spain and Portugal would negatively affect Greece, and especially its agricultural producers. Therefore, its proposal was for the creation of a new Community structural policy, in favour of the weaker member-states. This was how the Integrated Mediterranean Programs (IMP) were created, with the objective of strengthening the agricultural sector and the infrastructure of Greece, Southern Italy, Portugal, Ireland and certain areas of Spain and France. The time frame for the implementation of the IMP was from 1985 to 1990. These Programs were the start of Community policies for the improvement of cohesion among the EC economies. This policy was later continued with the Community Support Frameworks and various other Community Initiatives (Konsolas, 1992: 41-52).

The first period of Greece's accession to the EC coincided with some negative economic developments and found the country unprepared to face the very competitive environment into which it was thrust. Between 1981 and 1987, most economic indicators continued to worsen, restrictive and expansive policies alternated, unemployment became a major issue, real wages declined, and the trade deficit expanded. At the same time, public debt increased and the drachma was devalued twice.

GDP growth was reversed and an average annual decline of 0.4% was characteristic of the period (see Table 2.2). In 1987, GDP declined by 3.1%, mainly because of the stabilisation programme, which restricted home demand. The composition of the GDP again changed slightly in favour of services (that reached 55.6% on average), while manufacturing production and manufacturing capacity declined.

Investment, as a percentage of GDP, decreased from an average of 31.3% (1975-1980) to 24.8%, with manufacturing and agriculture mostly affected. Low investment coincided with the end of the migration trend of previous decades, and unemployment increased by 3.4% between 1981 and 1987, reaching 7.4%. It is worth noting that 40% of the unemployed were under 25 years old, and more than 50% were women.

The consumer price index's annual growth was on average 4.2% greater than that of the previous period, despite a decrease in 1987 when it went down to 16.4%. Another important indicator, which has now become very relevant due to the European Monetary Union (EMU), was the level of interest rates. Throughout this period interest rates increased, reaching 19.5% for the 1-year treasury bill rate in 1987. The average of 17%, however, was 3.4% lower than the average inflation of 20.4% and as this was evident in most of this period, it lowered the purchasing power of smaller depositors (Vamvoukas, 1991: 431-433).

Salaried employees also faced an increased tax burden as the state was trying to deal with the mounting fiscal difficulties. Public debt, as a percentage of GDP, doubled from 34.5% in 1981 to 62.2% in 1987, and the average for the period was 48.4%. The average trade deficit also increased, as a percentage of GDP, by 0.7% between 1975-1980 and 1981-1987 and the average current account deficit by 1% (1981-1987 averages: Trade deficit: 13.4%, Current Account deficit: 4.7%). During this period, Greece's trade relations with the EC were further strengthened, as 54% of Greek exports went to the EC and 51% of imports originated in EC countries.

The downward trend for most indicators and the continued macro-economic difficulties are the main characteristics of this critical period for Greece.

The 1988-1992 period This was a period of political uncertainty, resulting from three government changes in a short period of time (two in 1989 and one in 1990). Despite this fact, the implementation of an economic stabilisation policy since 1990 and the funds from the First Community Support Framework (1989-1993) helped the economy regain its growth potential.

The average annual increase in GDP between 1988 and 1992, was 2.3% (see Table 2.3). Investment, as a percentage of GDP, was around 25%, while unemployment rose further to 8.7% in 1992.

The trade deficit substantially increased throughout this period, reaching 14.1% of GDP in 1992, while the current account deficit improved to an average of 2.7% of GDP between 1988 and 1992, aided by the EU transfers.

Nevertheless, some of the main goals of the stabilisation policy were not met. Inflation rose again in 1990 and was 16.6% on average for the period. Interest rates continued to rise and in 1992 were much higher than inflation. The worst development of this period, that still in 2001 remains the major problem for Greek public finances, has been the huge increase in public debt. Specifically, public debt increased from 66.8% of GDP to 89% of GDP in just four years. This development was due to the huge increases in general government deficits that were 13.3% on average for the period, with highs of 14.4% and 16.1% in the politically unstable years of 1989 and 1990 respectively.

After the initial worsening of some indicators in this period, a promising sign emerged with the apparent consensus of both main parties towards the goal of stabilisation.

The 1993-2001 period The aforementioned consensus ensured a smooth transition of power in 1993, when the socialist party PASOK won that year's elections. A revised stabilisation programme was created with the goal of meeting all the so-called 'Maastricht criteria' or the criteria necessary for Greece's inclusion in the euro-zone.

Despite an initial decrease of 1.7% in 1993 (see Table 2.4), GDP growth resumed at a very high pace. Investment also increased, especially after 1996, while a negative development has been evident in unemployment that surpassed 10%. The trade deficit has again worsened (15.2% of GDP in 1997), while the current account situation has not improved substantially despite the positive contribution of the Second Community Support Framework (1994-1999).

Other economic indicators moved in line with Greece's goal of joining EMU in 2001. The March 1998 entry of the drachma into the Exchange Rate Mechanism, that was combined with a 13.8% devaluation and a series of anti-inflationary and privatisation measures, sent a clear signal of the government's commitment and satisfied the currency stability criterion for entry in the EMU. Inflation decreased 10-fold since 1990 approaching the level of the other EU members. Interest rates have also decreased, at a much slower pace, from their high of 24% in 1990 to 4.6% in December 2000, very close to that of the other euro members (Bank of Greece, 2001: 124).

Government debt, as a percentage of GDP, was at 111.6% in 1993 and despite the efforts to reduce it, it still remains above 100%. The budget deficits, another persistent feature of the Greek economy, have been tackled in the 1994-2001 period, with substantial reductions in government expenditure and a wide-ranging privatisation programme.

It is obvious that despite the great, and ultimately successful, effort to meet the euro criteria, a lot remains to be done. The prolonged stabilisation policy has created resentment from large parts of the population. There are, nevertheless, signs of a political consensus in terms of the measures necessary for development and the private sector is also responding positively to the improved economic environment.

The various indicators that were analysed in this section must be compared with those in other EU countries since economic convergence is considered a pre-requisite for further integration steps. Overall, the restrictive economic policies and the EU's fund transfers, have brought some indicators into line with most other EU countries. However, other indicators, and especially those related to the standard of living, are still behind those of most developed nations. Worth mentioning are the per capita GDP figures, adjusted for purchasing power parities. Between 1981 and 1998 Greece's per capita GDP has increased from 65% of the Community average to 68%, the lowest increase for all Community countries below the average in 1981. In fact, since 1990, Greece is the country with the lowest per capita GDP among the EU-15 (Epilogi - Statistics, 2000: 20-21). Despite the success of the Convergence Program in reducing inflation, fiscal deficits, public debts and interest rates, the long-term real convergence requires further positive developments in GDP and productivity growth, unemployment and other quality-of-life indicators.

Additional features of the economic environment A central feature of the Greek economic environment is public administration. After the changes that the dictatorship imposed on public administration, the return to democracy brought with it the pre-1967 structure. The international developments in public administration management were not incorporated in the Greek administrative system and the only major change was a reduction in the number of hierarchical levels, through the removal of some of the higher ones (Makrydimitris, 1996: 124).

In the 1980s, decentralisation was promoted and the role of regional administration was strengthened. In the 1990s, three important measures further increased this trend. The first one was the increased authority of the General Secretaries of the regions on a variety of local issues. The second was the direct election of Prefects by the electorate. The third, and most important, was the unification of small communities in larger municipalities, under the auspices of the 'Kapodistrias' programme (Konsolas, 1998).

The major problem of public administration is its dependence on political parties. This especially affects hiring and promotions, leading to a low quality of service and an over-inflated number of employees. A more transparent system for the hiring of all civil servants was introduced in the early 1990s and its use has been extended to most hiring decisions of the wider public sector. Its successful implementation was considered a major step towards achieving meritocracy in the public sector.

Another issue for the Greek economy is the systematic efforts of many businesses to conduct their transactions without having them appear in their records. This 'underground economy' has become a major problem, which decreases tax revenues and distorts most official statistics. The sectors mostly affected are small-scale manufacturing industry and most of the services industries.

Certain studies (for example, Pavlopoulos, 1987; and more recently Kanellopoulos et al., 1995) have attempted to estimate the size of the 'underground economy' as a percentage of GDP. The results for the mid-1980s were in the range of 25-35% of GDP (Vavouras and Karavitis, 1997: 129-130; Drakatos, 1997: 119). The recently introduced Revised System of National Accounts aims at capturing a large part of the 'hidden' transactions, so that at least the official government statistics will more accurately reflect the real situation (Vavouras and Karavitis, 1997: 135; Drakatos, 1997: 119-120).

Population and labour force In the sub-period 1975-1980, population in Greece rose at an average annual rate of 1.2%. Since 1981, however, annual increases have been much lower, never exceeding 0.9%. According to the official results of the 1991 census Greece had a population of 10,259,900 people, while the provisional results of the 2001 census show a small (6.6%) increase to 10,939,771 people (Kathimerini, 2001: 7). The share of urban population has been rapidly increasing in the post World War II years, and has recently stabilised around 59%. Rural population (28.3% in 1991) has been decreasing, more recently in favour of the semi-urban segment (those living in towns with under 10,000 inhabitants). The composition of the population is also changing in terms of the dominant age groups. Those aged over 70 are now 9.3% of the population (4.3% in 1951, 6.9% in 1971) and both the pension and health service systems are under increasing pressure. This problem will be exacerbated in the future as those ready to enter the labour force (under 20s) represent only 26.8% of the population, down from 39.1% in 1951 and 33% in 1971 (Epilogi - Statistics, 2000: 66-68).

Out of the approximately 3.85 million people employed in 1997, 14.7% are University graduates, while another 8.2% hold diplomas from other technical or vocational schools (Epilogi - Statistics, 2000: 80). The overall picture has improved substantially from previous decades (Glytsos, 1995). Employment statistics have been slow at reflecting the large number of foreign immigrants seeking work in Greece. In the 1990s their number has increased dramatically, especially after the changes in Eastern Europe, and they are now estimated at 600,000. The process of their legalisation, that started in 1997, has provided some useful data, a lot remains to be done however, if this immigrant population is to be fully recorded.

The employment statistics also reflect the changing importance of the different economic sectors. The agricultural sector has witnessed constant falls in employment and its share was in 1998 down to 17.8%, while the industrial sector, that was before 1971 the main recipient of those leaving agriculture and the rural areas, has had in the past three decades a slowly decreasing share of employment, 23.1% in 1998. The services sector is the only one registering constant increases, and in 1998 accounted for 59.1% of total employment (Epilogi - Statistics, 2000: 77).

Review of the Literature on Greek Industrial Competitiveness

This section contains a brief review of a number of published works that examine the competitiveness of Greek manufacturing and service industries. Particular emphasis is placed on those studies that explore the factors affecting the varied performance of different sectors.

Factor Conditions, Home Demand and the Government's Role

Researchers have used basic factors (especially raw materials and cheap labour), government policy and some aspects of the Greek market to explain the diverging development of many manufacturing industries. The industry definitions were usually aggregated (most often the 20 sectors in the National Statistical Service of Greece's classification), although some studies have used data on an expanded number of industries.

The first major study after the post-World War II reconstruction that dealt with these issues was provided by Coutsoumaris (1963) in one of the first publications of the newly established Centre of Economic Research. Coutsoumaris, in his introductory chapter, identified the factors that shaped the pattern of development of Greek industry as: resource availability, capital availability and allocation, skilled labour supply, indigenous entrepreneurship, domestic market nature and size, tariff protection and government intervention, social institutions and attitudes, and supporting services, such as power facilities and trade activities. He then examined several characteristics of each of the 20 major industrial sectors including number and size of producing units, mechanical power, output, employment (education, skill levels, wage, non-wage, family), investment, capital-labour mix, ownership form, and financial and cost structure. Also, the domestic and foreign markets were analysed in terms of their structure, their income elasticities of demand and some organisational aspects.

Geographical distribution and regional concentration was the subject of a separate chapter, where Athens was found to have more than its 'fair' share of most producer-goods industries, such as petroleum refining and metal manufactures, various durable goods industries, such as furniture, printing and publishing and some of the consumer goods industries, such as footwear and clothing. The performance of the 20 industrial sectors over time was the focus of the book's second section, where output growth, value added, labour and capital productivity, returns to labour and capital and capacity utilisation were used as measures. The industries considered to have an advantage for the future were material-oriented, labour-intensive and transport-extensive with low technical knowledge and skill requirements (for example, textiles, footwear, clothing, rubber articles) and a few transport-intensive or regionalised industries whose products had high material content.

In another subsequent publication of the Centre of Planning and Economic Research, Prodromidis (1976) adopted a more formal approach. He estimated export demand functions for 14 sectors and sub-sectors based on data from the 1960s. Exports were found to be linked to prices and domestic and foreign consumption growth. One of the most interesting findings of the study was that Greek supply conditions determined to a great extent exports of certain products, like textiles, machinery and mining products, while world demand conditions affected more Greece's traditional exports (food, beverages, tobacco and other agriculture-related products). His recommendations were in favour of improving the quality, and thus increasing the price, of Greek exports and focusing on expanding the domestic production of textiles, chemicals and certain agricultural products.

In a rather different approach, Negreponti-Delivani (1986) analysed a series of factors, responsible for the structure and performance of Greek manufacturing industry. Among those, were factors related to the domestic market, not so much in its size that she, of course, considered limited, but in its composition. The relative numbers of farmers, salaried employees and self-employed, their propensity to save or consume, and the different taxation levels for each group, were presented and their effects on exports and imports were estimated. Government policy was considered another major influence on Greek industry and the focus was on tax policy (and the related problem of tax avoidance), foreign direct investment policy and subsidies. In the second part of the book, the performance of Greek industry as a whole, as well as of 20 broad sectors individually was investigated. The major indicators used were: investments, productivity, firm size, exports, imports, persons employed, output and value-added for the period 1963-1980. While the relative position of most industries had changed within the time frame employed, the sectors with above average performance were: food products, textiles, apparel, non-metallic minerals and metal products and to a lesser extent beverages, tobacco, chemicals, petroleum and basic metallurgy.

In an attempt to analyse the correlation between export performance and some structural characteristics of 82 Greek industries, Giannitsis (1983) reached some interesting conclusions. His findings were that capital-intensive and low-wage industries were the ones where exports were rising; that there was little or no correlation between export performance and the degree of vertical integration, or the degree an industry was related to others further up or down the production chain, whereas there was a positive correlation of export performance with the concentration of domestic production in big units.

Greece was also one of the countries studied by Leamer (1984) in his detailed empirical study of comparative advantage and resource abundance profiles. Greece, in line with its resource profile that includes an abundance of land area in a Mediterranean climate zone, was found to export agricultural products in 1958, and mainly labour intensive manufactures in 1975, while importing machinery.

In the 1990s, Lolos and Papagiannakis (1993) examined factor conditions for several years and found that Greece exported capital-intensive products and imported skilled labour-intensive products. Over time the share of total exports of products requiring low or medium-skilled labour had increased. In terms of product groups, Greece, in the 1980s, had a comparative advantage in food, beverages and tobacco, textiles and apparel (including shoes, leather and fur) and construction-related products (mainly non-metallic minerals and aluminium), while in the 1970s some chemical, steel and metal processing industries also exhibited a high comparative advantage.

Baltzakis and Katsos (1996), in a wide-ranging study by the Centre of Planning and Economic Research, used export and import data to measure competitiveness and concluded that the most competitive sectors were: textiles, apparel, tobacco, petroleum and non-metallic minerals. Two of those sectors, however, apparel and tobacco, along with the less competitive publishing industry, had the greatest decreases in competitiveness between 1989 and 1994. Changes in unit labour cost and the effective exchange rate were also presented and a market shares analysis was conducted, showing that the slight drop in Greece's exports as a percentage of total OECD exports between 1980 and 1992, was due to the lack of major changes in the product mix or the recipients of Greek exports.

In-depth studies of individual industries are conducted by the Centre of Planning and Economic Research, the Foundation of Economic and Industrial Research and ICAP, a private data bank and consulting company. These studies focus especially on labour costs, resource availability, the size and structure of the domestic market and government policy. Moreover, an important survey, in the 1990s, of 30 broad sectors of Greek manufacturing and services (Patsouratis and Rossolymos, 1997) also emphasised factor costs, domestic market attributes, government policy and firm strategy.

Greece and the EU

The accession of Greece to the European Community had major consequences for both manufacturing and service firms. A number of studies conducted before or right after 1981 considered the effect of reduced protection on the size, export potential and productivity of Greek manufacturing industries. For some of the writers, full membership was seen as another step in Greece's continuing liberalisation, affecting, therefore, only slightly the established patterns of Greek industry. Others saw accession as a more fundamental change that would shape the development of the Greek industrial profile in the decades to follow (for a critical review of most of these studies see Giannitsis, 1988a: 37-74).

When the first data from the post-1981 period became available, many influential books and articles were published (for a list of the post-1980 works on Greece and the EU see Ioakeimidis, 1996: 154-160). These works also aimed at investigating a wider variety of influences on the development of individual industries.

Giannitsis (1988a) attempted to estimate the effects of accession on manufacturing industries and Greek trade. First, changes in tariffs were calculated and the EU countries' share of Greek exports and imports was presented at the 3-digit SITC level. Giannitsis found that, after 1981, Greek competitiveness in food, beverages and tobacco (with few exceptions, such as vegetable oils and fruits) had been reduced, especially in its trade with other EU countries, influenced by changes in protection and Greece's participation in the Common Agricultural Policy. In terms of other 'industrial' products, one-sixth of the 95 industries studied had improved their position after 1981, one-third did remain at the same level, while the rest (representing about 50% of value added among all industries) had seen their position worsen slightly or substantially. Again, changes in trade patterns with other EU countries have had very negative effects. Giannitsis also noted a reduction in average firm size after 1981.

Around the same time, Mitsos (1989) dealt with similar issues. Mitsos calculated in detail tariffs and non-tariff barriers for a list of products, presented the changes brought about by EC membership and correlated protection levels with imports and with certain characteristics of the domestic industries. He also analysed export data from 1980 and 1985, and Greece was found to have an especially high 'revealed comparative advantage' for both years in fruit and vegetables, fresh and preserved, other food products, cement, aluminium, other minerals, and apparel. Four groups of determinants were used in an attempt to explain Greece's comparative advantage in certain products. The first one was factors of production, where the most successful industries were found to be capital-intensive, while the correlation with skilled labour levels was inconclusive. The second group comprises of industrial structure variables (number and size of units, geographic concentration, domestic market shares), where only a possible positive relation with firms' size was statistically significant. The third group of determinants was related to the characteristics of the product, and Greece's advantage was concentrated in products also exported by countries with lower income levels. The fourth group were the tariff and non-tariff protection variables, where, although most results were not statistically significant, there seemed to be a negative correlation between protection and competitiveness.

In another comprehensive publication about Greece and the EU, Hassid and Katsos (1992) correlated the performance of aggregated industrial sectors with concentration ratios, capital/labour ratios, labour productivity, labour costs, investment levels and tariff levels. Performance was calculated in relation to output, prices, wages, returns on capital, import penetration and export volume. The best-performing group of industries was found to have had higher concentration ratios, higher capital/labour ratios, higher unit sizes and higher labour productivity and labour costs than the worst-performing and the 'intermediate' groups. Export subsidies and investment levels provided mixed conclusions and their role was not clear, while the correlation for some of the other factors was not very strong.

In two publications about Greece in the new millenium, a separate chapter was devoted to the competitiveness of Greece's manufacturing industry. Giannitsis (1988b) found that Greece was improving its advantage in traditional industrial products, while the advantage of agricultural and raw materials industries was slightly decreasing. Greece's advantage, was, however, very low in 'technologically advanced' products or products for which world demand was rapidly growing. These developments were attributed to lack of investment in these 'high-tech' industries, the low levels of R&D conducted by Greek firms, the absence of protection for 'infant industries' and the government policy on research promotion, education and infrastructure, which made most firms rely on labour cost advantages and government subsidies.

Kintis (1995) considered Greece's competitive advantage to be eroding in many industries. The factors that were causing this were grouped in two categories, one related to the structural deficiencies of Greek manufacturing industry and the second to the environment in which firms operated. The small size of firms and their orientation to traditional industrial activities were considered the most important structural deficiencies. In terms of the environment, the rapid liberalisation after 1973, coinciding with the world economic crisis, the macro-economic and tax policies of the State, the lack of mobility for skilled personnel and the low level of country infrastructure, were the major influences on firm's performance.

Porter's Diamond

Competitiveness and export performance have been the subject of an increasing literature, of which typical examples were mentioned above. There still lacks, however, a holistic framework to explore the competitiveness of Greek manufacturing industries. Also, the multitude of determinants in Porter's diamond are not all featured in this body of research. Nevertheless, the diamond framework is being increasingly noted and has been used in two relatively recent influential studies.

Hassid (1994) considered cost data and exchange rates as inadequate to explain the competitiveness of Greek industries. A questionnaire survey of Greek firms was then conducted, with Porter's framework as a basis for some of the questions. The areas where firms believe improvement is necessary for competitive performance were mainly related to human capital and production technology.

Pitelis et al. (1997) in his study on competitiveness, industrial strategy and the future of Greek industry, commissioned by the Ministry of Development, emphasised human capital, technology and innovation, transformation economies (that is, economies of scale, scope, learning, time etc.), infrastructure, natural resources and government policy as the determining factors of competitiveness. Greece was found to have a disadvantage in domestic market size, size of firms, lack of high multinational activity, specialisation in low- or medium-technology activities and high defence spending. However, this study envisaged ways of turning these characteristics into advantages, for example (and this, in fact, was one of its basic recommendations) by linking small businesses, especially those in geographic proximity, so as to enable them to retain their flexibility, while developing economies of scale and scope.

Although interest in Porter's diamond has been growing, there is still no comprehensive application for Greece, that would include an in-depth analysis of trade data at a disaggregated level and detailed case studies, following Porter's framework.

The Competitive Industrial Structure of Greece

This section presents the methodology for the entire study and the results of the primary data analysis. First, Porter's methodology is articulated and its use in the Greek case is explained. Then, trade and other data are used to identify the competitive Greek industries and group them in clusters. In the last section, the methodology for the conduct of the case studies is presented, along with the reasons for selecting the five particular industry case studies.

Porter's Methodology and its Application to Greece

As was previously mentioned, Porter (1990) studied ten, mainly developed, countries, six from Europe (Germany, Italy, United Kingdom, Denmark, Sweden and Switzerland), three from Asia (Japan, South Korea and Singapore) and the United States. Additional research on other countries has been conducted by teams headed by Porter, such as the widely available New Zealand (Crocombe et al., 1991) and Canada studies (Porter and Monitor Company, 1991). Independent researchers have also applied Porter's methodology for identifying competitive industries, for example, in the cases of Ireland (O' Donnellan, 1994) and The Netherlands (Jacobs and De Jong, 1992). In the original 1990 book, the internationally competitive industries were identified with the use of international trade, foreign investment and other data from three points in time (1971, 1978, 1985). Industries were defined as narrowly as possible, in an attempt to represent 'strategically distinct businesses' (Porter, 1990: 739).

The basic measure used to determine an industry's position in international competition was the industry's share of world exports. All industries in a country, at the 3-digit, 4-digit and 5-digit level of the Standard International Trade Classification, were included in the analysis.

The lowest level of disaggregation was used, that is, if data were available for the 5-digit level, at least for one industry, then the 4-digit industry was excluded and the share of the remaining 5-digit industries (if it was not available) was calculated as a residual. Then the exports of these industries were divided by the world exports for the particular years used, in order to calculate the world export share.

The list of competitive industries included, initially, those industries that had a world export share above the nation's cut-off. The cut-off was calculated by dividing a country's total exports (as given in the UN International Trade Statistics) by the world's total exports. The competitive lists were then modified according to additional trade-related criteria. Specifically, industries with a negative trade balance were excluded, unless their world export share was more than twice the country's cut-off. Also, industries that were among a country's top fifty in terms of export value for that particular year, with a positive or slightly negative trade balance, were included, regardless of their export share. Industries were kept off the list if their exports were exclusively to neighbouring countries or if exports were dominated by subsidiaries of foreign firms.

This list was extended to include industries where there was evidence of substantial outward FDI, if this investment was 'based on skills and strengths developed in the nation' (Porter, 1990: 740). Also, many service industries were added using published data and interviews. Other data, as well as the researcher's judgement, were used to modify the lists of competitive industries to a small extent.

In order to highlight the competitive patterns in each nation and identify the interconnections among its successful industries, the list of competitive industries was used to produce the cluster charts. All competitive industries were clustered into 16 broad categories that were further grouped in 'Upstream Industries', 'Industrial and Supporting Functions' and 'Final Consumption Goods and Services'. 'Upstream Industries' included the Materials/Metals, Forest Products, Petroleum/Chemicals and Semiconductors/Computers clusters. 'Industrial and Supporting Functions' included the Multiple Business, Transportation, Power Generation & Distribution, Office, Telecommunications and Defence clusters. The 'Final Consumption Goods and Services' grouping included the largest number of industries that belong to the Food/Beverages, Textiles/Apparel, Housing/Household, Health Care, Personal and Entertainment/Leisure clusters.

Within each cluster, industries were put into four categories in an attempt to capture vertical interconnections. The 'primary goods' category is the one where most industries were placed, as it includes both end-products and self-contained components. The 'machinery' category represents the industries producing machinery for the production of the primary goods, while 'specialty inputs' consists of the necessary inputs for this production process. The related 'services' industries form a separate category in each cluster.

The cluster charts for the years studied constituted the basis for the selection of the case studies. The case studies were a detailed illustration of the industry's history in the country examined and, briefly, in the rest of the world, in an attempt to identify the sources of competitive advantage or disadvantage. The industries selected were picked from a variety of clusters and included both service and manufacturing industries. They were a combination of well-known highly successful industries and some lesser known star performers with industries where competitive advantage had shifted over time. The emphasis on relatively successful industries can be justified by the fact that in an open economy the share of the competitive industries is increasing, while a study of non-competitive ones would offer insights into a small and shrinking part of the economy. Porter also mentions that examples of non-competitive industries were studied as a result of the extensive review of the world market for each case. Natural resource-dependent industries were mostly avoided, as Porter (1990) considers that their advantage is well explained through other theories.

The methodology has been criticised, along with the other parts of Porter's (1990) framework, and a summary of the criticism is available in Chapter 1. I would like to emphasise here three points that are relevant for the application of Porter's (1990) methodology to Greece.

The first one is related to the use of mainly export and, to a lesser extent, foreign direct investment data, which has been criticised by many scholars (among others Grant, 1991; Bellak and Weiss, 1993; Rugman and D' Cruz, 1993; and Cartwright, 1993). It should be noted that an alternative measure that would be internationally comparable and widely available at the level of disaggregation required is hard to find and that Porter used additional national and international data in order to modify the lists of competitive industries. A second point that has received a lot of criticism (especially by Rugman, 1991; Rugman and D' Cruz, 1993; and Bellak and Weiss, 1993) is Porter's treatment of foreign direct investment and the exclusion from the competitive lists of industries with exports dominated by subsidiaries of multinationals, when these subsidiaries lack autonomy in formulating strategy. The reasons behind this policy were not considered satisfactory by the above mentioned scholars and even Porter himself (1990: 740) admits that few industries were excluded with this rationale. The third point, that has been mentioned in the criticisms of Porter's framework (for example in Harris and Watson, 1993: 248), is the exclusive selection of successful industries to be studied. Although the rationale for that was explained above, the question of whether unsuccessful industries exhibit some of the same characteristics was not adequately addressed by Porter.

In the Greek case, trade data were mainly used to identify competitive industries, in order to obtain an objective view of the industries' positions in international competition. Other data were also used with the purpose of adding service industries to the list of competitive Greek industries. Personal judgement and interviews were helpful in verifying the overall picture of the Greek economy that was obtained; however, no additions or subtractions were made based on them. The only adjustments to the lists of competitive industries were made using export or foreign investment data, in accordance to Porter's (1990) various criteria.

Additionally, no industries were excluded from the competitive list because of significant multinational presence, due both to the controversy mentioned above and the lack of data. Export data at company level were not widely available and the degree of subsidiaries' autonomy was hard to determine. However, issues of ownership were given particular attention, especially in the case studies.

Moreover, in selecting the case studies, the objections regarding the emphasis on very successful industries was taken into account. One of the five industries studied, was uncompetitive (the men's outerwear industry) and its position has further declined in the last nine years.

Industrial Clusters in Greece

The years studied in the Greek case are 1978, 1985 and 1992. Selection was based on the availability of comparable and accurate trade data from the UN International Trade Statistics. The most recent year when accurate trade data was available at the required level of disaggregation, was 1992, while the 1978 and 1985 data were the focus of Porter's analysis. This, however, was not the only reason for the selection. These three years belong to three distinct sub-periods in the era after the restoration of democracy in Greece (1974-present). Specifically, 1978 was in the middle of the 1975-1980 period, when the effects of the democratic system of governance were already evident and the country was preparing for accession to the EU; 1985 was part of the first post-accession period of 1981-1987, and 1992 was the final year of the turbulent 1988-1992 period.

The industrial base of Greece is rather narrow, considering its level of development. Greece's share of world exports in 1992 was 0.26% and only five clusters of industries had a share above that figure. These clusters were: Food/Beverages, Textiles/Apparel, Housing/Household, Personal (all four belonging to the category 'Final Consumption Goods and Services') and Materials/Metals (from the 'Upstream Industries' group). The same five clusters exceeded Greece's average share of world exports in both 1978 and 1985. The complete cluster chart for 1992 is presented in Table

2.5, while the cluster charts for 1978 and 1985 are in Tables A.1 and A.2 respectively, in the Appendix.

The Food/Beverages cluster, according to Table 2.6, was the one with the highest share of world exports for 1992, with 0.7%. Its share has been constantly rising (it was 0.5% in 1978 and 0.6% in 1985 as seen in Table 2.7) as well as its importance among Greek clusters. The range of competitive industries was very wide in this cluster and Greece had a relatively strong position in both the primary goods and the specialty inputs categories, with world export shares of 0.7% in both. The lack of any competitive Food/Beverages machinery industries was not a characteristic of this cluster only, but common to all Greek industrial clusters. The Food/Beverages cluster included many of the industries with the highest world export shares among all Greek industries (among them the first one, olive oil, where Greece had a 30% share). Although agricultural products was where Greece has the highest world export shares, processed food and beverages represented a substantial part of the competitive exports from this cluster, that accounted for 27.5% of all Greek exports.

The second cluster in importance was the Textiles/Apparel cluster that had a world export share of 0.6% for 1992. This cluster saw a rise in its share between 1978 and 1985, when it reached 0.9%, the highest among Greek clusters at the time. This rise was due to the increased shares of the primary goods industries, mainly the apparel ones. Since 1985, these industries experienced a drop in their world export share, which was matched by an equal drop in the share of the specialty inputs industries. In 1992, the best performing industries in this cluster were cotton yarn (from the specialty inputs category), fur products and some of the women's apparel industries. Exports from the competitive Textile/Apparel industries represented 23.6% of total Greek exports in 1992, 3.4% less than in 1985, but still 1.6% more than in 1978. The other two important 'Final Consumption Goods and Services' clusters were the Housing/Household and the Personal, each accounting for approximately 5% of Greek exports in 1992.

The Personal cluster had the higher share of world exports (0.6%) but this was almost entirely the result of Greece's 20% share of non-Virginia type unstripped tobacco exports. Between 1985 and 1992, the range of competitive tobacco-related industries increased, to include stripped tobacco and cigarettes. There was also a rise in the cluster's share of Greek exports (from 3.8% to 5.3%).

The range of competitive industries in the Housing/Household cluster (share of 1992 world exports: 0.3%) was wider, and has remained so since 1978, despite the slight drops in Greek and world export shares. The strongest industries belonged to the specialty inputs category and were mostly related to building materials, although some competitive primary

Table 2.5 Clusters of internationally competitive Greek industries, 1992

Primary goods	**MATERIALS/METALS** IRON AND STEEL **Iron, simple steel coils** **Tinned plates, sheets** *Iron, steel, universal and other plates, sheets** *Iron, simple steel, wire* *Iron, steel, tubes and pipes* *Thin plate, rolled, of iron or simple steel* METAL MANUFACTURES *Aluminium transport boxes and iron, steel, aluminium compressed gas cylinders** NON-FERROUS METALS **Copper tubes, pipes** **Aluminium bars, wire etc.** **Aluminium foil** **Aluminium powders, tubes, tube fittings*** *Aluminium plates, sheets, strip* *Aluminium and alloys, unwrought* *Copper plates, sheets and strip* OTHER MATERIALS AND WASTE **Natural abrasives** **Asbestos** **Other crude minerals, exc. clay, asbestos*** *Other refractory construction material** Metaliferous non-ferrous waste Non-ferrous metal waste and scrap, exc. copper*
Machinery	
Specialty inputs	**Aluminium ores and concentrates** **Alumina (aluminium oxide)** *Zinc ores and concentrates*
Services	

Primary goods	**FOREST PRODUCTS** WOOD Plywood of wood sheets
Machinery	
Specialty inputs	
Services	

Primary goods	**SEMICONDUCTORS/COMPUTERS**
Machinery	
Specialty inputs	
Services	

Table 2.5 (cont.)

Primary goods	**PETROLEUM/CHEMICALS** **Spirit-type jet fuel and other light petroleum oils*** *Polyvinyl chloride in primary forms* *Halogenated derivatives of hydrocarbons*
Machinery	
Specialty inputs	
Services	

Primary goods	**MULTIPLE BUSINESS**
Machinery	
Specialty inputs	
Services	

Primary goods	**TRANSPORTATION** *Fishing vessels and other ships** Tugs and floating structures**
Machinery	
Specialty inputs	*Articles of rubber, exc. other articles of unhardened rubber**
Services	**Shipping#**

Primary goods	**POWER GENERATION AND DISTRIBUTION** *Insulated wire, cable, bars etc.*
Machinery	
Specialty inputs	
Services	

Primary goods	**OFFICE**
Machinery	
Specialty inputs	
Services	

Primary goods	**TELECOMMUNICATIONS**
Machinery	
Specialty inputs	
Services	

Primary goods	**DEFENSE**
Machinery	
Specialty inputs	
Services	

Table 2.5 (cont.)

Primary goods	**FOOD/BEVERAGES** BASIC FOODS *Fish, fresh or chilled, exc. fillets* *Fish dried, salted, exc. cod* *Rice in the husk or husked* *Rice, broken** *Groats, meal and pellets, of wheat** *Other cereal meals and flours* Edible nuts, fresh or dried** Crude animal materials, exc. gut, bladders* FRUITS AND VEGETABLES **Other vegetables*** **Oranges, fresh or dried** **Grapes, fresh** **Grapes, dried (raisins)** **Stone fruit, fresh** **Figs and other fruit, fresh or dried*** *Potatoes fresh, exc. sweet* *Mandarines, clementines etc., fresh or dried** *Lemons, grapefruit etc.* PROCESSED FOOD **Fruit, preserved exc. fruit juices*** **Vegetables, prepared, preserved** *Milk and cream, fresh** *Cheese and curd* *Shell fish, prepared, preserved* *Pastry, cakes, etc.* *Sugar candy, non-chocolate* Fruit or vegetable juice, exc. orange** EDIBLE OILS **Olive oil** *Soya bean oil* *Cotton seed oil* BEVERAGES *Wine of fresh grapes* *Spirits obtained by distilling wine or grape marc* Other alcoholic beverages or compounds*
Machinery	
Specialty inputs	**Nitrogen, phosphorus and potassium fertilisers** **Durum wheat, unmilled** **Maize (corn), unmilled** *Nitrogenous fertilisers, exc. urea** *Chemical potassic fertilisers exc. potassium chloride** *Seeds for other fixed oils, exc. copra** Beet-pulp, bagasse Feeding stuff for animals, exc. oil-cake etc.**
Services	

Table 2.5 (cont.)

Primary goods	**TEXTILES/APPAREL** **FABRICS** **Made-up articles, exc. linens and other furnishings*** **Pile etc. cotton fabrics** Grey woven cotton fabric **APPAREL** **Woman's coats and jackets, exc. of man-made fibres*** **Women's skirts** **Women's blouses, exc. of man-made fibres*** **Women's suits, exc. of cotton or man-made fibres*** **Women's dresses, suits, etc., exc. of synthetic fibres*** **Other outer garments, accessories*** **Under garments, knitted, of cotton, non-elastic** **Articles of furskin** *Men's suits* *Men's trousers, exc. of cotton** *Men's jackets, blazers etc.* *Women's dresses, exc. of man-made fibres** *Jerseys, pull-overs, of cotton or regenerated fibres** *Under garments, knitted, other than of cotton** **OTHER** **Hides and skins, raw, exc. bovine*** **Furskins tanned or dressed** *Leather, exc. of other bovine cattle**
Machinery	
Specialty inputs	**Raw cotton, exc. linters** **Cotton, carded or combed, inc. linters, waste*** **Cotton yarn, exc. 40-80 km per kg*** **Yarn of regenerated fibres** *Yarn of synthetic fibres, exc. polyamide and discontinuous synthetic fibres** Old textile articles, rags
Services	

	HEALTH CARE
Primary goods	
Machinery	
Specialty inputs	
Services	

Table 2.5 (cont.)

Primary goods	**HOUSING/HOUSEHOLD** **Floor coverings exc. knotted carpets and carpets of man-made materials*** *Coarse ceramic houseware* *Household equipment of base metal, exc. domestic type heating and cooking apparatus* Cutlery**
Machinery	
Specialty inputs	**Cement** **Building stone, worked** *Stone, sand and gravel* Lime and unfired mineral building products**
Services	

Primary goods	**PERSONAL** *Cigarettes* *Other articles of precious metal*
Machinery	
Specialty inputs	**Tobacco, unstripped, non-Virginia type*** **Tobacco, stripped, non-Virginia type*** *Tobacco refuse**
Services	

Primary goods	**ENTERTAINMENT/LEISURE** Coin-operated electric gramophones*
Machinery	
Specialty inputs	
Services	**Tourism#**

KEY

Times New Roman	0.26% world export share or higher, but less than 0.52% share
Italics	*0.52% world export share or higher, but less than 1.04% share*
Bold	**1.04% world export share or above**

*	Calculated residuals
**	Added due to significant export value in a segmented industry
#	Added based on in-country research

Source: Author's calculations based on UN, *International Trade Statistics Yearbook*.

Table 2.6 Percentage of Greek exports by cluster and vertical stage, 1992

	MATERIALS/METALS				FOREST PRODUCTS				PETROLEUM/CHEMICALS				SEMICONDUCTORS/COMPUTERS				UPSTREAM INDUSTRIES	
	SC	CSC	SW	CSW	SC	CSC	SW	CSW	SC	CSC	SW	CSW	SC	CSC	SW	CSW	SC	SW
PRI. GOODS	8.9	-3.4	0.3	-0.1	0.2	-0.5	0.0	-0.1	5.3	-6.2	0.1	-0.1	0.0	0.0	0.0	0.0	14.4	0.1
MACHINERY	0.0	0.0	0.0	0.0	0.0	0.0	0.0	0.0	0.0	0.0	0.0	0.0	0.0	0.0	0.0	0.0	0.0	0.0
SPE. INPUTS	1.1	-1.0	0.3	0.0	0.0	0.0	0.0	0.0	0.0	0.0	0.0	0.0	0.0	0.0	0.0	0.0	1.1	0.2
TOTAL	10.0	-4.4	0.3	-0.1	0.2	-0.5	0.0	-0.1	5.3	-6.2	0.1	-0.1	0.0	0.0	0.0	0.0	15.5	0.1

	MULTIPLE BUSINESS				TRANSPORTATION				POWER GENERATION & DISTRIBUTION				OFFICE				TELECOMMUNICATIONS				DEFENSE				INDUSTRIAL & SUPPORTING FUNCTIONS	
	SC	CSC	SW	CSW	SC	CSC	SW	CSW	SC	CSC	SW	CSW	SC	CSC	SW	CSW	SC	CSC	SW	CSW	SC	CSC	SW	CSW	SC	SW
PRI. GOODS	0.0	-0.1	0.1	0.0	0.1	-0.3	0.1	0.0	1.0	+0.4	0.1	0.0	0.0	0.0	0.0	0.0	0.0	0.0	0.0	0.0	0.0	-0.1	0.0	0.0	1.1	0.0
MACHINERY	0.0	0.0	0.0	0.0	0.0	0.0	0.0	0.0	0.0	0.0	0.0	0.0	0.0	0.0	0.0	0.0	0.0	0.0	0.0	0.0	0.0	0.0	0.0	0.0	0.0	0.0
SPE. INPUTS	0.0	0.0	0.1	0.0	0.1	+0.1	0.1	0.0	0.0	0.0	0.0	0.0	0.0	0.0	0.0	0.0	0.0	0.0	0.0	0.0	0.0	0.0	0.0	0.0	0.1	0.0
TOTAL	0.0	-0.1	0.2	0.0	0.2	-0.2	0.2	0.0	1.0	+0.4	0.1	0.0	0.0	0.0	0.0	0.0	0.0	0.0	0.0	0.0	0.0	-0.1	0.0	0.0	1.2	0.0

	FOOD/BEVERAGE				TEXTILES/APPAREL				HOUSING/HOUSEHOLD				HEALTH CARE				PERSONAL				ENTERTAINMENT/LEISURE				FINAL CONSUMPTION GOODS & SERVICES	
	SC	CSC	SW	CSW	SC	CSC	SW	CSW	SC	CSC	SW	CSW	SC	CSC	SW	CSW	SC	CSC	SW	CSW	SC	CSC	SW	CSW	SC	SW
PRI. GOODS	22.3	+1.5	19.7	-0.4	0.7	0.0	0.7	0.0	0.9	+0.1	0.1	0.0	0.0	-0.1	0.1	0.0	1.2	+0.7	0.1	0.0	0.0	-0.1	0.0	0.0	44.1	0.4
MACHINERY	0.0	0.0	0.0	0.0	0.0	0.0	0.0	0.0	0.0	0.0	0.0	0.0	0.0	0.0	0.0	0.0	0.0	0.0	0.0	0.0	0.0	0.0	0.0	0.0	0.0	0.0
SPE. INPUTS	5.2	+1.9	3.9	-0.4	0.7	0.0	0.4	+0.4	4.0	-0.6	1.3	-0.5	0.0	0.0	0.0	0.0	4.1	+0.8	3.9	+1.2	0.0	0.0	0.0	0.0	17.2	0.8
TOTAL	27.5	+3.4	23.6	-0.3	0.7	0.0	0.6	+0.4	4.9	-0.5	0.3	-0.5	0.0	-0.1	0.0	0.0	5.3	+1.5	0.6	+0.1	0.0	-0.1	0.0	0.0	61.3	0.5

KEY: SC Share of country's total exports 1992
CSC Change in share of country's exports 1985-1992
SW Share of world cluster exports 1992
CSW Change in share of world cluster exports 1985-1992

Table 2.7 Percentage of Greek exports by cluster and vertical stage, 1985

	MATERIALS/METALS				FOREST PRODUCTS				PETROLEUM/CHEMICALS				SEMICONDUCTORS/COMPUTERS				UPSTREAM INDUSTRIES	
	SC	CSC	SW	CSW	SC	CSC	SW	CSW	SC	CSC	SW	CSW	SC	CSC	SW	CSW	SC	SW
PRI. GOODS	12.3	-1.2	0.4	0.0	0.7	+0.4	0.1	+0.1	11.5	+0.1	0.2	0.0	0.0	0.0	0.0	0.0	24.5	0.2
MACHINERY	0.0	0.0	0.0	0.0	0.0	0.0	0.0	0.0	0.0	0.0	0.0	0.0	0.0	0.0	0.0	0.0	0.0	0.0
SPE. INPUTS	2.1	-0.3	0.3	-0.1	0.0	0.0	0.0	0.0	0.0	0.0	0.0	0.0	0.0	0.0	0.0	0.0	2.1	0.3
TOTAL	14.4	-1.5	0.4	0.0	0.7	+0.4	0.1	+0.1	11.5	+0.1	0.2	0.0	0.0	0.0	0.0	0.0	26.6	0.2

	MULTIPLE BUSINESS				TRANSPORTATION				POWER GENERATION & DISTRIBUTION				OFFICE				TELECOMMUNICATIONS				DEFENSE				INDUSTRIAL & SUPPORTING FUNCTIONS	
	SC	CSC	SW	CSW	SC	CSC	SW	CSW	SC	CSC	SW	CSW	SC	CSC	SW	CSW	SC	CSC	SW	CSW	SC	CSC	SW	CSW	SC	SW
PRI. GOODS	0.1	0.0	0.0	0.0	0.4	+0.4	0.0	0.0	0.6	-0.4	0.1	0.0	0.0	0.0	0.0	0.0	0.0	0.0	0.0	0.0	0.0	0.0	0.0	0.0	1.1	0.0
MACHINERY	0.0	0.0	0.0	0.0	0.0	0.0	0.0	0.0	0.0	0.0	0.0	0.0	0.0	0.0	0.0	0.0	0.0	0.0	0.0	0.0	0.0	0.0	0.0	0.0	0.0	0.0
SPE. INPUTS	0.0	0.0	0.0	0.0	0.0	0.0	0.0	0.0	0.0	0.0	0.0	0.0	0.0	0.0	0.0	0.0	0.0	0.0	0.0	0.0	0.0	0.0	0.0	0.0	0.0	0.0
TOTAL	0.1	0.0	0.0	0.0	0.4	+0.4	0.0	0.0	0.6	-0.4	0.1	0.0	0.0	0.0	0.0	0.0	0.0	0.0	0.0	0.0	0.0	0.0	0.0	0.0	1.1	0.0

	FOOD/BEVERAGE				TEXTILES/APPAREL				HOUSING/HOUSEHOLD				HEALTH CARE				PERSONAL				ENTERTAINMENT/LEISURE				FINAL CONSUMPTION GOODS & SERVICES	
	SC	CSC	SW	CSW	SC	CSC	SW	CSW	SC	CSC	SW	CSW	SC	CSC	SW	CSW	SC	CSC	SW	CSW	SC	CSC	SW	CSW	SC	SW
PRI. GOODS	20.8	-3.5	0.7	0.0	19.7	+6.1	1.1	+0.3	0.8	-0.7	0.1	0.0	0.3	0.1	0.0	0.0	0.5	+0.4	0.1	+0.1	0.1	-0.1	0.0	0.0	42.2	0.5
MACHINERY	0.0	0.0	0.0	0.0	0.0	0.0	0.0	0.0	0.0	0.0	0.0	0.0	0.0	0.0	0.0	0.0	0.0	0.0	0.0	0.0	0.0	0.0	0.0	0.0	0.0	0.0
SPE. INPUTS	3.3	+2.0	0.3	+0.2	7.3	-1.1	0.8	0.0	4.6	-1.3	1.8	-0.5	0.0	0.0	0.0	0.0	3.3	-3.0	2.7	-1.8	0.0	0.0	0.0	0.0	18.5	0.7
TOTAL	24.1	-1.5	0.6	+0.1	27.0	+5.0	0.9	+0.1	5.4	-2.0	0.4	-0.1	0.3	0.1	0.0	0.0	3.8	-2.6	0.5	-0.5	0.1	-0.1	0.0	0.0	60.7	0.5

KEY: SC Share of country's total exports 1985
CSC Change in share of country's exports 1978-1985
SW Share of world cluster exports 1985
CSW Change in share of world cluster exports 1978-1985

goods industries (metal household equipment and floor coverings) consistently had a high world export share.

The remaining two clusters in this grouping are the Health Care and Entertainment/Leisure ones, where 'isolated cases', as Porter terms them, were evident. The only Health Care industry with noteworthy exports was antibiotics which was competitive both in 1978 and 1985, but not in 1992. In Entertainment/Leisure the most important feature was the presence of a competitive service industry, tourism. Data from the World Tourism Organisation show Greece with a share of more than 0.5% of both tourist arrivals and receipts for many consecutive years.

Among the 'Upstream Industries' and the 'Industrial and Supporting Functions' clusters, the most competitive one was the Materials/Metals, with a share of world exports of 0.3% in 1992, a 0.1% decline from 1978 and 1985. This cluster included a large number of competitive industries, both specialty inputs and primary goods ones, although most of them were related to aluminium and iron and steel, where the highest world export shares were observed. Competitive exports from this cluster accounted for 10% of Greek exports in 1992.

The other noteworthy 'Upstream Industries' cluster was the Petroleum/Chemicals one, where Greece had a 0.1% share of the world market. The range of competitive industries in this cluster has narrowed over time. In 1992, the few remaining competitive primary goods industries accounted for 5.3% of Greek exports.

Among the other two 'Upstream Industries' clusters, Forest Products included one or two competitive wood or paper industries for each year studied, accounting for between 0.2 and 0.7% of Greek exports. Semiconductors/Computers was among the clusters where Greece had no competitive industries in any of the years studied.

The same was observed in most 'Industrial and Supporting Functions' clusters, as Greece had no presence in the Office, Telecommunications and Defence ones, as well as in the Multiple Business cluster for 1992. The Power Generation and Distribution cluster had consistently a 0.1% world export share and a share of Greek exports between 0.6 and 1%. However, this is mainly due to one industry, insulated wire and cables, whose products are related to the Materials/Metals cluster and the competitive wire industries there. The Transportation cluster included a few competitive industries in 1992, three of them related to sea transportation. The most interesting case was that of shipping, another competitive Greek service industry, where a large part of the world's vessel fleet is under Greek ownership, either registered in Greece or in other countries.

'Final Consumption Goods and Services' dominated Greek exports in 1978, 1985 and 1992. Primary goods from these clusters had a large and increasing share of Greek exports and a considerable share of the world market. Specialty inputs had a slightly declining share of Greek exports, though their world export share was still high in 1992 (0.8%). The presence of both primary goods and specialty inputs industries in all five of the very competitive clusters, was not accompanied by the presence of any machinery industries. Competitive service industries were also few, although the ones included in the competitive list were among the best performing Greek industries. The declining shares of the 'Upstream Industries' clusters were not associated with increasing shares of the 'Industrial and Supporting Functions' ones, as Porter expects in a country's development path. Indeed, out of the five clusters where Greece had no competitive industries in 1992, four belong to the 'Industrial and Supporting Functions' group.

Among the most important individual clusters, the Food/Beverages one saw its share of Greek exports drop in 1985 and increase sharply again in 1992, while the opposite was true for the Textiles/Apparel cluster. The Materials/Metals cluster experienced declines in its shares, although it remained a major component of Greek manufacturing industries. The same was true for the Housing/Household cluster, while the special case of the Personal cluster was entirely dependent on the performance of tobacco-related industries.

The Industry Case-Studies

The identification of the sources of competitive advantage for particular industries and the comparison of those sources with the determinants of competitive advantage included in Porter's diamond necessitates the conduct of in-depth case studies. In an attempt to follow Porter's methodology, in order for the results to be comparable to those presented in Porter (1990), the same types of sources were used, which included books, articles and other published data, unpublished company records and in-depth interviews with leading industry experts, representatives of trade associations and, primarily, high-level executives of the relevant companies. Studies considered influential in the development of the industry were given particular attention and research institutes associated with the industries were also contacted. Extensive use was made of the few existing Greek databases and especially the most comprehensive ones.

All the case studies were presented using a similar format. The first section of every case deals with the industry's product, certain aspects of its production process and recent trends in the world market and the European Union. Particular mention was made of certain developments in the European Union since all Greek industries are also part of a wider EU industry and EU countries are usually where the main customers and competitors of Greek firms are located. The next section describes the historical development of the industry in Greece, along with the essential facts regarding the enterprises and their financial status. The third and most important section aims to identify the relevant sources of advantage for the Greek industry and compare these sources with Porter's 'four plus two' determinants. The final, summarising section assesses the applicability of Porter's diamond framework for the particular Greek industry by providing a brief summary of the effects and interactions of the diamond determinants.

The selection of industries followed several criteria. The mix of industries was representative of the dominant clusters in the Greek economy and included a competitive service industry. The international positions of the industries selected reflect the positions of their respective clusters and vary from industries with low and declining shares to some of the best performers.

The first case study is the cement industry, the sixth Greek industry in terms of world export share, in 1992. The industry's extraordinary performance over the years and the recent foreign acquisitions in Bulgaria, Egypt, the Former Yugoslavian Republic of Macedonia (FYROM) and the USA reflect the performance of the whole specialty inputs category of the Housing/Household cluster. Moreover, Greece's particularly high share of world exports in cement has been the subject of research and speculation for many years. The particular attributes of Greek demand for the product also presented an opportunity to evaluate the relevant determinants in Porter's diamond.

The second case study, the rolled aluminium products industry, is again a relatively successful one, although much less so than cement. In 1992 it was the 50th among Greek industries, however, its world export share has been consistently high. This industry is a primary goods industry from the Materials/Metals cluster and its products are directed to industrial customers. It belongs to a wider group of aluminium-related industries that exhibit different characteristics. The case study for this industry was an opportunity to examine, in less detail, the other aluminium industries and gain insights into the role of related and supporting industries. This particular industry was selected among this wider group of industries for two reasons. First, its advantage is related to natural resources only to a very small extent, and second, the lack of domestic rivalry presented an opportunity to test Porter's relevant strong views.

A service industry, tourism, was selected for the third case study. The industry is more of an 'isolated case', as it is in the otherwise underdeveloped Entertainment/Leisure cluster. It is also an industry that includes a multitude of firms offering different parts of the complete tourist product, increasing the industry's complexity. The Greek tourism industry's development is closely associated with basic factors. However, as the industry matures, the role of advanced factors is strengthened, along with the influence of the other determinants. This was the only resource-related industry studied. Its selection was also considered necessary because of its importance for the Greek economy, as it represents more than 7% of Greek GDP and employment (GNTO, 1999: 8-12).

All the above industries have achieved high world export shares in the three years studied. The remaining two cases were selected because their performance was somewhat different, reflecting their cluster's status.

The Textiles/Apparel cluster is still central to the Greek economy, although the loss of export share has been very high between 1985 and 1992. An industry whose share has moved accordingly is the men's outerwear industry, the fourth one studied. Although part of the industry was still in the competitive lists for 1992, the downward trend has continued well into the 1990s. The perspective of this case study is towards understanding the role of the various determinants in an industry whose competitive position is declining. The industry was also selected because it is a producer of consumer goods.

As the Food/Beverages cluster rose to first place in both Greek and world export shares in 1992, new industries were added to the competitive list. A characteristic example is the fifth case study, the dairy industry. The industry's world export share was still low in 1992. Nevertheless, the magnitude of change since 1985 merits further examination. This is also an industry where the role of rivalry can be further explored as small firms are constantly entering the Greek market and the two leading firms are the best known rivals among Greek companies. Again this is an industry where Greece does not possess a particular advantage in natural resources, at least compared to most other food and beverages industries.

The five industries selected belong to the four major Greek clusters (that include most of the Greek competitive industries) and to a fifth, less developed one. Special effort was made to include a service industry in order to test the relative assumptions. The combination of five diverse industries, in terms of their products, export performance, firms' number and size and other characteristics, offers interesting insights into the sources of competitive advantage in the Greek case. Given the high level of detail required in the examination of each case and the extent to which the cases demonstrate trends throughout their clusters, I believe that the objectives of this study can be covered to a great extent with the use of these five cases.

3   The Greek Cement Industry

Introduction

The first industry selected for a detailed analysis is the cement industry, a 'specialty inputs' industry among the most competitive not only of the Housing/Household cluster but among all Greek industries. Greek cement exports have risen from $177 million in 1978 to $235 million in 1992, while Greece's share of world exports has remained exceptionally high, 9.21% in 1978, 8.68% in 1985 and 7.05% in 1992 (UN, International Trade Statistics Yearbook). The Greek cement industry has had a particular importance for the Greek economy, ever since it was created in the beginning of the 20th century. Its export potential, however, has been fully realised in the last thirty years.

Cement production has several phases. The raw materials (usually limestone and clay) are brought from the quarry, crushed, and ground together until they form a homogenous mixture. This mixture passes through a slowly rotating kiln where it is heated to very high temperatures, usually around 1500°C. The end product of this heating process is called clinker. Clinker is then fed in a grinding plant where it is ground with gypsum (which prevents too-rapid hardening) and other additives to form cement (ICAP, 1999g: 6-7).

Cement is almost 100% used by the construction-related industries, either on its own or mixed with other materials. The most common mixture is concrete, produced from sand, water, cement and other additives. Cement is primarily sold to ready-mixed concrete companies, that manufacture concrete, and to construction companies, that use it directly or mix it with other materials on the construction site. Cement is also bought by other companies that manufacture construction products (for example, blocks, bricks and tiles) from cement. It is primarily used in building construction, for example construction of houses, industrial buildings, and hotels. Demand is closely related to each country's preferences. Common substitutes are wood, aluminium, steel, plastics and other materials, especially in small houses and low-height buildings. Cement is also used in non-building construction projects (for example, various infrastructures), in conjunction with other materials, such as steel and aluminium (IOBE, 1982; Pheng and Bee, 1993: 3).

The European and North American cement industries were the first to develop and they remained the major producers until 1980. The rapid economic development of East Asian countries made the Asian cement industry the leading producer. In 1996, Asia produced 988 million tons of cement, with China being the leading producer (491 million tons). Europe had a production of 256 million metric tons and the American continent, almost 200 million metric tons (UN, Industrial Commodity Statistics Yearbook).

The countries of the European Union continue to play an important role in the world cement industry. Italy has been the largest European producer in the past decades with Germany, whose industry was given a boost after the German re-unification of the early 1990s, currently being second. The estimates for 1999 showed Italy producing 37 million tons, Germany 36.2 million tons, and Spain, after constant production increases in the 1990s, 35.8 million tons. France's production has stabilised, after serious reductions in the 1980s, around 20.3 million tons, while the fifth largest producer in the EU was Greece, which has kept production levels steady throughout the 1980s and 1990s, and for 1999 had an estimated production volume of 14.3 million tons. Other EU countries, with an estimated production volume of more than 5 million tons in 1999, were the UK, Portugal and Belgium. In 1999, it was estimated that Greece was the leading EU exporter with 5.7 million tons, followed by Spain (3.1 million tons), Belgium (3 million tons) and Germany (2.9 million tons) (Cembureau, 1997; Titan, 2000: 30).

The European market has a few major players that hold significant shares of their domestic markets and are trying, mainly through acquisitions, to enter the other EU markets. Among these companies there are two German ones (Dyckerhoff and Heidelberger), one Italian (Italcementi) and one French (Lafarge). A Swiss firm (Holderbank) and the Mexican giant Cemex, are also considered direct competitors to the firms mentioned above, as they have substantial cement interests in the EU (Cembureau, 1997: 9.36).

Demand for cement is closely correlated with the levels of construction activity, as cement is a primary input of the construction process. The levels of construction activity, in turn, are closely connected with economic growth rates. Therefore, demand for cement is very cyclical and heavily dependent on each consuming country's economic growth trends. The way that most cement companies deal with these fluctuations is to increase exports in periods of decreasing domestic demand. This strategy is not always easy, given the nature of the product. Cement is heavy, difficult to handle and, most importantly, its ratio of price to weight is low. Transportation expenses therefore are high, both in absolute terms and relative to the product's value. This factor has limited world cement trade to a small fraction of world production, recently 6%-7% (Cembureau,

1997: 9.34). Consequently exports require a willingness to accept lower profit margins in order to achieve economies of scale.

The Greek Cement Industry

Historical Development

The first cement factory in Greece (with a capacity of 2,000 tons) was established in Eleusina in 1902 by Nicholas and Angelos Kanellopoulos. In 1911 the company was named Titan SA and in 1914 the rotary kiln was introduced, as part of the factory's modernisation (Titan, 1992a). Around the same time (1911), a new company called General Cement Company was formed by D. Zamanos, D. Zavogiannis and others. By 1913, the company operated a factory (with the name 'Heracles') in Drapetsona near the port of Piraeus (Greece's main port). After a period of organisational difficulties, the company was sold in 1917. The new owner turned the situation around and increased enormously the company's production and domestic sales (Charontakis, 2000: D16). These were the only factories in the country then and their share of Greek consumption was high. In 1922, as refugees from Asia Minor arrived in the Greek mainland, housing needs increased and domestic consumption rose substantially. As a result, three new cement companies were formed. The first, Volos Cement Company 'Olympos', where the National Bank of Greece had a large share, started producing in 1925 and was bought by the General Cement Company in 1928. The second one, Halkis Cement Company, started operations in 1926 in Halkis, Evoia, while the third one, and last among the four major cement companies, was Halyps Cement established in 1934.

The Second World War brought to a halt all industrial activity and the ensuing Civil War restrained the country's productive capacity for three more years. Very soon, however, production surpassed the pre-war levels, covering the demand generated from the reconstruction efforts. Although a small part of the production was exported, more than 90% was directed to the domestic market. In the 1960s, Titan established two new factories, one in Nea Eukarpia, near Thessaloniki, in 1962 and the other in Drapano, Achaia, 15 km. from Patras in 1968 (Titan, 1992a). As a consequence, production surged to 4.9 million tons in 1970. The oil crisis of 1973 and the enormous increases in revenues for the oil producers in the Middle East and in North and West Africa caused demand for cement in these countries to rise. Greece's proximity to this area offered the Greek industry a great opportunity. Exports rose beyond expectations and production doubled between 1974 and 1983. Two new factories were established, in Kamari, Boiotia in 1976 by Titan, and in Milaki, Evoia in

1983 by the General Cement Company, that was renamed AGET Heracles in the 1970s.

The Greek cement industry was affected by the 1980s crisis in the world cement industry, which was mainly due to over-capacity and reduced demand from oil-exporting countries. Despite continued high sales, financial results were poor, coinciding with a period of price controls and lay-off restrictions in Greece. The Greek drachma's devaluation against the US$ was the breaking point for cement companies (especially Heracles and Halkis) who had a large part of their debt denominated in US$. Control of these two companies (Halkis and Heracles) passed to the State, they were, however, re-privatised, Heracles in the early 1990s and Halkis in 1996. Production volumes declined up to the early 1990s, as had export levels.

A major development in the 1990s was the foreign direct investment of the Greek company Titan in the USA and the Eastern Mediterranean. In 1992, after considering a number of options for its U.S.A. expansion, Titan decided to use the productive capacity of an existing factory, in Roanoke, Virginia. A capital outflow of $40 million was required and the factory was able to supply the American market with one million tons of cement. The company that owned this factory, Tarmac Inc., was bought by Titan in 2000 and some of its quarrying operations were sold off. In 1998, Titan acquired 48.6% of a Bulgarian cement company, Plevenski. In the same year, Titan, in co-operation with the Swiss giant Holderbank, acquired 83% of USJE, the largest cement producer in neighbouring FYROM (the Former Yugoslavian Republic of Macedonia). Finally, in August 1999, a joint venture between Titan and the French cement producer Lafarge bought a 76% share (later increased to 95%) of the Egyptian Beni Suef Cement Co. (Titan, 2000: 35).

The Major Firms

The Greek market is relatively concentrated. There are four major cement producing companies effectively accounting for the entire Greek production.

Titan Cement Co. SA was the first to be established as an SA in 1911, although its first factory was built in 1902. It now accounts for almost 40% of Greek production. It is part of a wider group consisting of quarrying, shipping and ready mixed concrete companies, as well as a porcelain maker. Since 1912, the stock is traded at the Athens Stock Exchange, where it is considered among the few 'blue chip' stocks. The descendants of the initial founders, the Kanellopoulos and Papaleksopoulos families, are still the major stockholders, with more than 20% of the outstanding shares.

Heracles General Cement Co. SA is the other major cement producer in Greece. It was established in Athens, in 1911 and is listed in the Athens Stock Exchange since 1919. It controls a large number of subsidiaries, mostly related to cement raw materials production and cement and concrete distribution. The firm was unprofitable for a short period of time in the mid-1980s, while carrying out an expansion and modernisation program. Thus, huge debts were accumulated. Control passed from the Tsatsos family to the State, through state-owned banks and specialised organisations. In 1992, the majority of the shares was sold to Cal-Nat, a company formed by the National Bank of Greece and the Italian concrete producer Calcestruzzi. Calcestruzzi's controlling share was transferred to a non-cement related company, Concretum, in 1996. In 2000, this company was sold to Blue Circle Industries, the major UK cement producer, which in turn was acquired by the French cement producer Lafarge. The National Bank of Greece remained the major minority shareholder after the sale.

The third Greek producer, Halkis Cement Co. SA was established in Athens, in 1926. In the 1980s, it ran into the same problems as Heracles and, after a long process lasting almost five years, was finally sold to Concretum. Effectively, Halkis is now controlled by Heracles, and a formal merger took place in 2001, with an exchange of existing Halkis shares for Heracles' ones.

Halyps, the fourth Greek company, was established as an SA in 1943, when it changed its legal status, evolving from a limited partnership formed in 1934. In 1990, the French producer Ciments Français bought a controlling interest in the company, and now owns almost 95% of the shares, while the rest are traded at the Athens Stock Exchange (originally listed in 1949).

The essential figures for 1999 for all Greek cement producers are given in Table 3.1:

Table 3.1 Financial results of Greek cement companies (1999)

Companies	Turnover (million Drachmas)	Net Income (million Drachmas)
Heracles	107,282	-2,597
Titan	107,147	30,471
Halkis	32,484	6,368
Halyps	16,209	2,803

Source: ICAP, 2001.

The two major producers, Heracles and Titan, have made significant sales, earning high profits throughout the last decade (although in 1999 Heracles had to write-off an amount higher than its operating profits of 32 billion Drachmas), among the highest for all Greek companies

(ICAP, 2001). The two smaller companies, Halkis and Halyps, have turned their financial situation around, from the huge losses of the late 1980s and early 1990s to modest profits of the mid-1990s and a financial situation comparable to that of the other two companies in the late 1990s.

Production - Exports - Imports

The Greek cement industry was established in the first decades of the 20th century and by 1938, all four Greek cement companies were in operation. Their combined production in 1938 was 308,000 tons. At around the same time (1935), the first Greek cement exports were recorded. During the pre-World War II years, imports had a fluctuating share of domestic demand. In 1920, 4,000 tons of cement were imported to cover 17% of domestic demand. Then, as the refugees from Asia Minor came to Greece in 1922, imports surged and by 1925 accounted for 55% of domestic consumption. However, because new Greek companies were being formed and the existing ones were investing in increased capacity, imports were reduced and by 1938 had reached the low levels of 22,000 tons (Association of Greek Cement Manufacturers, 1994).

Soon after World War II production rose sharply and then, from 1950 until 1970, output almost doubled every five years. Also, immediately after the war, in 1947, exports resumed, although at the very low level of 2000 tons. By 1955, exports had reached 232,000 tons, but, in the years that followed, expansion was greater in the domestic market while exports stagnated, and, by 1970, export volume had barely increased to 342,000 tons. During this period, imports were very low, starting at 2,000 tons in 1950 and stopping altogether in 1978 (Association of Greek Cement Manufacturers, 1994).

The favourable circumstances in the beginning of the 1970s caused a capacity expansion and, this time, all the extra production was exported. In 1975, cement production was 7.94 million tons, with Titan and Heracles producing about 3 million tons, Halkis producing 1.47 million tons and Halyps 386,000 tons. At the same time, exports surpassed the 3 million tons mark and by 1980 had reached 5.9 million tons, or 46% of production. All companies increased their production almost every year until 1983, when Greek production peaked at 14.2 million tons, with Heracles being ahead, with 6.2 million tons, followed by Titan with 5.5 million, Halkis with 2 million and Halyps with almost 0.5 million tons. The rise was also evident in export volume, up until 1983 when 7.8 million tons, or 55% of Greek production, were exported. All four companies participated in the export surge, with Titan leading in the 1970s and Heracles in the 1980s (Association of Greek Cement Manufacturers, 1994).

Then, as all companies ran into financial difficulties, production levels fell slightly. Capacity levels remained approximately stable and production reached a low of 12.5 million tons in 1989. The 1980s crisis also affected exports that fell to 5.1 million tons in 1989. The two smaller companies were hit harder, with Halkis halving its exports and Halyps stopping them altogether. Since then, production has been rising, having recently reached the 1983 levels, with Heracles accounting for approximately 43% of Greek production, Titan for 38%, Halkis for 14% and Halyps for the remaining 5% (Association of Greek Cement Manufacturers, 1994; Karsaba, 1997: 37).

The new export rise started in 1993, however this time only Titan and Heracles registered significant increases, with Halkis steadily exporting around 1.2 million tons. All three companies export around 40-50% of their production, while Halyps has resumed its exporting efforts in the late 1990s (ICAP, 2001). In 1991, some imports reappeared, but the quantities were still very small.

The destinations of Greek exports indicate the responsiveness of the companies involved. Although cement is not easy to transport and usually needs certain unloading installations in the destination country, Greek cement companies have been very adept at finding new markets. In the beginning of the export boom, between 1974 and 1976, Greek cement was essentially exported to three countries, Libya, Algeria and Saudi Arabia. Then in 1977, Greek exports reached most Middle Eastern countries and some other African countries like Egypt and Nigeria. In the first half of the 1980s, the two most important markets for Greek cement were Saudi Arabia and Egypt. However, both these countries developed their own cement industries and when oil prices started declining, major development projects in most Middle Eastern and African countries were scaled down. As soon as those trends were evident, the Greek industry changed its focus and without abandoning its traditional markets started exporting elsewhere.

The first major target was the USA market, which in 1988 received 38% of Greek exports, or 2.1 million tons. At the same time Greece exported to other EU countries, namely Italy and the UK. In the early 1990s, the shift was complete and European countries, along with the USA, accounted for most Greek exports. Although the slowdown of European markets in 1991-1992 caused an increase in the proportion of Greek exports going to the Middle East and Africa, to around 20% in 1993, the majority of exports still go to the USA and the big European markets of Italy (where, for certain years, Greece was the major importing country), Spain, France and Britain (Association of Greek Cement Manufacturers, 1994).

Investment in the industry has been high throughout its history. New factories were built and the productive capacity of the existing ones was increased many times, sometimes even as soon as two years after the establishment of a factory, as was the case in the Thessaloniki factory of

Titan (Titan, 1992b). Since 1970 two other major targets of investments were the creation of terminals for unloading cement in bulk in most export markets where Greece was present and the replacement of petroleum as the fuel used in the kiln. Before 1983, major investments in production capacity took place and investment from the cement industry registered year-to-year increases substantially higher than the whole of Greek manufacturing industries. Between 1983 and 1989, this trend was reversed, and only during the 1990s, when financial results improved, did investments pick up (Karsaba, 1997: 69).

Sources of Competitive Advantage

Factor Conditions

Cement is essentially a mixture of two minerals, one containing calcium chloride and the other silica. There are many types of materials that contain these substances, but the ones commonly used for cement production are limestone (as a calcium source) and clay (as a silica source) (Bianchi, 1982).

Greece has abundant deposits of both types of minerals, as do most cement producing countries. The Greek cement industry uses exclusively Greek raw materials and supplies are plentiful and easy to obtain. The cost of raw materials is usually around 15% of the cost of the final product (Kalloniatis, 1996a) and therefore the most important factor in sourcing raw materials is quality, with cost coming second. The quality and the exact composition of the limestone and clay used determine a number of parameters in the production process. Consequently, it is important that the properties of these materials are relatively constant and within certain limits.

As relevant studies (for example, Chrisochou, 1987; Karsaba, 1997: 23) and the interviews I conducted with managers in the industry indicate, Greek raw materials are of excellent quality and easy to extract. Also, since one source can provide large quantities of them, their properties are constant. Even more important is the fact that Greek industry has used, for over 90 years, limestone and clay with similar properties and has therefore made all the necessary adjustments to the production process. Additional materials, like gypsum, used in most cements, or other additives, used in special kinds of cements, are also easily obtainable in Greece.

Labour costs are a somewhat important cost component in cement production. However, cement manufacturing is not labour-intensive and total Greek employment in 1996 was estimated at 4,480 people (Karsaba, 1997: 26). The cement industry is considered highly competitive with steady employment prospects. Wages are substantially higher than the average for Greek manufacturing industries (Karsaba, 1997: 17). Therefore, the industry is able to attract top-level graduates from all educational levels. All employees, and especially workers and engineers, undergo some, mainly on-the-job, training before they are given full responsibility and are then periodically trained as needs arise. The industry was well known for years for the skills of its machine operators. They are now being replaced by highly automated production control systems, present in all Greek factories. The workers, however, are not laid off but their experience is used to fine-tune the automated systems. As they retire, the number of low-skilled personnel is being reduced. In fact, the proportion of low-skilled factory employees has decreased from 43% in 1980 to 22% in 1996 (Karsaba, 1997: 26).

Wages in the industry may be higher than in other sectors of Greek manufacturing, but are still lower than wages in most other developed countries. Data for 1996 show that Greek per hour labour costs in the non-metallic minerals sector are the second lowest in the EU, after those of Portugal (European Commission and Eurostat, 2000: 225). The same cost differential, at least with other EU members, has been observed throughout the 1980s (European Commission, 1988: 30). Total labour costs have also not dramatically increased in the past two decades, and this is due to the constant decreases in the number of workers. In 1981, the Greek cement industry employed 6,363 people, 1,883 more than in 1996 (Karsaba, 1997: 26). The huge capital investments, especially in the 1970s, as well as the personnel reductions, have made the cement industry in the 1980s and early 1990s (when investment resumed) among those Greek industries with an above average value added per employee (Giannaros, 1997: 561). Union activity has not changed this picture, as strikes are very few and most problems are solved through negotiations.

Capital requirements are high in the industry. However, as profits were rising before the 1980s crisis, the industry was able to finance its expansion through retained earnings and bank loans at competitive rates. In the 1980s, when needs became greater, capital was harder to find and, with the rise of inflation, nominal interest rates were high. Nevertheless, since the mid-1980s, the State, mainly through state-controlled banks, has been involved with two of the cement companies and funds were again available at competitive rates of interest. Halyps has also eliminated its financing problems as, since 1990, it is part of a larger group of companies. Titan has maintained a sound financial position for years, borrowing at low rates from Greece and abroad.

The infrastructure whose state affects the cement industry is the transportation network. Roads are the main network for inland transportation in Greece. However, the road network is not in a very good condition outside the main motorways that connect the major urban centres. Moreover, the roads inside and around the main cities, and especially Athens, are not sufficient for the huge traffic loads. The Greek industry is therefore disadvantaged in terms of road transportation. There are, however, three major infrastructure projects under way that would probably ameliorate the situation in the years to come. Specifically, the modernisation of the main national motorway connecting Patras, Athens and Thessaloniki, that is in its last stages, the creation of a new motorway in the north of the country and the new bridge linking the Peloponnese with the rest of Western Greece are expected to substantially improve the network's condition.

The way to work around the road network's problems has been to use the extensive ports' infrastructure in Greece. All cement factories are located near ports and all cement companies own ships (through a number of subsidiaries), as well as loading and unloading facilities. The long tradition of sea carriage in Greece has created an extensive port network, a large number of shipping companies and a large pool of highly skilled seamen. Sea transportation has not, therefore, been just a compensating factor for the road network problems. Greek companies have had a long experience in transporting the material by sea and operating port facilities, and have taken advantage of that experience in reaching foreign markets. This has been a major source of competitive advantage, since most of the exported cement in the world is transported by sea (Pheng and Bee, 1993).

Energy costs in the cement industry vary according to the parameters of the production process, but they usually represent 35-45% of the total production costs (Bianchi, 1982). These costs are split between the costs of operating the various grinding, mixing, drying, etc. plants and the costs of operating the kiln, where the main heating process takes place. In Greece, electricity is used for the operation of most of the machinery, apart from the kiln. Electricity prices in Greece are very close to the OECD average giving the Greek industry neither an advantage nor a disadvantage (IEA, 1996).

The kilns in all Greek factories used to burn oil that was 100% imported. However, since the first oil crisis it became evident that the costs of continuing that policy would be prohibitive. Greek companies, and mainly Heracles and Titan, experimented with various kinds of fuels, and finally decided that coal was the most cost efficient. The only drawback was that coal needed a number of special installations requiring high investments, which Greek firms undertook. Coal is also imported and its supply or prices can in no way be affected by the Greek cement industry, giving it therefore a slight disadvantage. However, the fact that firms are not exposed to the highly volatile prices of oil to determine their operating costs is an advantage.

The initial impetus for the expansion of the Greek cement industry in the beginning of the 1970s, when it developed an internationally competitive position, came in part from Greece's proximity to the Middle East and North Africa. As the countries of these regions were importing large quantities of cement, Greece became a major source. Transportation expenses for Greek companies were lower than those of most other European and Asian companies, as Greece was for some countries the closest cement exporter. Greek firms were able to offer very competitive prices and, consequently, capture a large part of the Middle East and West African markets.

However, since the drop in oil prices and the creation of domestic cement industries in most of these countries, Greece has changed its export orientation. The Greek industry is now mainly exporting to countries of the EU and the USA. Although Greece is not very far from EU countries, all of them have strong local industries and are also close to each other, engaging in cement trade among them. Also, Greece is further away from the USA than its European or Asian competitors.

The R&D requirements of the cement industry are not very high. The production process has experienced few major improvements and most research is made with the purpose of automating the process and conserving energy. Some important innovations, which have occurred in the industry in the last decades, are related to the product itself. New types of cement are being produced, either for specialised uses, or to replace other expensive or rare materials. Existing cement types are being improved, usually with minor changes to their composition in order to meet stricter specifications.

Laboratories are present in most cement factories, mainly for quality control purposes, since the product is tested by governments or independent authorities in most countries. In Greece, all companies have their own laboratories that continuously examine the product. Titan and Heracles, the two major Greek producers, have large research units that conduct all types of research. Because of the need for Greek firms to produce various types of cement that would conform with the regulations of all the countries where the Greek industry has an export presence, researchers have made useful observations on the product's properties. Research has also focused on production automation systems, resulting in substantial improvements in the production process. Heracles has a special subsidiary (Amber SA) that produces integrated industrial automation systems, and another subsidiary (Hellenic Cement Research Centre Ltd.) that conducts research relating to cement manufacturing and quality control methods in general. In the 1980s, the laboratories of Heracles were well-known for important discoveries. In the 1990s, Titan exhibited increased activity, participating in a number of EU initiatives, co-operating with companies in other industries and maintaining a close working relationship with most Greek Technical Universities.

The Departments of Chemical Engineering in two of the Technical Universities, those in Athens and Patras, are conducting extensive research, connected to the cement industry. In this research, they co-operate with Greek companies, mainly Heracles and Titan, and the results are used by these companies to improve production methods and manufacture cement of superior quality.

With the industry's initiative, the Association of Greek Cement Manufacturers has been established. In the past, up to the late 1980s when cement prices were regulated, the association was active in lobbying as well as in collecting data for the industry. The reduced State involvement in the industry and the sale of Heracles and Halyps to foreign owners in the early 1990s (and later of Halkis), have limited the scope of the association's actions.

Demand Conditions

Greek demand for cement mainly comes from building construction. Housing and non-housing construction accounts for almost 80% of cement consumption in Greece, while in most EU countries that number is usually around 75-80% (IOBE, 1982). Building construction is not only the biggest segment in most foreign markets but also the one where most of cement's direct substitutes are used. In addition, the profit margins in this segment are much higher, since public works contracts require big discounts. Greek manufacturers, therefore, have a slight advantage, since the building construction segment in Greece receives most of their output.

In terms of cement buyers, more than half of the cement sold in the Greek market goes to the ready mixed concrete industry, while the other half is divided among the precast concrete firms (about 6% of the total), the major construction companies (11%) and the building materials wholesalers and retailers (Karsaba, 1997: 16; ICAP, 1999g: 29-31). The percentage of cement sold to ready mixed concrete companies (55.5% in 1995) is comparable to that of other major cement producing countries (45.7% in Italy for 1995, 57% in Germany) or, in some cases, considerably higher (40.5% in France) (Eurostat, 1998). Therefore, the major segment of the market is where Greek firms are concentrating their efforts.

The ready mixed concrete industry manufactures fresh, unhardened concrete and then transports it to the production site. Although in Greece the first ready mixed concrete firm was established in 1968, later than in other EU countries, the industry has grown substantially and Greece was recently the sixth largest EU producer (ERMCO, 1997: 9.44). Ready mixed concrete is not a tradable product and, therefore, one cannot comment on the industry's competitiveness. There are more than 400 ready mixed concrete companies in Greece, both independent and subsidiaries of Greek and foreign cement firms (ICAP, 1999g: 22, 108). Competition is intense among these firms, although it is mainly price-based. However, the bigger firms are emphasising delivery reliability and product quality, having invested in automated production controls and modern concrete-carrying vehicles (ICAP, 1999g: 36).

Unlike the ready mixed concrete industry, the precast concrete industry in Greece is still very small compared to that of other developed countries. In 1999, there were less than 200 Greek firms producing construction materials from cement, most of them with under 10 employees (ICAP, 1999f: 18). External trade is negligible and most of the industry's capacity is located around the major population centres of Athens and Thessaloniki (ICAP, 1999f: 34). The construction industry is large and growing in Greece with many, independent buyers. Construction companies were considered competitive in the 1970s. More recently, however, their foreign contracts have been reduced. It seems that the nature of buyers of Greek cement can be considered a slight advantage for the Greek industry, since there are many independent competitive buyers with an adequate level of sophistication.

The Greek market is not among the major markets in the world. However, in the period between the 1920s and the 1980s it exhibited remarkable growth rates. Even in the pre-World War II period Greek consumption grew from 24,000 tons in 1920 to 330,000 tons in 1938. After the war, in 1947, consumption was at 175,000 tons. Then, demand took off, reaching 393,000 tons in 1950 and doubling every five years until 1965. In 1965, Greek consumption just surpassed the 3 million tons mark (Association of Greek Cement Manufacturers, 1994). This was also the period when investments, which increased productive capacity and the level of technological sophistication, were made in the industry.

After 1965, growth continued, at a slower pace. By 1970, the Greek market had expanded to 4.5 million tons, a level also characteristic of the next five years (Karra, 1985: 2). Then a further construction surge pushed consumption to 7.17 million tons by 1979 (Association of Greek Cement Manufacturers, 1994). This was also a period of increased investment in the industry and of creation of the very modern factory of Titan in Kamari in 1976, as well as the beginning of the construction of the Heracles II factory that was completed in the early 1980s.

After decades of impressive growth, the Greek market in the 1980s appeared saturated. In the beginning of the 1980s demand started decreasing and by 1984 it had reached 6.2 million tons (Karra, 1985: 110). In the late 1980s and early 1990s, demand was again increasing and in 1992 consumption reached a new peak of 7.7 million tons (Association of Greek Cement Manufacturers, 1994). Since then domestic demand has decreased to 6.7 million tons in 1994, when a new demand surge drove domestic consumption upwards (Karsaba, 1997). In 1999, it was estimated that 8.5 million tons of cement were used in Greece (Titan, 2000: 30).

Market saturation, observed in certain periods in the last three decades, has been a major incentive for the Greek cement industry to increase exports. The first export surge coincides with the slump in domestic demand between 1970 and 1975. Even after 1975, exports have consistently registered substantial increases in years when domestic demand has dropped. For example, between 1979 and 1982 annual consumption in Greece fell 11%, while exports increased almost 40%. The same trend is present in almost every year since 1978 as can be seen in Figure 3.1. Overall, market saturation has been a driving force behind the Greek companies' emphasis on the international market.

The Greek market reached its saturation point with very high rates of per capita demand. Even among developed countries, Greece had a very high per capita cement consumption. In 1984, Greece was third in per capita consumption among the EU countries, with 680 kg per inhabitant, almost three times the UK per capita consumption, which was the lowest in the EU (253 kg). However, even these numbers fail to show the true picture. In developing countries, in 1983, per capita consumption was even lower with 35 kg/inhabitant in India, 93 kg/inhabitant in China and 73 kg/inhabitant in Kenya, with similar numbers for most countries, apart from some oil producers and the South East Asian tigers (Sinha, 1990). Although Greek per capita consumption has not increased dramatically, reaching 710 kg in 1997 and estimated at 810 kg in 1999, it is still among the highest in the world, 50% higher than the EU average of 470 kg and third among EU countries, after Luxembourg and Portugal (Karsaba, 1997: 13; European Commission and Eurostat, 2000: 234; Titan, 2000: 30). Part of this difference in per capita consumption can be explained by Greece's development needs, and the associated demands for building and public works construction. However, the substantial differences with other countries must also be related to a general preference for cement as the building material of choice.

As was mentioned before, every country has its own regulations on the types of cement used within its borders. Greek firms have created cement to fit the regulations in all the countries they export to, without affecting these regulations. However, Greece has affected foreign demand for cement through what Porter (1990) calls 'mobile buyers'. This was done in the beginning of the industry's exports to the Middle East when some of the construction projects in these countries were implemented by Greek construction companies. Local cement factories were non-existent and these companies, having used, with excellent results, Greek cement at home, preferred to use cement manufactured in Greece. This fact gave the Greek cement industry an additional impetus to export.

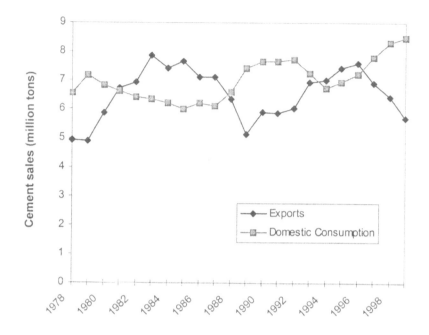

Figure 3.1   Greek cement exports and domestic consumption, 1978-1999

Source: Association of Greek Cement Manufacturers, 1994; Karsaba, 1997; Titan, 2000.

Related and Supporting Industries

The Housing/Household cluster, which includes the cement industry, represents a consistent part of Greek competitive exports. The cluster is among the four major competitive clusters of Greek industry, although usually its export shares are below the ones corresponding to the other three.

However, looking at the primary goods industries of this cluster, there are some, but not many, very competitive Greek industries. Therefore cement's success does not seem to be related to the 'primary goods' category of the cluster, something not surprising, since this consists mainly of products that furnish a house after its completion. The picture changes when observing the 'specialty inputs' category of the Greek Housing/Household cluster. In all the years studied, Greece had significant positions in most of the industries in this category.

Specifically, apart from cement, Greece had a very strong competitive position in 'worked building stone' and 'stone, sand and gravel', a significant industry since its output is used for concrete production. In the same 'specialty inputs' category, Greece had a substantial presence in the 'lime and unfired mineral products' industry. In fact, it is competitive in a number of industries that extract and process crude minerals with world market shares that often exceed 1%. Cement companies have acquired a number of quarrying firms that specialise in the kinds of materials that they require. Therefore, close co-operation between suppliers and cement firms is extensive including monitoring of the quality and composition of materials.

Looking at the related Materials/Metals cluster, Greece is very competitive in most steel and aluminium building materials industries. This clearly indicates that cement is not an isolated case but part of a competitive range of building materials industries. One must also stress here the importance of the Greek shipping industry that has been internationally competitive for many decades. Cement production and sales are related to sea transportation since it is common for cement to be transported by sea, sometimes even within a country. Greek companies have used shipping services since the early 20th century, benefiting from the competitive shipping industry, and establishing their own shipping companies.

The machinery industry for cement production is a global oligopoly. The market is controlled by a handful of German, Danish, French and Japanese firms. The Greek industry imports all of its machinery, alternating among the suppliers. Although Greek firms have used this equipment very productively and have been very adept at creating a smooth production flow, they have no direct or indirect involvement in machinery development and production.

Other equipment needed for production like storage tanks and bricks is mainly being supplied by Greek companies. Since the State took control of some of the cement companies, a conscious effort has been under way to use Greek suppliers, especially for more basic products.

Firm Strategy, Structure and Rivalry

Up to the early 1980s, all the Greek cement firms had a similar ownership structure, a mix of family and public ownership. All four firms were listed on the Athens Stock Exchange very soon after their creation. However, a significant and usually controlling number of shares remained in the hands of a few families who were also heavily represented in the Board of Directors, a fact common in most Greek enterprises (Chapman and Antoniou, 1998).

Titan is still essentially controlled by the Kanellopoulos and Papaleksopoulos families and Heracles was under the guidance of the Tsatsos family until 1983. The situation changed in the 1980s when control of two of the cement firms passed to the State. Nevertheless, their shares were still being traded in the exchange as the State essentially took over the interests of the controlling families. Currently (2001) major multinational cement groups (Italcementi and Lafarge) control Halyps and the recently merged Heracles and Halkis. Titan's ownership has not changed, although successive share capital increases have reduced the two families' share to less than 50%. It seems that the ownership structure in the Greek cement industry favoured tight control by a small group of individuals or the Greek State or, more recently, large foreign firms. This has probably eased the pressure for short-term results, enabling the industry to make substantial investments, not always, however, at the right time. Other results of the ownership structure are also not clear. The mix of family control and stock market discipline was an asset until the early 1980s, while the period of State control for Halkis and Heracles gave mixed results. Since their privatisation, these two companies have improved substantially their financial results and Heracles has kept its market share both in Greece and abroad. Titan has had a consistent positive record.

The fact that the industry has been successful for a long time has attracted top talent to it, especially engineers with solid knowledge in their field and a wider understanding of non-engineering issues. Also, the policies of few layoffs, aided by the fact that during a period in the 1980s and 1990s, two of the companies were state owned, created a situation of near-lifetime employment. In fact, in the non-state owned Titan the average employee has been with the firm for more than eighteen years and this figure is almost constantly increasing (Titan, 1996: 9). This has helped top management to push responsibility and authority downwards to middle managers and factory supervisors. Stock options and performance-related bonuses have provided an added incentive. The people rising to the higher managerial positions have a good understanding of the company's strong and weak points and a firm grasp of the peculiarities of the production process, something important for the cement industry. In fact, for Titan, as one of my interviewees claimed, most loan agreements have a covenant stating that the company's top management must not change substantially throughout the loan period.

The global cement industry is characterised by a vertically integrated structure (Pheng and Bee, 1993). Vertical integration has also been a conscious policy for all Greek cement companies, as they are all well integrated both upstream and downstream. Upstream, all cement firms own mining companies and the ones owned by Heracles and Titan are among the biggest in the country. Downstream, a lot of ready mixed concrete companies are owned by the cement manufacturers, providing a steady source of demand for each company's cement. In addition, sea transportation of the finished product is mainly carried out through fleets owned by the relevant subsidiaries of the cement companies. Road transportation is usually handled by independent operators. Nevertheless, cement companies provide drivers with financial incentives and organise safe-driving and other seminars for these independent drivers.

Greek cement companies have so far competed on lower costs and timely delivery of their product. This has forced them to invest in modern production technologies that would lower costs, especially energy costs, and improve loading and unloading facilities in many locations. The effort has been continuous, as investment in acquiring modern equipment, in using cheaper fuels with increased efficiency and in automating production has been going on for over forty years. The factories created in the 1970s and 1980s are considered among the world's most modern, at least according to the companies' annual reports. Titan has also built unloading terminals, sometimes in co-operation with local businessmen, first in the Middle East and Africa and then in Spain, Italy, France, the UK and the USA.

The export strategy of Greek companies has also been very successful. Although all companies claim that they give priority to the domestic market, they have shown considerable skill in penetrating foreign ones. All producers were quick to make the adjustments necessary in order to produce cement that would meet the quality and composition standards of many foreign markets. Then, they started shipping huge quantities to the rapidly developing oil producers of the Middle East and Africa as soon as petroleum prices increased. When oil revenues in these countries decreased, Greek companies were not satisfied with retaining their positions in these markets. While continuing to export to their traditional clients, they aggressively entered first the American and then the Western European markets, taking market shares from long established local companies. Titan has even taken the step of investing in the USA gaining a steady presence in the American market, where it also continues to export.

The strategy of being a low-cost producer, with a consistent-quality product, ready to be delivered anywhere in the world has proven well suited for the industry. The Greek industry's success is also documented by the efforts of many cement giants to enter the relatively small and mature Greek market, primarily intending to reduce Greek companies' domestic revenues. Given these efforts, and cement's transportation difficulties, the strategy of catering first to the domestic market also seems well founded.

The Greek market is characterised by an oligopolistic structure. The two major Greek producers, Titan and Heracles General Cement, have seen their market shares remain relatively stable for the last twenty years, ranging between 38% and 44% of the domestic market (Karra, 1985: 10; Karsaba, 1997). In the 1970s when one company's share increased, the other's decreased. However, for several years in the mid-1980s, as the other two smaller producers were experiencing difficulties, both companies achieved market shares close to the high end of the range. In the 1990s, the shares of the two large companies have slightly decreased and the smaller producers have rebounded with Halyps capturing 6%-7% of the domestic market and Halkis 13%-14% (Karsaba, 1997: 97).

The oligopolistic structure is not uncommon in most world cement markets. The huge investments required for a new cement plant, in addition to the reluctance of authorities to permit such investments, for environmental reasons, has left the number of producers, especially in developed countries, steadily decreasing. In the European Union, some smaller countries have only one domestic cement producer, while it is common even for larger countries that the (usually three or four) dominant producers capture a combined market share of over 60%. In Italy four companies control 65% of the market, in Germany the four largest producers have a 62% share and in Spain a 69% share. Ireland, Sweden, The Netherlands and Norway have one dominant producer, while Portugal has two, and Belgium three (Karsaba, 1997: 88). Acquisitions among these producers are common and the result is a market controlled by very few companies.

The acquisition trend is under way in Greece too, as Halkis' control has passed to Heracles. Although Halyps' share of the market is increasing and Halkis is following a relatively independent strategy, it is Heracles and Titan that now dominate the domestic market. This has also been the case in past decades, as Halkis and Halyps were never major players. However, the rivalry between Heracles and Titan has always been intense, without any market or price 'agreements' and with foreign expansion being a sign of superiority. It remains to be seen whether the recent changes in Heracles' ownership, that made the company part of a very large cement group, will have an effect on its foreign expansion plans and the resulting rivalry.

Porter considers geographic concentration a recurring fact in a number of competitive industries throughout the world. The Greek cement industry is no exception. All four companies have their headquarters and approximately 10%-20% of their employees in or very near the capital, Athens. Most of their productive facilities are also located in proximity to each other. Although a lot of factors, such as proximity of ports and quarries, influence the location of a cement factory, the eight Greek factories are located in six of the country's 52 prefectures. Even more than that, five of the eight factories are in Attica, Boiotia and Evoia, relatively close to each other and at a reasonable distance from Athens, two more are in Patras and Volos, again near major cities and at a reasonable distance from Athens, while the eighth is in Thessaloniki, the second largest Greek city. Specifically, the existing factories and their capacity can be seen in Table 3.2.

Table 3.2 Greek cement factories and their capacity

Greek Factories	Capacity (million tons)	1st Year of operation
Heracles – Halkis		
- Olympos Factory – Volos	4.80	1925
- Heracles II Factory – Milaki, Evoia	1.70	1983
- Halkis (or Heracles III) Factory	2.70	1926
Titan		
- Patras Factory	1.65	1968
- Boiotia Factory	2.65	1976
- Eleusina Factory	0.15	1902
- Thessaloniki Factory	1.45	1962
Halyps		
- Aspropyrgos Factory	0.80	1936
TOTAL	15.90	

Source: Karsaba, 1997: 32-34; Halyps, 1999.

Although geographic proximity exists, it is mainly related to the Athenian market. Titan followed a concentration strategy by creating the Boiotia factory, near its original base of Eleusina. The merger with Halkis has also enabled Heracles to follow a similar strategy. There was no mention of co-operation between firms due to proximity either in published studies, or in the interviews I conducted. However, the mere proximity to Athens, where the stock exchange, government agencies and sources of information for both the domestic and international markets are located, gives some credit to the geographic concentration argument, especially given the headquarters' location in Attica.

The Role of Government

The industry has not been a major target of trade policy. High import tariffs were abolished even before World War II and although some tariffs were existent, as with most products, until the mid-1980s, the cement industry has not benefited substantially from some form of protection. Export subsidies, common in many industries, were instituted very late, in the mid-1970s, and then abolished after Greece's full integration in the EU. Despite the industry's apparent competitiveness, its environmental impact and its relatively low number of employees have halted the creation of strong pressure groups for the industry.

The industry has of course benefited from certain measures like investment incentives and export subsidies. However, for the reasons mentioned above, these benefits were fewer than in most other Greek industries and the bureaucratic delays associated with them, made their impact even less pronounced. Some bureaucratic measures have also hindered the industry and my interviewees mentioned as examples the huge number of permits needed even for a minor investment in Greece or abroad and the usual bureaucratic delays. These delays are partly blamed for the late construction of Heracles' second factory that was decided during a period of high demand and completed in the beginning of a low-growth period. Another bureaucratic necessity mentioned in my interviews is the need to have all employees in quarrying operations registered with the police, because of the use of explosives in the mines.

The State's involvement in the mid-1980s, when it intervened to rescue the producers in trouble, was more active. When the huge investments, especially by Heracles and to, a lesser extent, Halkis coincided with a demand slump and rising dollar costs, it was the State's involvement that kept them from going bankrupt. However, most of the involvement consisted of capitalisation and restructuring of debts and there were no large scale subsidies. In fact, the prices paid by the new owners for the state-controlled companies were above world market average and the government and the state banks were able to recoup part of their investment.

The Role of Chance

The major chance event that contributed to the industry's international prominence was the first oil crisis in the early 1970s. In a short period of time, the accrued revenues of the oil producing countries raised the demand for cement. Greece was in an ideal geographic location, better suited than any other European country to satisfy the needs, particularly of Middle Eastern and certain North African customers. The Greek industry took advantage of that huge opportunity and expanded capacity to satisfy these needs. The industry was also able to quickly meet the quality standards of these countries and to ensure timely delivery by using Greek ships, usually company-owned, and specially made terminals.

As demand in these countries declined, a second chance event created serious problems for the Greek industry. The dollar's rise beyond any expectation in the 1981-1985 period increased tremendously the costs in an already cost-sensitive industry. Machinery needed for production modernisation, oil, that constituted almost a quarter of production costs, and other expenses were all paid in dollars. Revenues in dollars, however, were declining as cement prices fell and exporting opportunities became harder to find. The industry took steps to remedy the situation by seeking new export markets and establishing a presence in some very competitive markets, substituting oil for coal, and increasing the number of Greek suppliers of auxiliary equipment. Although the turnaround was successful, state assistance was necessary to guarantee the continued presence of two of the four cement firms.

Summary

The Greek cement industry is part of a global industry dominated by large companies that control, directly or through subsidiaries, the main regional markets. In the early part of the 20th century, the four Greek cement firms were established with the goal of satisfying the increasing home demand. Soon after the Second World War, the Greek market was firmly in their hands and the first attempts at expansion abroad were evident. Through a combination of factors this expansion was accelerated in the 1970s and the result was an internationally competitive industry able to hold its own, against companies with much higher production volumes. Despite the many changes since then, Greek firms remain among the world's major exporters and, while still controlling the Greek market, they aggressively seek market share in many foreign countries.

An analysis of this performance, using Porter's diamond framework, revealed a competitive advantage based on several sources. Factor conditions have been mostly favourable for the Greek industry. Basic factors, like good quality, cheap and abundant raw materials, as well as a good geographical position, were present in the case of Greece. These, however, were not enough and, as the industry evolved, it was able to use effectively more specialised factors, such as human capital and sea transportation networks. Other advanced factors, like R&D, are constantly being upgraded by the Greek industry and have reached a satisfactory level. Disadvantages in the availability of energy sources, the condition of the road network and, to a lesser extent, in the availability of capital and specialised institutions, still exist. However, their effect is not substantial, mainly because of the industry's efforts. Factor conditions can partly explain the Greek industry's success.

Demand conditions offer a more positive picture. In terms of buyers, there are many independent firms, especially in the most important ready mixed concrete segment, and their sophistication is adequate. One of the most important attributes of Greek demand is the very high per capita consumption, among the highest in the world, related not only to the country's development level, but also to the preference for cement. In addition, the Greek market fits perfectly Porter's description of a high growth market that eventually saturates, forcing the industry first to invest and then to expand to other markets. The lack of 'internationalisation' of demand patterns appears to be the only major part of demand conditions lacking from the Greek industry's case. Overall, demand conditions have contributed substantially to the industry's competitive position.

Related and supporting industries are also present in the Greek case. Competitive material suppliers are closely tied (often with ownership ties) to the cement industry. A number of other building materials industries are also competitive in Greece, making cement a non-isolated case. However, the success of these industries has not spurred the creation of a competitive cement machinery industry, a fact, nevertheless, common among all Greek clusters. Therefore, related and supporting industries can be considered a major source of advantage for the Greek cement industry.

Firm strategy, structure and rivalry had a positive effect on the Greek industry. Managerial skills, personnel policies and the companies' goals regarding domestic market share and foreign expansion played an important role in the industry's development and its success in foreign markets. The industry has also benefited from somehow strong domestic rivalry, in a, nevertheless, oligopolistic environment, a successful policy of vertical integration and strong geographical concentration.

Government involvement is a characteristic of most Greek industries. The cement industry is no exception, although, only in the 1980s was the State's direct or indirect role a major one, with the intervention to rescue the financially troubled producers. In most other circumstances, the cement industry was not considered a 'targeted' one and, in fact, certain bureaucratic obstacles have disadvantaged the industry. Chance events have affected the Greek cement industry in a positive way in the early 1970s and a negative one in the 1980s, while the overall effect has been slightly positive, with the government's help.

There is sufficient evidence to support the role of all four groups of determinants of competitive advantage in the Greek cement industry case. These four groups, along with the effects of government and chance, form a coherent picture of the industry's competitiveness. What is even more important, is that none of these groups is unrelated to the others. A self-reinforcing system seems to be at work, where an advantage in one factor, affects the status of several other factors and this, in turn, upgrades the status of the original factor, in a circular way. However, gaps do exist in particular aspects within each determinant.

4 The Greek Rolled Aluminium Products Industry

Introduction

The second case study examines an industry from the Materials/Metals cluster. This cluster contains a number of very competitive Greek industries, including many aluminium-related industries. Among these aluminium-related industries, the rolled aluminium products industry is a rather special case. Its competitive advantage is not directly related to the presence of bauxite in Greece as is the case with, for example, the alumina refining industry, so it cannot be classified as resource-dependent. Also, rolled aluminium products' trade is controlled by an oligopoly of large, vertically integrated firms. In this environment, the apparent competitive advantage of the Greek rolled products industry, merits further examination.

The production of metallic aluminium comprises several stages, each one being an industry on its own with specific characteristics. These stages are: the bauxite mining, the alumina refining and the aluminium smelting (Brown and McKern, 1987: 22-23). Primary (from smelting) and secondary (recovered from scrap) aluminium are then transformed into milled products and castings. The term aluminium fabrication is commonly used for the first stage in the production of aluminium products. This first stage is where aluminium is: a) extruded, to produce bars and rods, b) rolled, to produce sheets and plates, c) cast, to produce castings. Aluminium can also be forged, drawn, compacted and sintered or machined and joined, using a variety of methods (Bunker and Ciccantell, 1994: 50). The products of aluminium fabrication are then used in manufacturing plants, where they either undergo some minor modifications and are sold to the consumer (for example, as aluminium foil, or aluminium pipes), or are used as inputs in other industries, such as the automotive, construction and packaging industries. The properties of aluminium products have turned aluminium into the second most widely used metal in the world, after iron and steel (GATT, 1987: 2, 5).

The focus of this chapter is the rolled aluminium products industry. As a fabrication industry, it transforms aluminium into sheets and plates of various sizes. Hot and cold rolling are used to reduce the metal plates to the exact thickness required by each customer. Most end uses have their own specifications in terms of the sheets' or plates' size and the aluminium alloys used for their fabrication. The sheets or plates produced are delivered to the customers (or to a plant of the same company) usually in flat or coiled form. These industrial customers then paint, cut and shape these sheets to produce houseware, building materials, packaging products, automotive parts, etc.

Rolled products fabrication is dominated by big firms in developed countries. In 1996, out of the almost 10 million tons of rolled products manufactured, 4.3 million were produced in the USA, 3.4 million in Europe and 1.4 million in Japan (UN, Industrial Commodity Statistics Yearbook). The same developed countries, with the addition of Canada, are the leading exporters of rolled aluminium products (UN, International Trade Statistics Yearbook).

In the European Union, Germany accounts for more than half of the EU's 1996 production of 3 million tons. Italy, the UK, Spain, Belgium, Austria, Greece and France are the other major EU rolled aluminium producers (UN, Industrial Commodity Statistics Yearbook). The same countries are also the major EU exporters, with Germany and France being among the world's leading exporters (usually in the top three places along with the United States). Germany is also one of the world's largest importers of rolled products, as these products are used as inputs in a number of industries where Germany has a strong position (UN, International Trade Statistics Yearbook).

The European and North American firms of the traditional aluminium oligopoly (Alcan, Alcoa, Reynolds, Kaiser, Pechiney and Alusuisse) still dominate all stages of aluminium production and fabrication, aided by the concentration of bauxite reserves in a few countries, the use of bauxite of specific composition in most alumina plants, the need for access to huge amounts of cheap energy for aluminium smelting and the technological sophistication required for the production of most aluminium products. Capital requirements for establishing a new unit are also another entry-deterrent for aspiring firms. In order, however, to effectively control bauxite sources and overcome barriers to trade, most of the big firms have adopted, since the late 1950s, a joint ventures strategy as a means of expanding their presence outside their home countries (Bunker and Ciccantell, 1994: 58-62). Because of the lower capital costs at the fabrication stage, a lot of smaller firms have entered this stage. Nevertheless, large vertically integrated firms are still the major fabricators as a result of their ability to conduct extensive R&D and exploit the communication benefits of integration. Moreover, because of the technological demands of aluminium fabrication and the need for close contact with the customer, fabrication facilities are still mostly located in industrialised countries (Bunker and Ciccantell, 1994: 51).

The Greek Aluminium Industries

Historical Development

The first aluminium-related industry in Greece was that of bauxite mining. In the mid-1920s, I. and G. Barlos formed the first bauxite mining company in Distomon, followed by H. Eliopoulos in the nearby mountains of Parnassos and Giona, in Central Greece. Production reached 4,000 tons in 1927 and 6,000 in 1929 and by 1939, as the major companies grew substantially, 200,000 tons of bauxite were extracted from locations in Central Greece and the nearby islands. In the early 1950s, production reached high levels again, while discussions started for the creation of a processing operation in Greece. With this prospect, bauxite production rose to 1 million tons in 1961 (Athanassakopoulos, 1997: 1).

An agreement between the Greek state and Pechiney, the French giant, granting the company certain privileges mainly related to electricity prices, led to the creation, in 1961, of Aluminium of Greece. Production of alumina and primary aluminium started in 1966, growing at a rapid rate. At the same time, a number of aluminium fabricators were established, completing Greece's presence in all aluminium-related industries. A few of these firms were operating before 1966, either using other metals or having a small production. However, as Aluminium of Greece's production rose and the company was ready to offer technical assistance to upstart fabricators in Greece, the number of aluminium-related firms increased.

Extruded products, mainly for construction purposes, were the main focus of production during the 1970s. Most of the major Greek firms were established between 1972 and 1979. Even now, as construction needs are still high, the extrusion industry is where most of the Greek aluminium-related firms are found. The Greek rolled products industry appeared in 1973, with the incorporation of the only fabricator of rolled products, Elval. Its production rose rapidly, reaching and surpassing the production of all the other fabricators.

Greece also has a few firms in the aluminium cables industry and the die-casting industry. Their production is small, compared to the other industries, and the limited home demand for their products makes it unlikely that these industries will develop further. There is also one producer of secondary aluminium, Epalme, established in 1973, with 51% of its shares now belonging to Aluminium of Greece. In the 1980s an effort was made by the Greek Industrial Development Bank (ETVA), to create a new manufacturing facility in order to produce alumina. However, the whole project was based on an inter-governmental agreement with the Soviet Union. Its successor, Russia, was unwilling to fulfil its financial obligations and the whole project was abandoned in the late 1990s. The port infrastructure already built was sold to the Viochalco group of companies, the owners of Elval.

The Major Firms

In the bauxite mining industry the main competitors are two. The first one is Silver and Baryte Ores Mining Co. SA, having absorbed the Bauxites Parnasse company, which has extracted bauxite from the Parnassos mountain since the 1930s. Its shares are quoted on the Athens Stock Exchange, however a controlling share still remains in the possession of the Kyriakopoulos and Eliopoulos families. The other competitor is Delphi-Distomon SA, established in 1975 as a subsidiary of Aluminium of Greece. In 1987, it absorbed Bauxites of Delphi, one of the original Greek bauxite producers and in December 1989, it acquired Hellenic Bauxites of Distomon, a mining firm operating since 1967.

For the alumina and primary aluminium industries in Greece, a monopoly situation has developed. The only company active in both industries is Aluminium of Greece SA, one of the largest Greek manufacturing companies. The founding aluminium multinational, Pechiney, still controls 60% of the stock, while the rest is traded on the Athens Stock Exchange.

The fabrication industries that are most prominent in Greece are the extruded and the rolled products industries. In the extruded products industry, six companies accounted for slightly less than 65% of Greek 1999 production (ICAP, 2000: 49). Alumil Mylonas, with a 14% share of Greek production, was established in 1988 as a family enterprise by G. Mylonas, who still owns a majority of the shares, while the rest are traded on the Athens Stock Exchange since 1997. Profil Aluminio, the second largest producer (12% share of Greek 1999 production), is also a family enterprise owned by L. Tzirakian since its establishment in 1974. From the other four main extrusion companies, two are exclusively producing extruded aluminium products (Etem and Exalco) and two have also other industrial and commercial activities (Soulis and Albio Viokarpet). Etem is a member of the Viochalko group of companies and its shares are traded on the Athens Stock Exchange. Exalco and Albio Viokarpet belong to the same group, of which Albio Viokarpet has, since April 2000, become the holding company (ICAP, 2000).

In the rolled products industry there is only one fabricator, Elval, again a member of the Viochalko group. Elval Hellenic Aluminium Industry SA was incorporated in 1973 and is quoted on the Athens Stock Exchange since 1996, as a result of a merger with a company of the same group, Vepal SA. Still, a majority of the outstanding shares is owned by Viochalco, the holding company, Aluminium of Athens (a financial services company of the same group), and the Stassinopoulos family, the founders of the Viochalco group.

A picture of the aluminium-related firms' performance and of the differences among the various Greek industries can be obtained from an overview of the main companies' financial results for 1999 in Table 4.1. Elval has reached a very high level of sales, slightly less than that of the six major extruded products fabricators combined. The high increase in sales over the last decade has also been accompanied by impressive profit growth. In 1999, Elval was 13th among all Greek industrial firms in terms of both profits and sales (Tortopidis, 2001: 338).

Table 4.1 Financial results of Greek aluminium-related companies (1999)

Companies	Turnover (million Drachmas)	Net Income (million Drachmas)
Aluminium of Greece	109,121	7,012
Elval	86,694	12,045
Silver and Baryte Ores Mining Co.	30,613	4,211
Alumil Mylonas	19,216	1,719
Albio Viokarpet	17,972	3,412
Soulis	14,126	678
Profil Aluminio	12,980	1,000
Etem	12,929	2,105
Exalco	11,497	1,013
Delphi-Distomon	6,308	1,159

Source: ICAP, 2001.

Production - Exports

Production of bauxite was at its highest in 1980, a few years after the creation of the Greek aluminium fabrication industries. The 3.2 million tons extracted ranked Greece eighth among world bauxite producers. Since then, Greek production has followed international trends, decreasing slowly and in 1999 it stood at approximately 1.8 million tons. Aluminium of Greece uses 60% of the Greek bauxite, while the rest is exported, making Greece an important bauxite exporter (Christodoulou, 1995: 2; Tsekrekos, 1998: 93; Greek Mining Enterprises Association, 2000: 16).

Aluminium of Greece is the only alumina and primary aluminium producer in Greece. Using Greek bauxite, it started production in 1966 and by 1968 was producing 223,000 tons of alumina. Production rose until

1980, when it reached 494,300 tons, and then fluctuated until 1990. Since then a further increase has pushed alumina production to about 650,000 tons annually. Half of that amount is exported, constituting 3% of world exports, while the other half is used by the company for the production of aluminium (Athanassakopoulos, 1997: 3).

Primary aluminium's production has followed the same trends as alumina, starting at 78,450 tons in 1968 (two years after the firm started operating) and reaching 146,500 tons in 1980. After a small decline in the mid-1980s, production reached 148,000 tons in 1988 and remained steady until 1998, when it increased to 158,000 tons (Athanassakopoulos, 1997: 4; Aluminium de Grèce, 1999: 22). In 1999, it is estimated that a further 8% increase has brought primary aluminium production to around 170,000 tons (ICAP, 2000: 2). Around 50,000 tons were exported in the early and mid-1990s, while in 1998 this quantity was increased to 62,400 tons and in 1999 it is estimated to have reached 70,000 tons (Aluminium de Grèce, 1996: 6; Aluminium de Grèce, 1999: 6; ICAP, 2000: 2). The rapid rise in the fabricators' production and their need for supplier diversification have necessitated significant aluminium imports, although the aluminium trade balance is still positive.

The fabrication industries had a production of 20,000 tons in 1969, one year after Aluminium of Greece started producing at normal levels. Since then, production has been rising, especially in the extruded and rolled products industries. Exports took off in the 1970s and have been growing since, with minor setbacks in the 1985-1986 and 1988-1989 periods. Until 1983 the main export markets for Greek aluminium products were the countries of the Middle East. Since then, the European Union has become the primary market for these products (Christodoulou, 1995: 6).

Until about 1979, both rolled and extruded products had almost the same shares of Greek production. In the years that followed, extruded products took a larger share and, in 1985, rolled products only accounted for about 40% of Greek production (with 36,000 tons), while the output of the extrusion industry was at 52,000 tons. The situation was reversed since the early 1990s and in 1999 rolled products production was 130,000 tons, 20,000 tons more than the extruded products production (ICAP, 2000: 46, 51). Exports of aluminium fabricated products have been rising throughout the 1980s, especially for extruded products. In the 1990s it was the rolled products that took the lead, with exports rising from 52,865 tons in 1993 to 96,000 tons in 1999 (ICAP, 1998: 94; ICAP, 2000: 62). Extruded products exports have increased to 39,000 tons in 1999, after a period of stagnation in the early and mid-1990s (ICAP, 2000: 54). Imports were approximately 10% of exports in 1999 (ICAP, 2000: 54, 61).

Sources of Competitive Advantage

Factor Conditions

Greece has very high bauxite deposits, 120 million tons of known reserves and another 500 million tons of possible reserves, which are the eighth largest for any country in the world (Christodoulou, 1995: 1-2). Greece is also the major bauxite producer in the European Union and one of the few European producers (ICAP, 1998: 3; UN, Industrial Commodity Statistics Yearbook). Both these factors provided the initial impetus for the creation of all aluminium-related industries in Greece. Another advantage of Greek bauxite is its high content in alumina (aluminium oxide) that is commonly around 57%, while it ranges between 30% and 62% in various deposits all over the world. There are, however, some peculiarities with Greek bauxite.

The first one is that it is very hard and therefore requires more energy for its treatment. The second one is that a lot of the Greek reserves are underground and can only be recovered by digging tunnels, while in other countries, like Australia or Jamaica, bauxite is mainly recovered by open pit methods. Some open pit mines still exist in Greece, but reserves there are being depleted and environmental objections to this method are growing (Christodoulou, 1995: 2). The declining use of open pit mining raises the cost of extracting bauxite and is added to the higher labour costs, which are around $6.7/ton, compared to a low of $0.7/ton for Brazil. Total net operating cost per ton in Greece is around $14, while in Brazil it is $3 (Bunker and Ciccantell, 1994: 43). These disadvantages, however, are not a major threat to the rolled aluminium industry as mining and milling of bauxite constitutes only about 1.9% of aluminium production costs and Aluminium of Greece has made the necessary adjustments in its alumina plant to deal with the hardness of Greek bauxite.

The price of the aluminium for the rolled products industry is determined in the world market. Therefore, the industry draws no price advantage from the presence of bauxite mines and alumina and aluminium plants in Greece. In fact, for diversification reasons and because Greek aluminium is not sufficient to cover Greek production, the industry imports part of its raw materials from several countries, both European (France, Germany, Norway, Russia) and Asian (Japan, Taiwan).

Elval is the only major company in the rolled products industry. It employs 670 people, 80% of which work in the plant and 20% are considered administrative employees. However, most of the administration functions are located in a building adjacent to the plant in Oinofyta, Boiotia, a fact permitting close contact between the production workforce and the administration staff. The closest contact is between the production planners and the sales people, since all of the production is made on order.

One of the great advantages of the company is its sales department. The personnel there is highly qualified in marketing activities, with appropriate University degrees, and employees are also encouraged by the company to pursue further studies. The sales department also includes some engineers to provide clients with the necessary technical expertise.

The workers in the factory perform strenuous tasks. It was mentioned in my interviews that finding qualified personnel, willing to do the particular work required, is hard. However, the fact that the company is not far from Athens (about 45 mins. drive) or some other towns (a lot of workers come from the nearby town of Halkis) has provided it with a good pool of applicants. Wages are satisfactory, given the company's excellent sustained performance, but are not considered exceptionally high relative to the average manufacturing firm. As far as labour relations are concerned, no major problems have been observed over the years and it is to be noted that a Union does not exist in the company. There is also a lot of personal contact with the main shareholders, the Stassinopoulos family, preventing any conflicts from escalating.

The company is very active in the area of training. The head of every department is responsible to ensure that all of his employees receive adequate training. The company has also sought funding for its training programs from the EU, ever since these became available. There are usually two seminar periods every year, with 30-50 employees trained in each period, while on-the-job training is also being offered, mainly to newcomers.

Elval's financing needs have so far been covered by bank loans, funds provided by the Viochalco group and, more recently, by equity issues. The fact that the company belongs to a group of very successful and profitable firms has helped it a lot. In fact, Viochalco is considered to have 'an excellent reputation in the local market and good relations with financial institutions' (ICAP, 1997b). The company's debt load is by no means excessive and the loan terms are usually favourable compared to the average Greek firm. Therefore, capital availability can be considered an advantage for the Greek rolled products industry.

The road infrastructure was mentioned in the previous case study as a disadvantage for the Greek cement industry. In the case of rolled aluminium products it is still a disadvantage but its effects are smaller. Raw material comes either from Aluminium of Greece, located in the same prefecture as Elval's plant, or arrives from abroad in a nearby port. The same situation is repeated in the transport of finished products. Most of the Greek customers of the company are located in Boiotia (Alouman), neighbouring Attica (Aluminium of Attica) or in Patras (Alucanco, now part of Hellas Can) and Korinth (Hellas Can), again not far from Elval's factory and in the part of Greece with the best motorways. The only problems with the road infrastructure are evident in the transport of products exported to European countries.

The remaining exports are shipped through the port of Piraeus, again not more than an hour's drive from Elval's factory. Shipping has not been as important for the development of the rolled aluminium products industry, as it was in the cement case, since the product is easier to carry, requires less specialised equipment and has a high price/weight ratio.

Energy requirements in the industry are not as high as in the cement industry or the primary aluminium industry. Therefore, the fact that Greek electricity prices are close to the OECD average (IEA, 1996) means that the Greek industry is not very disadvantaged. However, it is true that electricity prices in Greece are higher than in some of the main developed competitor countries (for example, Canada) and most of the developing competitor countries.

The Greek rolled aluminium products industry has benefited initially from geographical advantages. In the early stages of its development, exports were directed to the nearby markets of the then booming Middle East. Specifically, in 1976, 54% of rolled products exports went to the Middle East, while in 1983 the Middle East's share of Greek exports was 27% (Ghekas, 1985: 34). Very soon, however, the European Union became the main export target (48% of exports in 1983) and geographical advantages became less important. Since the mid-1980s Elval has had customers all over the world, from Japan to the United States, and geography seems to offer little advantage.

R&D for aluminium industries is concentrated in the research laboratories of the few major multinational competitors. There is little R&D done outside these huge firms and therefore Elval cannot be expected to have a significant R&D contribution. However, the company has a team of engineers that deals both with maintaining the product's quality and with exploring the properties of various aluminium alloys, making some worthwhile discoveries and innovations in the process. It also has some know-how transfer agreements with Pechiney, the owner of Aluminium of Greece, and other foreign aluminium firms. Therefore, the disadvantage of the lack of extensive R&D has not been a major one for the industry. Efforts are also under way to enhance the company's R&D capabilities by hiring personnel with experience in research outside Greece. Furthermore, Elval is participating in certain European Union initiatives, related to aluminium research and co-operating with the Technical Universities of Athens and Crete.

The industry has greatly benefited from the work of the Aluminium Association of Greece. Although there have been many contacts among all Greek aluminium-related industries since their establishment, it was only after the Association was founded in 1985 that firms in all these industries, from bauxite mining to aluminium fabrication, instituted a systematic co-operation. The Association has been adequately funded from its very start, mainly from Aluminium of Greece, and has been very active. It organises seminars for employees as well as workshops to present recent developments in the aluminium industries to the general public, government agencies and private organisations. It collects statistical data on all aluminium industries and conducts relevant studies. It also helps promote Greek aluminium products by organising international expositions in Greece, participating in such events abroad and establishing contacts with Commercial Attachés of most foreign embassies in Athens. The Association has also operated, since 1986, an extensive recycling program, for the benefit of the industry and its image. In the late 1990s fabricators have decided to create the Aluminium Manufacturers Association of Greece, which, in co-operation with the Aluminium Association, will promote further the fabricators' interests.

Demand Conditions

Greek rolled aluminium production is mainly intended for use by the packaging industry. In 1999, from the 130,000 tons produced, 98,500 were for packaging use, while a further 22,300 were to be used by the construction industry (ICAP, 2000: 52). The packaging segment is also the biggest one in most developed markets, with construction coming usually second (ICAP, 2000: 100). Therefore, the Greek rolled aluminium products industry benefits from an emphasis on the segments that are also the major ones in foreign markets and especially in EU ones where half of Greek fabricated aluminium exports are directed (ICAP, 2000: 66). The reduced emphasis, however, on the mechanical and electrical equipment and the transport-related segments, which are only slightly less important to construction in the EU markets, has been a relative disadvantage of the Greek demand structure, especially given the sophistication of certain industrial customers in these segments (ICAP, 2000: 100).

The Greek aluminium packaging industry is the major local customer for the rolled products industry. Most of the output is used for the production of aluminium foil and cans, with a smaller amount used for other packaging products (ICAP, 1998: 86). The number of buyers is relatively small as the aluminium packaging industry is capital intensive and the Greek market is limited. Aluminium packaging companies are very dynamic and have exhibited solid financial results. During the last decade these firms have also had an impressive export performance. The major ones are: Alouman (family owned, exported 94% of its production in 1999), Sanitas-Sanitas (the major foil producer, operating since 1975), and Hellas Can (publicly traded, controlled by the Carnaudmetalbox group, among the top 40 Greek firms in both sales and profits, exported 50% of its 1999 production) (ICAP, 1998: 75-84, ICAP, 2000: 40-43). The combined sales of these companies for 1999 were 53 billion drachmas, with profits of 7.7 billion drachmas (ICAP, 2000: 45; ICAP, 2001). The interchanges between Elval, the aluminium fabricator, and these manufacturing companies are obvious as, according to estimates, 70% of the manufacturers' production costs can be attributed to the raw materials, that is, mainly the aluminium plates and sheets (IOBE, 1993: 23).

Historically, the Greek market has not been a major one for aluminium products. This is, first of all, evident from the per capita consumption of aluminium. Due to the absence of major mechanical and electrical engineering industries in Greece, the per capita consumption of aluminium has been among the lowest in the European Union (ICAP, 1998: 4; ICAP, 2000: 97). The initial development of the rolled products market was due to demand from the Greek construction and household products industries, which between 1976 and 1980 used 33% and 26%, respectively, of the rolled products sold in Greece. The packaging industry used 26% of rolled products sold in the Greek market in this time period (IOBE, 1983: 19). By 1983, Elval had been able to produce more sheets appropriate for packaging products, and that shift in Elval's production coincided with a world-wide trend of increased use of aluminium in packaging. That year Elval sold 13,000 tons to the Greek market, 36% of which to the packaging industries, and, adding the 4,600 tons of imports, Greek per capita consumption of rolled products was 1.8 kg (Ghekas, 1985: 28-34).

The Greek market for rolled products remained stagnant between 1985 and 1989, registering increases of 1.1% per year (Christodoulou, 1996: 4-5). Since then the Greek packaging industry has shown significant growth and Elval has been supplying it with all the necessary inputs (for example, in the 1970s there was no Greek production of aluminium cans, while in 1997 26% of rolled sheets went to the production of cans) (IOBE, 1983: 19; ICAP, 1998: 86-88). However, there is no indication that Greek demand for new and improved products has been anticipatory of world trends.

The 1989-1993 was again a high growth period and in 1993 home demand reached 43,757 tons (IOBE, 1993: 14; ICAP, 2000: 73). In 1994 and 1995 consumption remained stable, while since 1996 it has been around 49,000 tons. The share of imports in recent years has consistently been below 50% (ICAP, 2000: 73). At the same time, since 1989 one can observe the phenomenon of rising exports in the years when Greek demand declines. It is striking that in 1992 Greek demand decreased by 18%, while exports increased by 34%, while in 1993 Greek demand increased by 37% and exports decreased by 6% (ICAP, 1996: 136-137). Stagnation in the Greek market also coincided with the export surge of 1994-1995 and 1997 (ICAP, 2000: 73). According to industry experts, part of the favourable export performance since 1992 can be attributed to the apparent saturation of the Greek market (Christodoulou, 1996: 5; Athanassakopoulos, 1997: 6).

In terms of 'mobile buyers' some of the initial export expansion to the Middle East was probably due to the strong presence of Greek construction companies there. Since the 1980s this presence has diminished and the bulk of rolled products is used for packaging. The 1990s saw a re-emergence of 'mobile buyers' in the form of beverages companies which used aluminium cans manufactured in Greece for their sales to the Balkan countries, either directly or through local bottling facilities and packaging companies, which sell part of their output to the same countries.

Related and Supporting Industries

The Materials/Metals cluster is the third most important for the Greek economy, both in terms of the number of competitive industries and in terms of the share that these industries' exports represent, which in some years exceeds 10% of all Greek exports. The two main groups of industries in this cluster are the iron and steel one and the aluminium one, with some copper industries completing the picture. The competitiveness of all these groups is, to a certain extent, related, as they use similar technologies and machinery, especially in the fabrication stage. Moreover, in Greece there is a lot of cross-ownership among these industries, something certainly true for Elval, which is part of a larger group of metal processing companies. Elval's competitiveness can also be linked with the satisfactory performance of the other main fabrication industry in Greece, the extruded aluminium products industry.

The data previously presented, show a very competitive industry, with strong financial performance, increasing sales, for the main 18 extrusion firms, from 37 billion drachmas in 1992 to 72 billion in 1995 and 98 billion in 1997, increasing production (49,500 tons in 1993, 81,000 tons in 1997) and high profits (ICAP, 1996; ICAP, 1998: 33, 35). Exports of extruded products have also been high, for example in 1978 Greek products accounted for 2.33% of world trade of aluminium bars, wire etc., while in 1992, Greek aluminium firms exported 1.59% of world exports of bars, wire etc. and 2.6% of tubes and tube fittings (UN, International Trade Statistics Yearbook). Both aluminium fabrication industries have benefited from the satisfactory performance of the construction industry, especially in the 1970s and 1980s. The rolled products industry, in particular, has also gained from Greece's strong position in the processed foods, beverages and tobacco industries, which use aluminium packaging extensively.

The competitiveness of the bauxite mining, alumina and primary aluminium industries, which were established before the rolled products industry, has been another positive factor for the industry's development. Figure 4.1 shows the entire group of Greek aluminium-related industries.

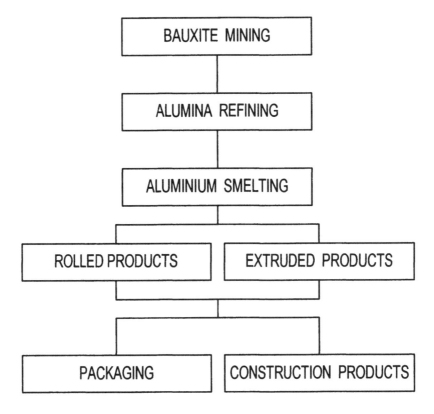

Figure 4.1 Competitive Greek aluminium-related industries

Greece is essentially the only bauxite producing country in the European Union and the mining firms have exhibited sound financial results and exports that represented 3.82% of world exports in 1992 (UN, International Trade Statistics Yearbook). The Greek alumina plant accounts for 9% of the European capacity, and while Greece exports almost half of its production, capturing 3% of 1992 world exports, the rest of Europe imports 35% of the alumina used in aluminium production (Christodoulou, 1995: 3).

Aluminium of Greece, the only Greek aluminium producer and the only domestic supplier to Elval, has consistently been among the top 20 Greek manufacturing firms in terms of assets, sales, market capitalisation and, usually, profits. Aluminium exports, almost 1% of world exports in 1992, are given attention by the company but the domestic market is not neglected either. In their early stages, fabrication industries have also benefited from direct technical assistance from Aluminium of Greece, while now co-operation exists mainly through the Aluminium Association.

Similarly to the cement case, there is no aluminium machinery industry in Greece. However, factory personnel is adequately trained to make even large scale adjustments to the machinery, if needed for particular orders.

Firm Strategy, Structure and Rivalry

Elval, the only company in the Greek rolled products industry, is part of the Viochalco group of companies, one of the largest and fastest growing industrial complexes in Greece. Established in 1937, the group comprises a large number of manufacturing firms, mainly active in metal industries, and some trading companies, engaged in the sale of metal and fabricated metal products. Elval's ownership structure seems to have had a positive effect on the company. One of the reasons for this is that Elval is not part of a huge conglomerate of unrelated firms, but of a group of companies with closely related activities. In fact, the other main manufacturing firms in the Viochalco group are very successful and among the leaders in their fields. Sidenor (active in iron and steel) is one of the largest Greek metal-processing firms, with 1999 profits of 11.65 billion drachmas, that ranked the company 14th among Greek industrial firms. Chalkor, the major Greek copper-processing firm, produces both rolled and extruded copper products, and its profits for 1999 were 13 billion drachmas (12th among Greek industrial firms). Hellenic Cables is the only Greek producer of certain kinds of cables with a 30% share of Greek cable sales and 1999 profits of 1.95 billion drachmas (62nd among Greek industrial firms). Etem, the extruded aluminium fabricator is also a member of the same group (Viochalco, 1997; Tortopidis, 2001: 338, 346, 348). The group is committed to the metal industries and that partly explains the fact that it has been successful in most of its ventures in these industries.

Belonging to such a group has also another advantage. Sound management practices and able managers can be transferred from company to company, especially since they all are in related sectors. Elval, in particular, is considered well managed, certainly above Greek manufacturing firms' average, by all the industry experts interviewed. The same experts consider especially good the quality of the engineers managing the production line, as well as the sales managers. In creating a competent sales department, the company has benefited from its interactions with the trading companies in the Viochalco group.

Elval is facing tough competition from vertically integrated aluminium producers as well as independent fabricators which have appeared in most parts of the world. Rolled aluminium products are traded at high volumes and account for a large part of aluminium trade. The fact that Elval holds consistently a significant share of world exports (more than 0.5%, some years well above 1%) demonstrates a successful export strategy. In fact, from its very start Elval realised the limitations of the Greek market for an industry requiring large production volumes. Therefore, it sought to achieve the production levels necessary in order to be cost competitive through increasing exports, that in 1999 represented 75% of total production (Dokas, 2001: 36). Cost reduction has been a major target for the company. Investment in new machinery has been consistently high, although old machinery is not discarded but is used for auxiliary purposes. In terms of personnel, hiring is kept at precisely the levels appropriate for the company's needs, and the total number of employees is rising very slowly despite significant rises in output. Consideration is also given to transportation costs and if the company can secure low rates for a particular destination, then that destination is targeted by the sales agents.

Quality has also been instrumental in the company's foreign sales. Quality controls are performed throughout the production line and any products not meeting the specifications required are being re-melted and used for raw material. The combination of good quality and low prices has enabled the company to follow its aggressive export strategy.

Another part of that strategy has been the establishment of wholly-owned trading companies in many foreign markets, especially European, and the co-operation with well-established trading companies in other markets, mainly the distant ones such as Japan and Singapore. This dual strategy reflects the market conditions in every country, but is also a reflection of the company's export goals. Elval seeks to have a continued presence in major European markets, where its competitors are operating and where product innovations occur as well as in the Balkan markets, where geographical advantages are important. At the same time, it targets countries where the market is growing, such as the Middle East in the 1970s and Asia in the 1990s, with the flexibility that co-operation with a local company offers.

In terms of the geographic concentration of aluminium-related firms in Greece, the location of bauxite reserves in Central Greece dictated the location choices for the mining companies, with Silver and Baryte Ores Co. exploiting the mountains of Parnassos and Giona and Delphi-Distomon operating in Boiotia and Fokida, while some smaller companies are operating in the same prefectures (Boiotia, Fokida, Fthiotida). The alumina and aluminium plants of Aluminium of Greece are located very close to the bauxite sources, at Distomon, in the Boiotia prefecture. In the extruded products industry, some firms are located in Boiotia (Profil Aluminium and one of Etem's facilities, both very close to Elval's main factory) or in Attica (Etem's other unit, Alco Hellas, Vioprofal, Deco, Katal and others), near the aluminium plants and the Athens market. Most of the others, and among them Almaco and Aloumil Mylonas, are in the north of Greece, usually not far from the second largest Greek city, Thessaloniki. Another big firm, Exalco and the new factory of Exalco's owners, Albio Biokarpet, is located in Larissa, Thessaly's largest city, not far from Central Greece.

The fact that the rolled products industry essentially comprises one firm provides limited scope for analysing geographic concentration. However, some facts do provide support for Porter' geographic concentration argument. Elval has its main facility at Oinofyta (Boiotia). That main factory is close to the Aluminium of Greece facilities in Boiotia, where more than 50% of the raw material is produced, and also close to the bauxite mining firms, many of the extruded aluminium products firms and the only secondary aluminium producer (Epalme in Aspropyrgos, Attica). Elval's main domestic clients are also at a reasonable distance, either in Oinofyta (Sanitas-Sanitas and one of Alpack's and Alouman's factories) or in nearby Attica (the second unit of Alouman), Korinth (one of Hellas Can's units) and Achaia (the former Alucanco factory, now part of Hellas Can). Only two factories (Hellas Can's newest unit and Alpack's second unit) are based in the north of Greece (ICAP, 2000: 37). Of course, all these firms are located in prefectures in close proximity to Athens, the major population centre in Greece. However, there is close co-operation with the geographically concentrated firms, both between Aluminium of Greece and Elval and between Elval and its clients, who often visit the factory to discuss product specifications.

The Role of Government

The government has been neither a major help nor a major hindrance to the rolled products industry. Its direct involvement has been minimal, as the industry is capital-intensive and is little affected by government regulation.

Of course, all aluminium industries are considered internationally competitive and, therefore, their reasonable demands are usually satisfied. Moreover, the existing incentives scheme supports the industry's investments. However, general bureaucratic obstacles, mainly related to delays in investment plans approvals, and local government objections to new facilities are thought to be important obstacles to Greek aluminium firms (Kalloniatis, 1996b: 94).

The Role of Chance

The Greek rolled products industry was started under favourable circumstances. Despite the fact that the Greek market was small and demand for aluminium products low in the 1970s, this was a time when the use of aluminium was increasing rapidly in every developed country, as well as in part of the developing world. Also, given the fact that the Greek market could not probably support more than one competitive firm, the setting up of that firm by a large industrial group, which provided funding and expertise in metals' processing, proved a positive circumstance.

Summary

Aluminium has been in use for a little more than 100 years. During that time, because of its properties and the intense research and marketing efforts of the major aluminium multinationals, aluminium production and consumption have risen substantially, making it the most widely used metal in the world after iron and steel. From the various aluminium-related industries, such as bauxite mining, alumina refining and aluminium smelting, the one analysed here in detail is the rolled products fabrication industry. As with most other aluminium-related industries it is controlled by a few large, integrated multinationals, based in Europe and North America. However, in the last thirty years, a number of smaller fabricators, both from developed and developing countries, and, in some cases, state-owned, have emerged.

The history of aluminium-related industries in Greece starts with the establishment of the first bauxite mining companies in Central Greece, in the mid-1920s. The creation in 1961 of Aluminium of Greece, a subsidiary of the French multinational Pechiney, that would produce both alumina and aluminium, was also the starting point for the Greek fabrication industries. The rolled aluminium products industry appeared in 1973, when its only firm, Elval, was incorporated. Since then the industry has experienced rising production levels, increasing exports to more destinations and impressive financial results. The examination of the industry's sources of competitive advantage using the 'diamond' framework reveals several major interrelated sources of advantage coming from all sides of the diamond.

Factor conditions were important from the very beginning. The availability of abundant bauxite with high alumina content and of alumina and aluminium plants in Greece spurred the industry's creation. Geographic proximity to the rapidly developing Middle East markets provided an additional impetus for growth. However, aluminium is now a commodity traded all over the world and the Middle East markets have stagnated since the mid-1980s. Today, more specialised and advanced factors are important for the industry. These are the quality and productivity of human capital, good labour relations, favourable terms for the supply of capital, proximity of ports and the very active Aluminium Association of Greece which organises seminars, workshops, expositions, recycling programs, and many other activities. The only gap in specialised factors is the lack of extensive R&D.

Demand conditions are the weakest side of the industry's diamond. The only major source of advantage is the quality, competitiveness, and size of independent buyers in Greece, essentially the Greek aluminium packaging industry. The segment structure of the Greek market, with demand mainly from the packaging industry, the presence of 'mobile' buyers as well as the market's high growth and saturation patterns have affected the industry positively. Nevertheless, none of these attributes of Greek demand can be considered an important source of advantage. The size of the Greek market and the lack of early demand for improved products are two attributes that affect adversely the industry's competitive advantage.

Related and supporting industries represent a pivotal source of competitive advantage for the rolled products industry. The Materials/Metals cluster includes many of Greece's most competitive industries (iron and steel, aluminium and copper products). Moreover, all supplier aluminium industries, namely the bauxite mining, alumina refining and aluminium smelting industries, are internationally competitive with impressive export performances and satisfactory financial results. Even the related extruded products industry and the loosely connected food and beverages, tobacco and, to a lesser extent, construction industries are among the competitive Greek industries. The only gap is the absence of an aluminium machinery industry, a common feature for all competitive Greek groups of industries.

Firm strategy, structure and rivalry is a side of the diamond with two major sources of advantage, structure and strategy. The industry's only firm, Elval, is owned by the Viochalco group, a group of well-managed, fast-growing firms, all committed to metal processing industries. Moreover, the company's strategy has been appropriate for the industry, pursuing exports vigorously and constantly targeting costs, without compromising quality. Geographic concentration, that in this case can be viewed as extending to all aluminium-related Greek firms, has also been to Elval's advantage. The third attribute of this group of determinants is domestic rivalry, which in this case is non-existent.

The role of government has not been a major one for the rolled products industry. The help to the industry, coming from the government's positive attitude towards it, has been counterbalanced by the numerous bureaucratic obstacles to investment. Chance events, mainly in the form of foreign markets growth, have been relatively positive during the development of the industry, but since then have played an insignificant role.

What is evident from this case is again that competitive advantage has a multitude of interrelated sources. For the rolled aluminium products in Greece, the presence of competitive related and supplier industries and the structure and strategy of the industry's only firm have worked to the industry's advantage in ways similar to what Porter expects. Factor conditions have also been important, with advantage shifting from basic factors to more specialised, advanced ones, although the transition is still not complete. Demand conditions are the only side of the diamond where results do not fully support Porter's views. The other gap, the absence of domestic rivalry, can also be attributed to the shortcomings of Greek demand, mainly its size and nature. Government and chance have only had a neutral to slightly positive effect on the industry's competitive advantage.

5   The Greek Tourism Industry

Introduction

The third case study is selected from the Entertainment/Leisure cluster, a cluster less developed than most other 'Final Consumption Goods and Services' clusters. The tourism industry is an exceptional case, as it is not only among the few competitive industries in its cluster but also among the few Greek competitive services industries. In 1999, according to the World Tourism Organisation, Greece was 15th in the world in terms of tourist arrivals and 14th in term of receipts. The 12 million tourists that visited Greece in 1999, generated receipts of $7.2 billion, giving Greece a 1.6% share of total world tourism receipts (World Tourism Organisation, 2000).

The tourism industry is a major part of the Greek economy, with a share of GDP that exceeds 7%, while it employs 8-10% of the total Greek labour force (GNTO, 1999: 8-12). These numbers do not reveal the full extent of tourism's role in the economy as they do not show the regional spread of tourist activity. Indeed, most tourist spending is directed to regions where tourism constitutes the main source of income and employment.

The tourism industry is a widespread complex network of businesses engaged in providing the tourist product. The producers in the industry are broadly grouped in four categories. The first one contains those dealing with accommodations, such as hotels/motels, villas, camping sites, apartments, etc. The second category comprises those involved in transportation, i.e. air carriers, sea carriers, railways, car rental enterprises, etc. The third category consists of those involved in managing and maintaining the attractions, both natural (beaches, mountains, etc.) and man-made (archaeological sites, museums, art galleries, theme parks, etc.). The fourth category is much broader and includes both public sector support services (ports, national tourist organisations, local information offices) and private sector support services (catering, financial services, etc.) that are not exclusively operating within the tourism industry (Foster, 1985: 51).

Despite the peculiarities of the production process, the distribution chain is similar to that of many other products. The producers can sell either directly to the consumer or go through middle-men, wholesalers or retailers. Tour operators are the wholesalers in the tourism industry, buying a range of products in bulk and combining them in 'package' tours (Holloway, 1998: 68). 'Package tours' often have their own brand-names separate from those of their components (Zacharatos, 2000: 119). These tours are then sold to travel agents, the retailers in the tourism industry, or directly to the customer-tourist. It must be stressed that the tour operators play an important role, since they combine the goods and services they purchase in a unique way, and some theorists even consider them as real 'producers' of the tourist product (Holloway, 1998: 68). Travel agents can choose whether to sell the ready-made 'package' tours or offer to the client a custom-made combination. Customarily, they do not charge for providing their services, since they receive fees either from producers or tour operators. They do not usually purchase goods and services in advance but on demand from the customer. In any type of purchase, the customer-tourist plays an important part in the definition of his/her tourist product (Foster, 1985: 50-64; Holloway, 1998: 69).

The last fifteen years have been a period of impressive growth for the tourism industry. Tourist arrivals reached 698 million in 2000 and tourism receipts totalled US$476 billion, according to preliminary data of the World Tourism Organisation (2001). Total tourist arrivals have increased more than 20-fold since the 1950s, when the modern tourism industry started growing (Archer, 1989: 594; Coccossis, 1995: 21). While the market shares of the major European and North American destinations have been slightly decreasing, especially in the last fifteen years, these two groups of countries still account for the majority of tourist arrivals. In 2000, Europe had a 58% share of international tourist arrivals (World Tourism Organisation, 2001). The second major tourism destination, the American continent, has seen its share remain steady in the last decades at around 20% of arrivals. A third group of countries, whose tourism industry is rapidly growing, consists of the countries of East Asia and the Pacific that in 1999 captured almost 15% of arrivals, 5% more than their share in 1985 (World Tourism Organisation, 2000).

It is expected that in the near future increased importance will be placed on 'special interest' tourism and new ways of distributing the tourist product. Examples of 'special interest' tourism include agro-tourism or farmhouse tourism, cultural tourism, health tourism and ecological tourism.

The European Union has remained by far the world's major tourism destination for many decades, ever since the phenomenon of mass tourism appeared. This is due to the fact that European Union countries combine tourist infrastructures and political stability with extraordinary cultural monuments and a wide variety of natural attractions. In the two decades between 1967 and 1987, Europe doubled its number of tourist arrivals. The greatest individual increases during that period were Greece (500%) and the United Kingdom (168%) (Lavery, 1989: 141). The period from 1987 to 1991 was still a period of growth, despite the fact that growth rates in the EU were lower than those in America or East Asia. Since then, EU growth rates have been around 2% for arrivals, lower in fact than those for Europe as a whole, while receipts are rising faster, since tourists in the EU spend more per capita (European Commission, 1997: 22.1).

In 1997, the EU accounted for about 40% of international arrivals in the world and a similar proportion of world tourism receipts. Eleven of the EU's fifteen member-states are among the world's top 25 tourism destinations. These figures do not account for domestic tourism and same day visitors, which are estimated to generate a large proportion (about two-thirds) of holidays taken by EU residents (European Commission and Eurostat, 2000: 427). These eleven EU members and their international tourist arrivals for 2000 are: France (74.5 million), Spain (48.5), Italy (41.2), the UK (24.9), Germany (18.9), Austria (17.8), Greece (12.5), Portugal (12), the Netherlands (10.2) and Ireland (6.7) (World Tourism Organisation, 2001).

Tourism is an important economic activity for the European Union. Its contribution to GDP is, on average, 5.5% and the tourism industry accounts for 6% of EU jobs. The countries with a relatively high degree of specialisation in tourism are Spain, Portugal and Austria (European Commission and Eurostat, 2000: 425).

Tourist firms in the EU increasingly invest towards the creation of larger establishments and the reinforcement of partnerships. Still, however, out of over 1.3 million enterprises involved in hotel and restaurant activities, 96% employ less than 9 persons. The main trends in all the establishments' strategies have recently been the targeting of niche markets and the creation of innovative products to appeal to specific segments of the vast tourist market (European Commission, 1997: 22.4 - 22.5).

The economic characteristics of the tourism industry are related to its nature. The tourist product is formed by a number of elements, and can take a great variety of forms. It is composed of a series of products and services offered by independent or co-operating producers. These products and services are complementary to each other and this creates the need for co-ordination among the producers. Sometimes tour operators and travel agents assume such a co-ordinating role. Other times, mergers, acquisitions and strategic alliances between companies offering these complementary products and services become necessary for effective and inexpensive co-ordination. Consolidation and vertical integration of the industry are on the rise, as opportunities for cost savings through integration increase (Dimakouleas, 1996: 52-54; Pappas, 1997: 75; European Commission, 1997: 22.5; Holloway 1998: 73-77).

Another important characteristic of the tourism industry is the way it is affected by external, uncontrollable circumstances. Although all industries are affected by external factors, in the case of tourism some external factors (such as the weather conditions) are part of the tourist product and therefore any major disturbances are felt sooner and with greater intensity. Also, tourism is strongly linked to a country's infrastructures and political stability, issues where the industry can only marginally intervene.

A central feature of the tourism industry, is seasonality. For reasons related to climate, tradition, common vacation periods for schools and workplaces, etc., tourists tend to travel more in specific times of the year with the result that there is an over-concentration of tourist arrivals during two or three months of the year (peak season). The peaking of tourist demand at certain times of the year creates a range of problems for the industry in the 'shoulder' and especially the 'off-season' periods, the most serious of which is the under-utilisation of capacity and the consequent decrease of revenues. So, a major challenge facing the industry is how to increase the number of people willing to take vacations in the off-season by developing and promoting new, attractive packages, targeting niche markets, making more efficient use of information channels, etc. (Fitzpatrick Associates, 1993).

The Greek Tourism Industry

Historical Development

Organised tourism first appeared in Greece around 1895, when a non-profit organisation, called 'Cycling Society', started organising excursions throughout Greece, that were also advertised in the British and French press. Tourism was further developed by the creation of many similar Societies, which were intended to provide specialised tours, like walking tours, tours for observing the natural attractions of a region, etc. A number of tourists, mostly domestic, chose the various spas (Loutraki, Aidipsos, Methana, Kammena Vourla), principally near Athens, where the water had healing qualities. Later, in 1922, the Greek government established the Office for Foreign Visitors and Exhibitions to promote tourist development. In 1929, as tourist flows slowly increased, a separate National Tourism Organisation was founded by the Greek State, to oversee tourist matters (Varvaressos, 1998: 135-136).

In the first post-World War II decade, the State intervened directly in the expansion of the, then still small, tourism industry. Emphasis was placed on reconstructing and improving the country's road network and, through a short-term credit policy, on modernising hotels units, especially in tourism centres well known before the war (Konsolas and Zacharatos, 1992: 58). These improvements were the impetus for the establishment of several tourism-related firms.

International tourist arrivals became a factor in the industry's development after 1954, as the 1953 currency devaluation and other liberalisation measures made Greece a cheap and politically and economically stable destination. This was the time when the state re-established the Greek National Tourism Organisation (GNTO) and designated it as the basic policy agency in the tourism industry. The GNTO encouraged private investments in the industry, and at the same time assumed a leading role in promoting public investments in superstructure, including accommodation facilities (the Xenia hotel chain), especially in regions where the private sector was reluctant to invest (Konsolas and Zacharatos, 1992: 58-59).

An increase in tourism investments became evident, mainly between 1958 and 1963. Political instability in the following years was a restraint for tourist activity. However, since 1970, investment resumed its previous levels and has been considerable ever since, despite the periodic fluctuations (Lagos, 1996: 256). An important characteristic of this period, as well as of the following decade, was the shift of the weight of public investments vis-a-vis private investments from a ratio of 1:1.5 to a 1:8 ratio (and later 1:10) (Chiotis and Coccossis, 1992: 134; Lagos, 1998: 52). The investment boom resulted in the construction of many new hotels and other forms of facilities (camping, bungalows, etc.) which covered to a great extent the growing demand for tourist accommodations, especially in coastal and island areas. This investment surge in the 1970s was not matched by a corresponding improvement in infrastructures, such as transportation networks (Chtouris, 1995: 52).

In 1970, the nights spent in Greek hotels were 11.8 million and Greek citizens accounted for half of them. The first major increase was observed in 1976, two years after the restoration of democracy in Greece, when nights spent by Greeks doubled, compared to 1970, while nights spent by foreign tourists quadrupled, to a total of 31 million. Foreign arrivals were increased from 210,301 in 1956 and 741,193 in 1963 to 1.6 million in 1970 and 4.2 millions in 1976 (Lagos, 1990: 174).

Increases in the numbers of foreign arrivals and nights spent continued until 1980. The early 1980s was a period of stagnation for Greek tourism, which only recovered in 1984 and 1985, when tourist arrivals reached 7 million for the first time. Total nights spent reached 47 million, with Greek tourists accounting for 11 million. Nowadays, Greece has become a major destination, especially for European travellers and tourist arrivals reached 12.5 million in 2000 (World Tourism Organisation, 2001). Although the high growth of all indicators of tourist activity in the 1960s and 1970s has been followed by slower growth in the 1980s and 1990s, the industry continues to expand, undeterred by occasional declines.

A closer look at the composition of foreign arrivals in Greece is essential for understanding the basic features of the Greek industry.

American tourists constituted the major source of income and growth for Greek tourist enterprises in the 1950s and 1960s. Even as late as 1971, USA tourists represented 25% of foreign tourists in Greece. Subsequent growth, however, in tourist numbers came from European countries that in 1981 accounted for 80% of foreign arrivals (Leontidou, 1991: 87). Greece's entry in the EU and the advantages this offered to EU travellers meant that the EU countries would subsequently provide the major sources of incoming tourists. Since 1985, EU tourists account for more than two thirds of foreign arrivals in Greece. In 1999, 20.1% of foreign tourists came from Germany, 20% from the UK, 6.1% from Italy, 10.4% from the Scandinavian countries, 7.8% from the Benelux countries and 4.5% from France. The rest of the foreign tourists come mainly from other European countries, while arrivals from the U.S.A. represented 1.9% of total arrivals (GNTO, 1996: 2; RIT, 2000: 96).

Another characteristic of foreign tourist arrivals in Greece is their seasonality. Although this is a characteristic of tourism industries in most countries, in Greece the problem is particularly acute. Greek hotels, in most major resorts, open in March and close in October or early November. During the 1990s, about 40% of arrivals and nights spent were observed in July and August, while June accounted for around 12-14%. September was also a popular month (up to 15% of total arrivals and nights spent), while the bulk of the remaining arrivals and nights spent took place in October, April and May. The only improvement from previous decades was the slightly reduced importance of July and August, in favour of June and September. Between 1975 and 1995 arrivals in the May-October period had increased by 290.5%, while arrivals in the 'off-season' months (November-March) only by 79.1% (GNTO, 1996: 3-6; Tsitouras, 1998: 4-6; ICAP, 1999c: 23, 25).

The Major Firms

The major developments in the Greek tourism industry took place after 1950. This is when the first major travel services companies were established in the country. Since then, their number has grown enormously and it is now estimated that there are 5,313 travel agencies. In fact, Greece has the highest per capita number of travel agencies in the European Union (DRI Europe, 1997: 22.42, 22.46). Five agencies accounted for about 27% of 'package tours' 1998 arrivals in Greece (ICAP, 1999c: 92-93). Their financial results are presented in Table 5.1.

What should be noted is that most travel agencies dealing with incoming tourists, are either subsidiaries of foreign, mainly European, tour operators or depend on these operators for a large part of their business. It is common for foreign tour operators to define exactly the 'package' sold to the customer and then use the Greek agencies in order to carry out the bookings. The major foreign tour operators and the number of tourists they sent to Greece in 1994 were: Thomson (588,000 tourists), TUI (330,000), Neckermann (295,000) and First Choice (290,000) (Pappas, 1997: 82).

Table 5.1 Financial results of Greek travel agencies (1999)

Companies	Turnover (million Drachmas)	Net Income (million Drachmas)
TUI Hellas	11,865	1,076
Zeus Krete	4,478	318
Hellenic Tours	4,251	19
Plotin Travel	3,943	81
Nouvelles Frontieres	3,795	-17

Source: ICAP, 2001.

Another important part of the Greek tourism industry is lodging. It comprises establishments that vary widely, in terms of size and services provided (large or medium-sized hotels, small family-run hotels, houses or rooms for rent, etc.). In 1999, Greece had 8,244 hotels, according to the Hotel Chamber of Greece, while 510,869 more people could be accommodated in 27,764 licensed non-hotel lodging units (GNTO, 1999: 16; Papanikos, 2000: 29). Of the major Greek hotels, a few are part of big international chains. These are mainly situated in Athens and the chains represented are: Intercontinental, Hilton, Marriott and Sheraton. Hyatt is operating a hotel in Thessaloniki, with a casino and a conference centre. A number of other big hotels are members of international marketing organisations, such as Best Western, Relais & Chateau and Leading Hotels of the World (Arthur Andersen, 1997: 168).

There are also some domestic chains of which the most important are: Xenia (government owned, some of its hotels have been privatised), Grecotel, the largest and most dynamic Greek chain that owns or operates twenty-two hotels in most major Greek tourism destinations, Aldemar (with hotels in Crete, Rhodes and Olympia), Chandris (with big hotels in Athens, Chios, Corfu and Mykonos), Divani Hotels, Maris Hotels, Helios and Sani (ICAP, 1999d: 79-82). The financial results of the major Greek hotel enterprises for 1999 are presented below, in Table 5.2. It should be noted that some of the major chains have their hotels in separate companies, for example, Grecotel, which is represented in the table by Daskhotels that includes only three of its hotels.

Table 5.2 Financial results of Greek hotel enterprises (1999)

Companies	Turnover (million Drachmas)	Net Income (million Drachmas)
Hyatt Regency	29,832	11,317
Athenaeum (Intercontinental)	9,764	277
Esperia	9,651	313
Ge.To.Xe.K. 'Aldemar'	9,485	680
Astir Palace	8,027	1,224
Helios Tourist Co.	7,598	1,512
Daskotels	7,397	608

Source: ICAP, 2001.

Another part of the tourism industry is the yachting companies and cruise ships operators, of which Greece has 105. Most of these companies are small, with only five of them having more than 100 employees (Arthur Andersen, 1997: 171). Other parts of the industry cater to the needs of both tourists and non-tourists. The most important is the one that includes the restaurants, bars, cafes, and other eating places. There are 19,200 such establishments in Greece, employing 50,980 persons (Fitzpatrick Associates, 1997: 22.10). In terms of transport-related companies, the passenger ferries market in the Aegean is very concentrated, with Minoan Lines, MFD, Anek, Nel and Strintzis Lines being the major players. There are also many small and larger car rental companies, with Hertz and Avis dominating the Greek market. In the airlines market, the local dominance of Olympic Airways is threatened by some private companies (Aegean and Cronus among others).

Sources of Competitive Advantage

Factor Conditions

The climate and morphology of Greece are its main basic factor advantages for the tourism industry. The mild Mediterranean climate, in most parts of the country, ensures long, sunny summers with little rainfall and relatively short, mild winters. This is especially true for the southern part of the country, where the 'sand, sea and sun' tourism season lasts for more than six months.

The morphology of the country is another major advantage. The large number of inhabited (227) and uninhabited islands is one of Greece's main attractions. Each group of islands has developed its own local character and tradition and has different types of landscape. Within each group there is still a wide variety, with several islands well-known for their cosmopolitan character (Rhodes in the Dodecanese, Mykonos in the Cyclades, and Corfu among the Ionian islands), while others are ideal for a quiet vacation. Some of the bigger islands even combine both, enabling the tourist to create his/her own mix.

The coastline, both of the islands and the mainland, is 15,000 km long, an impressive size given the country's total area of 131,957 sq. km. This includes a large number of beaches suitable for swimming, aided by the calm, warm Mediterranean water. The mainland, has also other things to offer. A series of mountains, ideal for climbing, hiking, and winter sports, dominates a great part of mainland Greece. In addition, the 3,500 caves and the 17 major spas offer the necessary variety, especially for repeated visits to Greece.

The multitude of Greece's cultural attractions is another major factor advantage for the industry. The significant monuments from its long past number in the thousands and their spatial distribution covers every region of the country, although in some regions there are greater concentrations of monuments and sites of particular types or periods. These monuments range in date from the 7th millennium BC to the 19th century, but the most important ones belong to the prehistoric period (Minoan, Mycenaean, etc.), the great classical era, the years of Alexander the Great and the Macedonian Dynasties, the Roman period and the Byzantine one and from the times when Greece was under Turkish or Frankish rule. As every part of Greece developed its own character, or was occupied for a certain period by different rulers, even monuments within the same time period can have wide variations (Konsola, 1993: 23). Greece is among the seven countries with more than ten sites in UNESCO's prestigious World Heritage List (Konsola, 1995: 89-91). Traditional clothing, artefacts, food and beverages and a multitude of customs are also characteristic of particular places and are important as part of a 'complete' cultural experience.

Greece is not very far from three of the top five tourist-generating countries (Germany, UK, France). However, a number of other countries (Spain, Italy) offering similar tourist products are even closer and access to them is much easier. Greece has no geographical advantages related to the other two major tourist-generating countries, the USA and Japan, and again it is other destinations, like Mexico or China, that benefit most from their geographic location. Greece's land borders are with low-income countries, which generate only a tiny part of the world's tourists.

By far, the majority (77% in 1997) of all visitors to Greece arrive by air transport. About 60% of tourists use charter flights, almost exclusively operated by foreign firms (ICAP, 1999c: 13). The Greek network of airports includes five major international airports (Athens,

Thessaloniki, Rhodes, Heraklion, Corfu) and 22 smaller ones (GNTO, 1999: 19). Despite the recent modernisation efforts the airport network is still not a major source of advantage for the Greek tourism industry. Some of the airports in small cities that have become popular destinations (Rhodes, for example) are still under great strain by having to handle more than one million arrivals every summer, mostly on charter flights (GNTO, 1996). Even the old Athens airport of 'Hellinikon' was unable to effectively handle its constantly rising traffic. A new airport, 'Eleftherios Venizelos', is now in operation and it is expected that it will be able to handle larger numbers of passengers and offer improved services. A small number of tourists (5.3% in 1997) prefer to enter Greece by boat (ICAP, 1999c: 13). A very modern and efficient ferry system, exclusively operated by Greek ferry companies, is in place, between Patras and Igoumenitsa, in Greece and the major Italian ports in the Adriatic Sea, providing a reliable, fast and relatively cheap service.

Transportation infrastructures inside the country are of a lower standard. The road network, while extensive especially around tourism destinations, is rather out-dated. It is to be noted, however, that huge projects in the country's main arteries, partly funded by the EU, will soon alter the picture, by linking most major mainland cities with a modern road network. Only 36,752 tourists arrived in Greece by rail in 1997 (ICAP, 1999c: 13). The very limited rail network, and its rather poor condition, does not allow it to be used extensively for tourist traffic, even within Greece.

Sea transport compensates for the road and rail networks' problems. As most tourists are directed to the islands, or certain seaside mainland locations, the condition of sea transport is very important. This was realised very early, and regular ship lines have been operating between Athens, Thessaloniki, Patras and most islands. Recent investments in new ships or in refurbishment of old ones, meant that the majority of ships are now in good condition. Fares are also kept at reasonable levels and the major problem of sea transport in Greece is the condition of ports on some tourist islands.

Besides the problems with the road network, the telecommunications and information technology infrastructures are not at an entirely satisfactory level. Telecommunications have improved substantially within the last ten years. The former state monopoly (OTE) has invested heavily in digital technology, and the three mobile phone companies (Panafon, Telestet, Cosmote) have also been very dynamic in their expansion. The liberalisation of fixed-lines telephony is expected to add to OTE's competition and force a new wave of investment in modern technologies. Already, in 2001, OTE is promoting its ISDN lines and a wide array of other services. The information technology network is at a worse stage. Most small, family-operated hotels and lodging establishments outside Athens lack the IT infrastructure to process bookings. Even shipping companies have only recently introduced an integrated system for ticket sales. These shortcomings are important for a tourism sector dispersed throughout the country.

As far as the cultural heritage is concerned there are problems in its preservation and management. Apart from the major archaeological sites, the focus of mass tourism, which are well preserved and properly organised, the majority of sites remain a non-exploited resource and their state of preservation is not satisfactory. The same holds true for the numerous archaeological museums. There are several large or medium-sized museums with important works of art exhibited in modern halls, while tens of smaller museums function at a substandard level, because of lack of space, equipment, personnel, etc. (Konsola, 1993: 23-24).

It is estimated that 285,000 people are directly employed in the Greek tourism industry. Of those, 41% work in hotels and 33% in rooms and other lodging establishments. Almost 80% of them are low or medium-skilled and that figure is even higher in some parts of the industry, such as rented rooms (Mylonas, 1996: 727). Low or medium-skilled labour in Greece earns considerably less than in most Western European countries, even those with whom it directly competes in the tourism industry, like Spain or Italy. That advantage is, however, lost over other low-wage countries, for example the North African ones. Nevertheless, the structure of many Greek tourist establishments partly compensates for that. Family employment is common in many small hotels and houses offering rooms, restaurants, bars and cafes, and other small tourist enterprises. This reduces wage and insurance costs, while providing a 'family atmosphere' for tourists. Other employees work seasonally, only in the summer, and therefore see tourism as a way to supplement their income, demanding lower wages and providing employers with a flexible pool of labour. In any case, the proportion of low or medium-skilled labour is rather high and many of the employees, especially the seasonal ones, receive little or no training.

Highly skilled labour is much harder to find, since demand is high from many competitive industries. The seasonality of tourism revenues and their dependence on external factors are not enticing to those wanting to join the industry. Despite the fact that a number of tourism-related education institutions produce graduates to fill most of the posts, only 60% of them end up working in the tourism industry, creating a shortage of specialised personnel (Mylonas, 1996: 728-729).

Capital availability is another problem for the Greek tourism industry, as commercial banks are reluctant to extend large loans to tourist firms and very few of these firms seek funds through the stock market. However, the state has created two development banks - ETVA (the Hellenic Industrial Development Bank), and Ktimatiki (the Mortgage

Bank) - that were required to help not only the manufacturing industry, where guarantees were higher, but also all parts of the tourism industry, from hotels to yachting companies, trying to judge the prospects of firms, rather than the assets they had available for guarantees. Also, all state incentives schemes, for locating in less developed areas, were specifically extended to include all forms of tourists enterprises, although some saturated areas were exempt. The most recent development law (Law 2601/1998) offers grants for building and expanding luxury and high class hotels, modernisation of hotels in certain areas and establishment, expansion and modernisation of conference, skiing, spa, golf and thalassotherapy facilities, as well as marinas (ETVA, 1999: 16).

One of the most important institutions for the development of the tourism industry has been the Greek National Tourism Organisation. Since 1951, when it took its present form, with wide-ranging responsibilities on all tourism-related matters, it has been directly involved in creating and promoting the Greek tourist infrastructure. The GNTO remains the owner of many important tourist properties, as well as the institution responsible for advertising the Greek tourist product abroad. In 1935, a special division of the police, called the Tourist Police, was also established.

Other state-related or independent institutions have helped the Greek tourism industry. The Hotel Chamber of Greece, and its localised chambers for every major tourism destination, have contributed to an integrated private and public approach on tourism issues. There are, also, many trade associations, for all tourist enterprises (Association of Greek Tourist Enterprises) and for every part of the industry, such as the hotel-owners and operators, the travel agents and the ferry companies. Some of these organisations also have specialised research institutes that are constantly collecting data on the industry and producing publications. The proposed establishment of a Tourism Chamber of Greece will further increase the number of specialised institutions dealing with tourism-related issues.

Moreover, there is a number of higher education institutions that are related to tourism. Most Universities include tourism-related courses in their business and management curricula and some of the professors responsible are among the leading experts in tourist research. Specialised Master's programs have also been created along with the option of a tourism management concentration in certain undergraduate programs. At the level of Technical Educational Institutions (TEI), there are seven specialised departments for Management of Tourist Enterprises. There, students selected after a pan-hellenic examination (as for all other state Universities and Technical Educational Institutions), follow a specialised program, offering a mix of theoretical and practical courses.

In addition, there are a number of Schools for Tourism-Related Professions, owned by the GNTO, independent of the rest of the state education system. Initially, these schools were designed to offer additional training to employees in the industry. However, since 1960, they have also administered a three year full-time course, with each year consisting of eight months of classes and four months of practical training. Private institutions (IIEK and EES), which are allowed by the state to offer specialised educational courses, also have one, two or three-year programs leading to various certificates on tourism-related subjects. There is also a state-operated School for Guides, and only graduates (many of them with archaeology degrees) of this two-year, intensive program are allowed to work as guides in archaeological sites or museums.

Demand Conditions

Greek demand for tourist products is similar in many ways to demand from foreign customers. Greeks, like foreign visitors, are mainly attracted to the islands and especially the well-known ones like Rhodes, Corfu and Crete (Falirea and Kapsi, 1996: 15). They seek the same 'sand, sea and sun' combination and concentrate their vacations in the period from mid-July to mid-September. They are very important to the industry since, in periods when external factors limit foreign arrivals, they act as a buffer to fill part of the extensive capacity in the major destinations. They are also considered high spenders, stay for extended periods and favour the 'personal touch' in their dealings with tourist establishments. However, their sophistication is in question, as they do not demand very high standards of service.

   Some other characteristics, however, of Greek demand are not so favourable for the industry's further development. Greeks, when travelling inside the country, favour independent travelling to 'package' holidays (Falirea and Kapsi, 1996: 15, 19). Even the 'packages' developed by Greek travel agencies are often for locations not preferred by foreign tourists. New forms of tourism are slow to develop in Greece and Greek tourists do not seem to favour them. Business and conference tourism are also not highly developed, as most Greeks travel for holiday purposes or to visit friends and relatives. Industry experts, however, expect that these and other 'special' forms of tourism will develop quickly as they fit well with the Greeks' preferences for independent travel.

   The initial development of the industry was a result of home demand. The islands, beaches and cultural monuments attracted Greeks and their desire to visit villages from where their family originated was, and still is, strong. In the 1950s and 1960s home and foreign demand moved at the same pace, and by 1970, the number of nights spent were the same for Greek and foreign tourists. Very soon after that a significant change occurred as foreign demand was increasing at a much higher pace than home demand. By 1976, foreign visitors accounted for 67% of nights spent and that figure has recently (1998) reached 75% (GNTO, 1996; GNTO, 1999: 6). Greek demand was at 10,480,070 nights spent in 1976 and by 1991 it had barely increased to 11,594,471 (GNTO, 1996). Since then, however, increases have been small but relatively constant providing the Greek industry with a steady source of income, regardless of international circumstances. In 1995, nights spent by Greek tourists reached 12,542,011, while in 1998 they had almost reached the 14 million mark (Falirea and Kapsi, 1996: 24; GNTO, 1999: 6).

The level of trip taking in Greece is still lower than that of many major European tourist-generating countries such as Germany or the UK. However, Greeks favour home to foreign destinations to a much larger extent. In fact, according to a 1985 European Travel Commission survey, only 7% of Greeks travelled abroad, compared to the EU average of 32% (European Commission, 1993: 14, 15). In a 1997 NSSG survey, out of the 10,512,309 trips taken by Greek tourists, only 354,454, or 3.4% were to foreign destinations (ICAP, 1999c: 37). Even using an earlier (1995) survey that reported only trips with a duration of four days or more, a more accurate approximation given Greece's distance from the major European tourism destinations, 90.1% of trips were taken within Greece (ICAP, 1999c: 34). Again, these are indications that Greek demand is still important for the Greek tourism industry, although its sophistication (given the reduced scope of comparisons with non-Greek destinations) is somewhat questionable.

Related and Supporting Industries

The highly competitive Greek cluster of Food/Beverages has been a major supplier of various parts of the tourism industry. The international competitiveness of many food and beverages industries has contributed to the tourism industry's success by providing high quality products at reasonable prices, especially those considered 'healthy' like fruits, vegetables, yoghurt and olive oil. These inputs were also differentiated from those of many other countries, helping to create a 'unique' image for Greek food, as well as for many of the beverages (for example, ouzo), and stress the well-known Greek culinary identity.

The shipping industry has also been important for the development of the Greek tourism industry. In the early stages of the industry's history, when ships were essential for the transportation of tourists, the extensive network of shipping lines was instrumental. Despite the relatively decreased reliance on sea transport, the competitive shipping industry is still a source of advantage for most parts of the tourism industry.

The construction industry, and especially its capacity to handle large volumes of work, has contributed to the rapid development of the tourism industry in Greece. After the Second World War, Greek construction companies provided the tourism industry, and especially hotels, with easy access to construction services and a qualified pool of engineers and architects.

A contribution to the Greek tourism industry has also been made by the Textiles/Apparel cluster. Its output of traditional and modern fabrics and apparel, has often been part of the Greek tourist product. A number of other industries have also complemented well the Greek tourist product. The most important ones have been the arts and crafts and housewares industries, some of which (rugs and carpets, silver jewellery) are very competitive.

Other related and supporting industries have not yet developed to a large extent. This has been a disadvantage to the Greek tourism industry, as, for example, a competitive travel agency automation industry would have helped the industry's organisation.

Firm Strategy, Structure and Rivalry

Greek tourist enterprises in all parts of the industry are relatively small. In terms of hotel enterprises, only 7% of Greek hotels have more than 100 rooms, while 43% have less than 20 rooms and a further 37% between 21 and 50 rooms. Average employment in Greek hotels is 8.83 employees (Papanikos, 2000: 29). Licensed units offering rooms and apartments are even smaller, with an average of 15 beds per unit (GNTO, 1999: 16). Travel agents, on average, employ three people, while the same figure for restaurants, bars and cafes is 2.5 people (Fitzpatrick Associates, 1997: 22.10; DRI Europe, 1997: 22.42, 22.44). It is estimated that more than 95% of Greek tourist enterprises are small and medium-sized (GNTO, 1999: 20).

This structure was initially well-suited for an industry where the product is usually produced and consumed in the same location, where multiple offerings are essential and where the 'personal touch' and the opportunity to understand the culture through the employees in the industry is highly appreciated. However, recent world trends are pointing to the consolidation of the industry.

A series of mergers and acquisitions have created huge hotel and restaurant chains that are taking advantage of common services, such as centralised bookings, and the opportunity to transfer management expertise from one establishment to the other. This trend has made a small but noticeable impact on the Greek industry. The rapid expansion of the Grecotel chain of hotels, the acquisitions of a few major hotels by other Greek chains are signs that some Greek enterprises are moving towards that direction. In other parts of the industry there has been a recent consolidation of ferry boat firms, leaving essentially three main competitors in the market. Certain fast food chains have also expanded rapidly and the Greek firm Goody's, is not only the market leader in Greece, but also one of the major European chains with a number of stores in other European countries (Fitzpatrick Associates, 1997: 22.14).

The small size and reduced co-ordination of Greek tourist firms has led to lack of strategic vision. Although several factors enable Greece to offer a differentiated tourist product, Greek firms have done little to enhance that differentiation. They have been very cost conscious and that has given the industry some cost advantage. However, this is not sustainable, especially as upward pressure on wages is already becoming evident. Most enterprises lack the scale and resources to mount extensive advertising campaigns in the major foreign markets. The Greek National Tourism Organisation is, almost exclusively, organising marketing campaigns in other countries. However, a national organisation seeking to promote the interests of all national firms cannot effectively target the specific segments of the population that certain groups of firms need to attract. Marketing was also considered product-oriented and there were few attempts to segment the market (Apostolopoulos, 1990: 232).

The reduction of Greece's cost advantage has not led most of the enterprises to place increased emphasis on service quality. This is evident by the per capita spending figures, where Greece in 1994 had an average of $364, much lower than in some of the direct competitors, such as Spain ($505), Italy ($870), Portugal ($419) and others (RIT, 1997: 70). The lack of product differentiation, and the emphasis on the mass tourist segment, along with the quality of service can explain the large gap in per capita spending. In terms of hotels, it is important to note that only 10% of units belong to the two highest categories, accounting for about 30% of hotel beds (ICAP, 1999d: 17-18). Moreover, the large number of licensed and unlicensed rooms is not included in these statistics.

My interviewees, along with recent studies (GNTO, 1999: 21), emphasise the emergence, especially in the last 10 years, of several Greek firms, that consider customer satisfaction as their primary goal and seek to increase average tourist spending. For example, some major hotel enterprises have developed large areas, equipped them with high-standard accommodation facilities and are also offering specialised products like thalassotherapy and golf courses. There is also an improvement in the quality of yachting services offered and the establishment of a large number of new marinas (GNTO, 1999: 17-18). All these firms are hoping to attract quality-conscious tourists, with a higher spending capacity.

There is also scope for the further development of the mass tourist segment, which, after all, is the largest one internationally. The strategy of relatively competitive costs and easy access to natural attractions and cultural monuments can be effective if combined with the provision of services of a standard comparable to that of other countries. The increasing number of training seminars conducted by both the state and private firms, even smaller ones, is evidence that many firms are moving towards that direction. There is still, however, much room for improvement, as, for many firms service is not among the highest priorities.

There is intense rivalry among all Greek tourist firms, and especially those dealing with incoming tourists (ICAP, 1999c: 86). The pressure by foreign tour operators has led to increased price competition among all firms involved. Rivalry is also intense among the airlines, as well as the ferry companies, where the few existing competitors are trying to outwit each other, often using government restrictions as a tool (Koumelis and Karantzavelou, 2000: 82-84; Tsamopoulos, 2000: 33-37). There are also cases of 'personal' rivalry among firms with similar activities within the same destination. Another level where strong rivalry is observed is between the small and the large firms in the industry, with the fiercest rivalry among hotels and rooms for rent. A good example is the proposed investment of a shipping tycoon in the creation of an Integrated Tourist Development Area (that would include hotels and other recreational facilities) in the prefecture of Messinia. Small businesses in the area viewed this as a way of expanding their sales through the increased number of incoming tourists, while large firms saw the huge addition in capacity as a direct threat to their hotel businesses.

Geographic concentration is a defining feature of the Greek tourism industry. The presence of archaeological sites, natural attractions or a developed infrastructure have led firms to concentrate in a few resorts and urban centres. A small number of islands and the cities of Athens and Thessaloniki account for the majority of hotel capacity and most other tourist firms are also located in these areas. Specifically, the Southern Aegean region (including the Dodecanese and Cyclades prefectures) accounts for 21.3% of total beds available in Greece in 1997, and 27.6% of nights spent in 1998. The region of Crete, with its four prefectures, accounted for 17.4% of total beds in 1997 and 20.9% of nights spent in 1998, while the Ionian Islands region for 7.5% and 10.5% respectively. Central Macedonia (including the Thessaloniki and Chalkidiki prefectures) and Attica account for 8.3% and 16.9% of 1997 capacity respectively, while capturing 7.5% and 13.9%, respectively, of 1998 nights spent (ICAP, 1999d: 65-69; GNTO, 1999: 13). In terms of specific destinations, Athens' share is slowly declining, while the Aegean islands, and especially Crete, registered increases in capacity and nights spent in the last decade (Mylonas, 1996: 740-742; ICAP, 1999d: 65-69). Overall, the proportion of beds accounted for by the top regions has been slowly rising for more than three decades. Crete, Athens, Thessaloniki, Rhodes and Corfu, are also where most luxury hotels are located, with more than 70% of them in these five areas, while lower-rated, smaller establishments are slightly more dispersed. The Dodecanese is where the highest number of beds per 1000 inhabitants can be found (439.5), followed by Corfu (283.6) and the

Cyclades (224.5) (Mylonas, 1996: 734, 746). More than 50% of travel agents are based in Athens, Macedonia and Crete, and most car rental and yachting companies are located in Athens, Thessaloniki and the major tourist islands (Arthur Andersen, 1997: 169-171).

The Role of Government

The government's official involvement with the industry started in 1914, with the establishment of the Office of Foreign Visitors and Exhibitions. Major intervention, however, was evident after 1950 when the economic situation permitted it and the National Tourism Organisation became an autonomous agency. The 1950s and 1960s saw great investments in public infrastructures, to facilitate communications and create opportunities for the private sector, as well as in accommodation facilities. The Xenia chain of hotels, operated by the National Tourism Organisation, served as model hotels at the time, but are now being privatised after running into financial difficulties. In 1962, private investments surpassed public investments for the first time, as the state focused on providing loans and other incentives to private enterprises, mainly through the Industrial Development Bank, ETVA (Leontidou, 1991: 88-89). Initially, these financial incentives led to the creation of facilities close to the major cities, as these were the only locations where land values could offer sufficient guarantees. Then, during the 1967-1974 dictatorship, an approach favouring the subsidisation of any type of tourist investment, increased the rate of creation of tourist facilities throughout the country. However, large units were built in areas with inadequate infrastructure or other limitations on tourist capacity and often by investors with little or no knowledge of the industry (Katochianou, 1995: 64; Mylonas, 1997:12).

Since ·1974 the approach of the state has been more cautious. Incentives schemes and other similar laws have been in effect throughout the last 25 years (eight such laws since 1976, with seven more between 1953 and 1973) (Varvaressos, 1998: 207-209). They all had specific targets related to the areas favoured to receive grants or subsidised loans. This became especially important in the late 1970s when most tourist areas started to face over-capacity problems as a result of the continued surge in investments. The result was the passing of the law 1262/1982 which reduced financing for larger units, leading to the creation of small, lower-class hotels (ICAP, 1999d: 14). Also, the restrictions on new facilities in 'saturated' areas favoured the creation of most of the unlicensed 'rooms' and of other types of semi-legal facilities (Katochianou, 1995: 64; Mylonas, 1997: 13). Another series of measures, taken between 1975 and 1982 with the goal of reducing the high seasonality of arrivals, had a negligible effect (Varvaressos, 1998: 51-52).

In the 1990s, laws aimed at promoting investment have used past experience and moved in the right direction by providing support to the modernisation of existing hotel units and the construction of luxury and high-class hotels, as well as, the creation of 'Areas of Integrated Tourist Development' and other specialised facilities (golf, thalassotherapy, marinas) (ETVA, 1999: 7-60). The presence, however, of an effective state strategy for tourism is still a point of debate by many experts, despite the government's assertions (Katochianou, 1995: 64; Kouzelis, 2000: 73). The changes in GNTO's structure announced in 2001 and the increased emphasis on market research, integrated marketing and the promotion of quality, demonstrate once again the state's interest in promoting tourist development (Aggelis, 2001: 4-5).

Since the 1980s, EU funding through the various initiatives has been available to Greek tourist enterprises, including the large amounts dispensed during the 1994-1999 Second Community Support Framework, that linked spending on cultural and tourism-related measures and promoted new forms of tourism, especially sea-related activities, as well as the modernisation of hotel units, staff training and the creation of an IT infrastructure (GNTO, 1999: 25). Also, marketing efforts for the Greek tourist product have been undertaken by the GNTO. All these measures, however, have had limited results due to the less than expected industry participation and co-ordination difficulties. The industry, and especially the small and medium-sized enterprises, need government support to modernise and upgrade their product. At the same time, there needs to be a conscious effort by these firms to develop their own strategies, without counting on the 'patron' state as a source of limitless funds, whenever any financial difficulties arise (GNTO, 1999: 21-22).

The Role of Chance

Chance events have affected the Greek tourism industry for short periods, without however major long-term implications. The first decrease in the number of tourist arrivals was observed in 1967, coinciding with the start of the dictatorial regime. Soon after, in 1969, tourists started coming back to Greece in increasing numbers and Greek firms were benefiting from the dictators' policy of promoting tourist development. The fall of the dictatorship in 1974 caused a 31% drop in arrivals as the political situation was considered unstable. Again, however, it was not long before growth in both arrivals and receipts was resumed.

The beginning of the 1980s was the most difficult period as the threat of terrorist activities prevented people, especially North Americans, from visiting Greece. The North American tourists never came back in the numbers witnessed before 1980. Nevertheless, European arrivals increased dramatically compensating for any other reductions, possibly aided by

Greece's 1981 entry in the EU. In 1991, the Gulf War had a short-lived negative effect but in 1993 and 1994 the number of arrivals rebounded sharply. Then in 1995 and 1996 further decreases were partly attributable to the unstable situation in the Balkans. These developments in the Balkans also had a positive side since some popular destinations near Greece were considered not safe for travel.

Summary

Greece is among the top 20 world destinations and the importance of tourism for its economy is evident from its high share of GDP and the labour force. The Greek tourism industry appeared at the turn of the century but its development for the first few decades was very slow. After the 1950s, due to the political and economic climate, both the public and private sectors invested heavily in all parts of the industry. Since then, Greece has retained a steady and, most of the time, increasing flow of tourist arrivals which has provided large sums of foreign exchange and determined the economic development prospects of many regions in the country.

The initial advantage for the Greek tourism industry came from certain basic factors. The large number of picturesque islands, the mild Mediterranean Sea, the extended coastline and Greece's exceptionally rich cultural heritage provide a unique and sustainable advantage for the Greek tourism industry. Other basic factors like the sea transport network, the variety of available destinations and sites in the country and the climate conditions have also been advantageous for the industry's development. The availability of capital and skilled labour, the road, telecommunications and information technology infrastructures, the country's location relative to the major tourist markets and the lack of a major Greek charter operator are sources of disadvantage despite serious efforts by the state and private companies to address most of these issues. Nevertheless, specialised factors, such as the activities of educational and research institutions, trade associations and chambers, as well as many other state-owned or private tourism-related organisations, are affecting the industry in a positive way.

Demand conditions have also been slightly favourable for the tourism industry. Early demand for certain destinations and the subsequent saturation have contributed to the industry's rapid expansion. The nature of home demand has also been advantageous with its emphasis on the same time periods, attributes and locations with foreign demand. Other characteristics of home demand have given a mixed picture, with positive effects from the high spending and long stay patterns but negative ones from the lack of emphasis on service quality and the reduced importance of 'package' tours.

The fact that the tourism industry has essentially incorporated most related activities reduces the magnitude of the effects of related and supporting industries. In the Greek case, the very competitive food and beverages and shipping industries have assisted the tourism industry in many ways. The construction, textiles/apparel and some of the household products and arts and crafts industries have also complemented well the tourism industry's product. However, other industries, especially the ones offering services, such as travel agency automation, are not adequately developed.

The strategy and structure of Greek firms have been favourable in the initial phase of the industry's development. The small, family firms enabled growth in many destinations and gave an extra 'personal touch', while the emphasis on low costs caused a rapid increase in foreign arrivals. The recent trends of industry consolidation and the required pursuit of quality, as the cost advantage is reduced, have not yet made their full impact on Greek firms. While some of them have adjusted and new entrants with high-quality, differentiated products have appeared, the majority of firms are still changing at a very slow pace. Rivalry has been intense in many cases, while geographic concentration is present and increasing constantly.

The role of government has also been very important during the industry's initial development in the 1960s. Investment in tourist infrastructures, the building of the Xenia chain of hotels and the availability of loans on generous terms have been important for a growing industry. In the later period, state involvement concentrated mainly in providing incentive schemes and, despite the negative impact of some policy measures, the results of the intervention can be considered rather satisfactory.

The role of chance events has been mixed. Political turmoil and terrorist threats have taken their toll, especially on tourist arrivals in the few years following them. However, the political stability after 1974 and Greece's entry into the EU in 1981 have had positive implications.

The Greek tourism industry developed because of the country's advantage in basic factors, which is still one of its major assets. Other determinants, such as early domestic demand, related and supporting industries, the firms' strategy, structure and rivalry, geographic concentration and government support have also affected the industry's competitive position in these early stages. More recently the developments are mixed, especially regarding firms' strategy and structure and some aspects of home demand. Also disadvantages in basic factors (such as the country's infrastructure), and specialised factors (such as the availability of skilled labour) still persist, despite recent improvements. Overall, though, all four groups of determinants continue to support the Greek tourism industry's competitive advantage.

6   The Men's Outerwear Industry in Greece

Introduction

This fourth case study examines an industry whose fortunes have changed dramatically throughout the last thirty years. The men's outerwear industry is part of the Textiles/Apparel cluster, one of the two largest Greek clusters. Its importance was heightened during the first part of the 1980s when output, employment and exports were at their highest levels. Since then, declines in production, employment losses, and a worsening trade balance have changed the cluster's position in Greek manufacturing.

The men's outerwear industry has followed a path similar to that of the other Greek textiles and apparel industries. After a period of sustained export growth that characterised the 1970s and most of the 1980s, decline has been swift. In 1992, a part of the industry (overcoats and other outerwear) had already been excluded from the lists of competitive industries. Since then, exports of the industry's products have been consistently decreasing and according to the 1996 data the entire industry can be characterised as uncompetitive by Porter's criteria, because of a negative trade balance of US$52 million (as opposed to a positive balance in 1992) and an overall share of the world market that has fallen from 0.5% in 1992 (almost double the country's average for that year) to 0.26% in 1996, making Greece the 48th world exporter (from 37th in 1992) (UN, International Trade Statistics Yearbook). This slump in export performance has been accompanied by disappointing financial results for many of the firms in the industry, and lower production and employment levels, while industry experts consider its prospects as limited.

The products that are the focus of this case study are men's outerwear. These typically include suits, trousers, jackets, overcoats, raincoats, etc. The apparel manufacturer commences the production process by producing or acquiring the basic design pattern. Then follows the cutting phase, where the various parts required by the pattern are cut from the fabric. These parts are sleeves, pockets, front and back panels, etc., and their number can be relatively high. Some of these parts of men's outerwear are then fused with an interlining. Subsequently, all parts are sewn together in the assembly phase of the production. Finally, the fully assembled garment goes through the finishing process, that usually includes pressing, inspection and other operations (Hoffman and Rush, 1988: 51-59; ILO, 1994: 6-7).

The world trade in men's outerwear is dominated by Western European countries, the USA and Japan, as well as by a number of other competitors, primarily Asian countries with lower labour costs and increasing labour productivity. In recent decades, European and North American producers, in response to competitive pressures, have targeted the high-fashion, niche segments, which are less price-sensitive, taking advantage of the increased fashion orientation of consumers. Firms from countries with high wage costs have also followed sub-contracting strategies, where the labour intensive assembly process is designated to smaller domestic firms that often use under-paid home labour or to foreign firms based in lower-wage countries.

The introduction of automation in almost all stages of production was also seen as an appropriate measure by these countries. R&D initiatives, with government and private funding, especially in Japan (like the Technology Research Association for Automated Sewing Systems) but also in the USA (National Apparel Technology Centre) and the European Union, produced important automation innovations that include the use of Computer-Aided Design systems, computer numerically-controlled cutting systems, robotic handling of fabrics, etc. However, these innovations have mostly affected the pre-assembly stage and have not altered the fundamentally labour intensive processes, primarily sewing (despite the limited application of automated sewing machines), which remain central in garment production (Eumoiridis, 1990: 65; ILO, 1994: 3-4). Moreover, these automation technologies have now spread to producers in the NICs, and the European and North American producers are seeking further advancements that seem still a long way ahead.

A more direct role was played by governments, especially in the USA and Europe, after constant lobbying by the apparel industries since the early 1960s. The result was the MultiFibers Agreement (MFA) that went into effect in 1974 and has been extended three times since. The agreement still governs part of the world trade in textiles and apparel but it is being slowly phased out and the textiles and clothing sector is expected to be fully integrated in the WTO regime by 2005.

In terms of specific products the picture is as follows. In men's jackets, European countries produced 31.8 million units in 1996, while Asian countries produced 85.9 million units, out of a total world production of 135 million units. In men's trousers a more balanced picture was observed with Europe's output of 164.6 million units being close to Asia's 178.1 million units and higher than North America's 138.5 million units. The same was true for men's suits, where Asian 1996 production was the highest with 22 million units, while Europe's (18.4 million units) and North America's (11.3 million units) share was considerable. Overcoats is the only segment where European 1996 production (9.2 million units) is still greater than Asian (4.3 million units) (UN, Industrial Commodity Statistics Yearbook).

The EU besides being the major producer among developed countries, is also the major exporter accounting for 28.1% of the industry's 1996 world exports. In terms of individual countries, Italy and Germany are still the major EU exporters, ranked third and fifth in the world respectively for 1996 (following China, Hong Kong and the USA in fourth place). Italy has restructured its industry, focusing on flexibility and speed and offering a differentiated 'fashion' product. This has enabled it to increase the value of its exports, despite falling from first place in the 1980s to third in 1996. Germany's export share has also fallen, while its export volume in US$ has remained stable. Belgium and Portugal are also among the EU countries that have effectively restructured their production holding (respectively) a 3.2% and 2.6% share of the world market in 1996 (UN, International Trade Statistics Yearbook).

The main destination of EU exports are other developed countries and European brand-names still generate considerable demand. Nevertheless, the industry is suffering from a slump in domestic demand, throughout the EU markets. It is also attempting to adjust to a more demanding marketplace, where styles changes are required almost every year and flexibility is necessary for a producer to maintain its market share (OETH, 1997: 4.20-4.21).

Despite the continued exports, production in the EU has been steadily declining in the 1990s among all segments of the men's outerwear industry. A large number of firms, both small and large, have withdrawn from the industry, while others, especially the larger ones, have transferred the more labour-intensive processes to lower-cost countries close to the EU (OETH, 1995: 14.15).

The Men's Outerwear Industry in Greece

Historical Development

The appearance of an organised men's outerwear industry in Greece coincides with the end of the Civil War, in 1949. Initially domestic demand was sluggish as the quality of ready-made garments was not considered very high. The market gradually developed as more and more people abandoned the traditional tailors in favour of the manufactured products.

The combination of low wages and available capital enabled the formation of a number of relatively large enterprises during the last part of the 1950s. These firms initially sought to supply the Greek market, but as their products were price-competitive, they turned to exporting from the mid-1960s on.

The 1970s was a period of high growth for the industry. Most of the firms, which still account for contemporary Greek production, were established during this period. Exports surged from 1972 onwards. Much of this export growth, however, was due to sub-contracting arrangements concluded by these firms, mainly with large German producers. By the early 1980s more than 50% of exports were made as part of sub-contracting arrangements (Patsouratis, 1985: 74-75).

Output growth slowed down after 1980, affected by a stagnating domestic demand. However, exports continued to rise, due to Greece's accession to the EU in 1981, as all barriers to trade with the major European markets were eliminated and Greece obtained a privileged position over other relatively low-wage countries (Singleton, 1997: 19).

This phenomenal growth in exports continued until 1991. Then increased competition from the restructured Western European industries and from other countries (that took advantage of reduced tariff levels), constant wage increases without corresponding improvements in design or quality, as well as decreasing demand in the EU markets, caused a decline for the first time in exports and a sudden surge in imports. Output had already declined to levels far lower than those of 1980 (Kalloniatis, 1995: 38). By the mid-1990s these trends resulted in a reversal of the industry's fortunes as exports constantly declined and imports continued to rise. Exports dropped by almost 30% between 1992 and 1996, while imports during the same years increased by the same magnitude (UN, International Trade Statistics Yearbook). Many firms, even some of the older and larger ones, went into bankruptcy, faced with fiscal difficulties and small prospects of recovery.

The Major Firms

The major firms that dominated the Greek industry have changed over time and these changes have been even greater during the last ten years. The Greek industry consists primarily of small establishments and large firms are few. The average number of employees in a men's outerwear manufacturing unit is 3.8, among the lowest for Greek apparel industries (Kazabakas, 1997: 210). The dominant firms, with more than 50 employees, which also carry out their own production, are analysed below.

The major exporter, Katerina, is producing almost entirely under sub-contracting arrangements, mainly with foreign firms. It was incorporated in 1973 and is based in the town of Katerini, in the prefecture of Pieria, in Northern Greece. Most of its production is carried out in its main unit in Katerini, where 490 people are employed. A small part is produced under sub-contracting arrangements with Bulgarian firms. It manufactures the whole range of men's outerwear, while it also imports other men's and women's clothing items (ICAP, 1999e: 17, 25). Since 1993 it has started producing garments under its own brand name which are sold mostly locally (ICAP, 1994).

A firm producing for the Greek and Cypriot markets, as a sub-contractor of other domestic firms and, to a lesser extent, under its own brand name of Boston Tailors is Evete. Established in 1970, the firm has 230 employees in its production facility in Markopoulo, close to Athens.

Best Form is also a firm located in Athens, supplying the Greek and Cypriot markets since its establishment in 1988. About 30% of its men's outerwear is produced under contract with other domestic firms. Eurotextilia is a relatively new firm (established in 1994 in Edessa, in Northern Greece) producing exclusively for the wholesale market (ICAP, 1999e).

Again producing mainly under its own brand name and based in Thessaloniki is Gruppo Bizzaro. It employs 75 people and exports a small part of its production to Cyprus, Yugoslavia and Hungary (ICAP, 1999e).

Other major firms, operating in the 1980s and early 1990s have now been closed or have discontinued their production activities, concentrating instead on importing apparel (ICAP, 1994: 7). Between 1997 and 1999, four major men's outerwear firms have gone bankrupt (ICAP, 1999e: 13-14). The same trend is evident throughout the apparel and footwear sector where from a high of 1532 manufacturing units that employed more than 10 people in 1992, only 910 are still operating in 1996 (Epilogi, 1998: 286).

The financial results of some of the major men's outerwear companies are outlined in Table 6.1:

Table 6.1 Financial results of men's outerwear companies in Greece (1999)

Companies	Turnover (million Drachmas)	Net Income (million Drachmas)
Evete	3,845	-211
Katerina	3,382	4
Gruppo Bizzaro	1,110	29
Eurotextilia	659	37
Best Form	406	1

Source: ICAP, 2001.

The financial results outlined above are characteristic of the performance of most businesses in the industry. Although often heavy losses in a year are then turned into profits, the overall profitability level (net profits/turnover) for the industry has remained around 3% since 1992 (ICAP, 1994; ICAP, 1999e).

Sources of Competitive Advantage

Factor Conditions

The basic raw material for garment production is fabric. In the case of the Greek men's outerwear industry, 80% of the fabric used is imported and only 20% is domestically sourced. All of the major enterprises, use almost exclusively imported fabric (ICAP, 1994: 5; ICAP, 1999e: 8).

Fabrics are imported mainly from Italy, France and Germany but also from England, Portugal, Belgium and other countries. The reasons for this preference for foreign fabrics are related to their consistently good quality and the availability of a wide range of designs and patterns. Although Greek suppliers are considered price competitive, they are not able to offer the same range of fabrics and usually produce the most modern styles with a considerable time lag (ICAP, 1994: 5; ICAP, 1999e: 8). Timely delivery is also an attribute mostly found in foreign producers (ICAP, 1999e: 7).

All my interviewees agreed on the prevalence of foreign fabrics for the reasons mentioned above. Moreover, they emphasised that the crisis in the domestic fabric industry has forced many firms to discontinue their operations, thereby limiting both the range of suppliers and the range of fabrics available. Also, as capacity in the fabric industry has declined, the ability of domestic producers to execute repeat orders in a short amount of time is limited, something very important as retailers and producers maintain lower stocks (OETH, 1995: 14.19). These developments have shifted the men's outerwear industry towards imported fabrics in the last ten to fifteen years.

Labour costs are the second largest component of costs for the men's outerwear industry, after raw materials. For the Greek industry, labour costs were estimated at around 20-22% of total cost and this proportion was among the highest in the EU (Drimoussis and Zissimopoulos, 1988: 23).

In the industry's first stages of development, labour costs were a major source of advantage. In 1965, wages in the apparel industries were 2.5 times lower than those in all Greek manufacturing sectors. Since the mid-1970s this gap began to narrow and in 1980 the apparel industries' wages were about 40% lower than the Greek manufacturing average. Even after these high increases, in 1981, the hourly wages in the Greek apparel industries were far lower than those in most developed countries, and even

15% lower than those in Spain and Ireland. Greek wages were closer in range to those in Mexico. In 1984, some changes came about as Greek wage increases were much higher than those in most other developed countries (Patsouratis, 1985: 56-59).

Throughout the 1980s Greek wages were rising in nominal terms at around 18% per annum. In real terms, they did not rise substantially, or, according to some calculations, they might have dropped slightly, and, in the beginning of the 1990s, Greece was still among the low-wage developed countries in the apparel sector. Nevertheless, the real and nominal increases had driven Greek wages well above those in the Asian NICs, as well as those in Portugal and Turkey, countries that compete directly with Greece in the same segments and markets and for the same sub-contracting arrangements (Kalloniatis, 1995). The integration of Eastern European countries in the international trading system, brought on a new group of competitors with wages in the apparel industries only a fraction of those in Greece. Therefore, wages have now become a disadvantage for the industry, despite the fact that increases have been modest throughout the 1990s.

The availability and quality of skilled personnel is another area of concern for the Greek industry. In the 1960s and 1970s only low-skilled labour was required, as the entrepreneurs that started most of the firms essentially carried out the management tasks. As firms grew larger and automation was introduced, at least in the initial stages of production, the need for specialised personnel increased. According to my interviewees and other researchers (Patsouratis, 1985: 124; Eumoiridis, 1990: 46; ICAP, 1994: 7; ICAP, 1999e: 122), skilled personnel is still difficult to find and requires substantial training. The only way around this problem is to attract personnel from other competitors, although these employees demand much higher wages.

Capital has been available since the very first firms of the industry were established. As the initial capital required for production was low and went to buildings and machinery, banks were willing to lend at the prevailing interest rates. In recent years, as the companies' profitability declined, the guarantees required by the banks have increased. Moreover, interest rates for working capital, which is essential for the industry, have increased disproportionately after 1990 according to my interviewees (see also Kalloniatis, 1995: 71; ICAP, 1999e: 122), placing a further burden on the industry's firms.

The location of production is influencing the destination of exports of finished products to a small extent. Location seems to matter more in the cases of large firms in developed countries that are sub-contracting the labour-intensive phases of the production process. In most cases, USA firms have used Mexican and Pacific Rim sub-contractors, while Western European firms have used Southern European sub-contractors. This was an advantage in the 1970s for the Greek industry and it became even more important after Greece's accession to the EU. In recent years, though, countries that are geographically close to Greece, such as Eastern European and North African countries, have been able to develop men's outerwear industries. As these countries have the advantage of substantially lower wages, they have attracted a large and increasing number of these sub-contracting arrangements, putting Greece's geographical advantage in question.

Very little research and development is being carried out in the Greek men's outerwear industry and by a very small number of relatively dynamic firms (Sefertzi, 1998: 103-104). The small scale of the enterprises and the lack of any co-ordinated schemes has not allowed firms to devote any funds for research into automation techniques (Sefertzi, 1998: 113). Fabric colours and designs are coming from other countries and Greek firms simply try to use the most modern ones. The actual design of the garments is also following international trends. A very small number of specialised firms operating at the higher end of the market are able to offer some innovations in design (Sefertzi, 1998: 110). Apart from these firms, most of the others make few adaptations to designs bought from foreign sources (ICAP, 1999e: 7).

Training for most of the workers in the Greek industry is rudimentary and there are only certain seminars offered by the government-operated Organisation for Employment (OAED). There is also a small number of departments in the Technical Educational Institutions (TEI) where design-related skills and techniques are taught. Most of the employees in the industry receive only on-the-job training and very few firms are really able to offer substantial skills to their workers, through this process (Kazabakas, 1997: 220-221). Very few institutions related to the industry are active to the point of affecting the industry's advantage. In fact, despite the presence of certain apparel associations, co-operation among the firms in the industry in the form of organised institutions is not a source of advantage for the industry.

Demand Conditions

Consumer spending on clothing in Greece has been high, although it has dropped substantially in the last fifteen years. This trend has been evident throughout the EU, as consumer spending on clothing has fallen from 8.4% of total spending in 1980 to 7.4% in 1993 (OETH, 1995: 14-18). However, Greece has experienced even sharper declines throughout the last thirty years. In 1970, 10.4% of consumer spending went to clothing items, while in 1980 this proportion fell to 8.6%, still higher than the EU average. In 1993, consumer spending on clothing was 7% of total consumer spending, 0.4% below the EU average for the same year. Furthermore, the proportion for clothing expenditure per household spent on men's outerwear has declined, from 29% in 1982 to 25.7% in 1988 (Kalloniatis, 1995: 19, 21).

These developments in consumer expenditure for apparel are not uncommon, and are often observed in countries that experience sharp increases in incomes. Rises in income levels, however, are also associated with higher degrees of consumer sophistication that forces domestic producers to emphasise quality and fashion (Singleton, 1997: 63). This appears to be the case in Greece only to a small extent.

Although customers were characterised by my interviewees as discerning in their purchases, they do not usually seek the best quality products and price is their most important consideration. In addition, the high fashion segment in Greece is still very small, much smaller than that of other developed countries. It appears that consumer demand has not pushed manufacturers towards creating new styles and upgrading to high-quality products.

Demand for ready-made men's outerwear first appeared in the 1950s, much later than in most developed countries. This first decade was a period of slow growth as domestic manufacturers expanded slowly. During the 1960s demand grew at a much higher pace, prompting the creation of new and larger firms. The 1970s was a period of high growth, with demand increasing every year and doubling between 1970 and 1980, along with most other apparel products. This was also the period when the industry constantly increased its production, as well as its exports, and in 1980 it had reached very high levels. The first years of the 1980s was the time when the market started to saturate and demand dropped slightly (Patsouratis, 1985).

Exports continued to rise in the 1980s, and the industry increased the proportion of its production to be exported. Nevertheless, production volume decreased along with domestic demand and the slight increases between 1987 and 1989 corresponded with increases in domestic demand (Kalloniatis, 1995). Since then demand for all men's outerwear products has been decreasing at a slow pace, with the exception of small increases between 1994 and 1995 (ICAP, 1999e: 71-77). From 1991 on, production has followed the same trend with a steady decline, especially during the 1991-1994 and 1996-1998 periods (ICAP, 1999e: 34-39). Between 1992 and 1998, exports have declined substantially, while imports rose almost at a steady pace (ICAP, 1999e: 71-77).

These production and export decreases were due to the fact that the Greek industry targeted new export markets to a smaller extent than was required as a response to its shrinking share of the slightly decreasing Greek demand. Germany has been the traditional export market for all Greek apparel products, with France coming a distant second (Kalloniatis, 1995: 76). The same situation is observed in the men's outerwear industry (ICAP, 1994: 71). The 1997 data show that exports to Germany still represented more than 50% of the total exports in terms of value. The Balkan countries have recently become a significant export destination, however exports to these middle-income countries have not counterbalanced the loss of market share in most EU markets (ICAP, 1999e: 68-70).

Greek demand has not had an effect on preferences in foreign markets. Greek designers have not set any trends in the men's outerwear industry and the products sold in Greece are mostly of the same type as those in other European markets.

Related and Supporting Industries

The men's outerwear industry belongs to a group of apparel industries that are responsible for a large part of the exports from the Textiles/Apparel cluster, the second largest cluster in Greek manufacturing. The women's outerwear industry is the one with the most similar production process. In fact, some of the firms active in the men's outerwear industry are also producing women's outerwear, in smaller quantities. The growth in output and exports of women's outerwear mirrors that of men's outerwear. High and growing exports in the 1970s and a share of over 1% of the world market in the 1980s made the women's outerwear industry even more successful than the men's outerwear one. In the early 1990s the decline was slower, but after 1992, it has become evident. In a similar path to that of men's outerwear, women's outerwear exports have fallen by 35% between 1992 and 1996, while imports have increased by 25% at the same time period. Despite a still positive trade balance in 1996, the industry's competitive position has deteriorated in the 1990s causing financial distress to many of its firms (UN, International Trade Statistics Yearbook).

The other apparel industries have also grown throughout the 1970s and among them the knitted products industries have proven the most successful. These industries, along with fur products, have maintained their high export shares throughout the 1980s, with slight decreases in the 1990s. Nevertheless, both competitive and uncompetitive apparel industries have experienced worsening trade balances in the 1990s as a result of rapidly increasing imports (UN, International Trade Statistics Yearbook).

Greece is a major producer of raw cotton and this has given rise to an extensive yarn industry. Although various types of yarn are produced by the industry, the largest proportion is cotton yarn (about 77% of total production). The yarn industry has experienced declines in exports in the last few years, especially in non-cotton yarn. It remains, however, among the most competitive of the textiles industries. Nevertheless, the phenomena common in all other textile and apparel industries have appeared in this industry too. Bankruptcies have become more common after 1990, and production has declined from 213.000 tons in 1986 to 176.000 in 1990 and 140.000 in 1997 (Karagiannopoulou, 1988: 39).

The situation is much worse for the direct supplier to the men's outerwear industry, the Greek fabrics industry. Although some parts of it were competitive in 1978 and 1985 (see Tables A.1, A.2 in the Appendix), only two kinds of cotton fabric were still in the competitive lists in 1992. Moreover, the industry has been characterised by the closure, throughout the 1980s, of some of its biggest firms. The firms that remained have attempted to invest in new technologies. Nevertheless, the Greek fabrics industry is considered the least modern among the EU industries (ICAP, 1997a).

The lack of a competitive machinery industry in the Textiles/Apparel cluster is not surprising given that it is a common feature of all Greek clusters. Moreover, more than 60% of world trade in textile and leather machinery is controlled by three countries, Germany, Japan and Italy (Singleton, 1997: 79).

Firm Strategy, Structure and Rivalry

Greek firms are consistently following a low cost strategy. The advantage of low labour costs in the 1960s and 1970s and the opportunities to conclude sub-contracting arrangements based on that advantage, especially throughout the 1980s, favoured this approach, that initially led to a rapid expansion of the industry, with a high export component. As Greece started exhibiting characteristics and wage costs similar to those in many developed countries, the same firms failed to make the necessary adjustments.

The differentiated, fashion-oriented strategy that was mentioned in previous sections as a response of industries in developed countries was only followed by a few traditionally up-market firms and a handful of companies, established in the 1980s and 1990s. These relatively new companies often rely on a recognisable Greek brand-name and offer a high-quality, differentiated product with an emphasis on design (Lyberaki, 1992: 284). The traditional major producers have only recently started to develop and promote their own brand-names. Their name recognition, however, has not reached that of the newer firms.

The lack of a 'Greek' fashion in men's outerwear (Patsouratis, 1985: 67-68) and the use of foreign design patterns by most firms (ICAP, 1999e: 7) and especially the larger ones (Lyberaki, 1992: 286) is still forcing the industry to compete on costs. Greek firms have recently been more successful at controlling labour costs, however, their investment in automation procedures is still limited (Lyberaki, 1992: 286; ICAP, 1994: 7). Overall, the organisation of the production process and the equipment used by most firms are considered outdated (ICAP, 1999e: 122). Marketing and distribution are also among the activities receiving relatively little attention from Greek firms (Sefertzi, 1998: 108).

With the emergence of other low cost competitors in neighbouring countries (Eastern Europe, North Africa), Greek producers need to offer a differentiated, branded product. The sustainability of the low-cost strategy will be seriously questioned in the coming years and the alternative strategies must produce results in a restricted time-frame. All apparel industries are now characterised by the need to manage efficiently the production and distribution technology required to develop and sell new products to new markets. The lack of emphasis on quality and distribution are areas where Greek firms must take the steps necessary to adjust to the competitive pressures (Almantarioti, 2000: 8-9).

The prevalence of small, family-owned and operated firms has been a characteristic of the Greek industry in its early stage of development. During the 1970s the average size of the enterprises increased and a degree of separation between owners and managers appeared. However, most large Greek firms in the 1980s suffered from a lack of market knowledge, difficulties in raising capital and attracting qualified managers (Patsouratis, 1985). Even the largest among these firms failed to reach a size comparable to that of the major European players in the industry. They also failed to create design or R&D departments (Lyberaki, 1992: 282). Authority remained concentrated on the top, reflecting on the centralised nature of firms and the abilities of the middle managers and supervisors (Fotinopoulou and Manolopoulos, 1991: 26).

Small firms in the 1970s and 1980s suffered as a result of their own shortcomings and the pressure of larger firms. The ones that survived were the ones that exhibited more dynamic characteristics and were located near the larger cities (Lyberaki, 1992: 282). A response to the increasing competitive pressures on small Greek firms could be the creation of networks combining producers, designers and distributors. This prospect is also supported by the Greek government's clustering initiatives, partly funded by the EU. So far, however, these efforts have had a limited impact on the Greek industry (Sefertzi, 1998: 115).

Geographic concentration is present in the men's outerwear industry but to a lesser degree than in other industries. The Athens region is where 34% of productive units are operating, employing 31.5% of the workforce (ICAP, 1994: 9). The second largest concentration of firms is in the Thessaloniki area, where a lot of the major enterprises are located. Given that these two cities, along with their surrounding areas, account for almost 50% of the Greek population, the concentration of men's outerwear firms is hardly surprising. Nevertheless, there are some large firms situated near other, smaller Greek cities.

There is intense rivalry among men's outerwear firms in Greece. The five leading firms in terms of sales, account for less than 40% of the total sales in the industry (Isotimia, 1997). Market shares are even more dispersed in the largest segment of the market, the men's trousers one, where even major firms have less than 1.5% of the market (ICAP, 1999e: 83). Greek firms are co-operating mainly in various forms of sub-contracting arrangements. Nevertheless, competition remains fierce as the shrinking size of the market, the increased import penetration and the large number of small, independent producers does not allow for collusion or any type of agreements distorting competition. Price is the most important element of domestic competition as it is the main factor affecting both subcontracting arrangements and, although to a lesser extent, customer's choices.

The Role of Government

The Greek government was relatively active in the first decades of the industry's development. Although there was no 'grand scheme' for the industry, the high tariff levels and the considerable export subsidies helped and protected the industry in the 1960s, 1970s and part of the 1980s (Sefertzi, 1998: 100). All types of export subsidies were discontinued under EU rules by the mid-1980s along with tariffs for EU products. Tariffs for non-EU producers have also been lowered in the last ten years, allowing increased import penetration from Asian countries. The firms in the industry can still take advantage of the various investment schemes and EU initiatives aimed at assisting modernisation, although it is only the largest firms that are adequately informed to do so. Moreover, the need for investing the firm's own funds along with the public money has prevented some firms from fully exploiting these resources.

The Role of Chance

Chance events have not been favourable for the Greek industry. In the mid-1980s as the industry was increasing its productive capacity and again in the early 1990s, the country faced a series of stabilisation programs that restricted domestic demand. In the early 1990s, the industry was also faced with a severe recession in its major export markets, those of the EU. As it was unable to substantially change its export orientation (more than 50% of Greek exports still go to the EU) this Europe-wide demand slump led to a decline in export volumes and contributed to the subsequent declines in production and the financial distress of the men's outerwear companies. The changes in Eastern Europe, in the early 1990s, have been a relatively positive development for the industry, as they opened up a new set of markets and the possibility of sub-contracting arrangements with Eastern European firms. The lack, however, of an established Greek design capability has limited the extent to which the Greek industry could use this advantage. At the same time, new competitors emerged from these countries, targeting the same low end of the market as some of the larger Greek firms.

Summary

The men's outerwear industry is in many ways a typical apparel industry, where competitive advantage is closely related to labour costs. Despite the relative automation of the pre-assembly procedures, such as garment design and cutting, the assembly phases of production remain labour-intensive. Asian producers have capitalised on that characteristic of the industry and are now the dominant force both in terms of production and exports. Nevertheless, European Union countries are still controlling a considerable part of the world trade through a combination of differentiation strategies, investments in technology, and sub-contracting agreements with firms in countries near the EU's borders.

The men's outerwear industry appeared in Greece in the early 1950s with the establishment of small units. Larger firms were formed in the 1960s and 1970s and, taking advantage of Greece's relatively low wages, targeted not only the domestic but also many foreign markets. Export growth continued into the 1980s mainly through sub-contracting arrangements with German firms. A combination of increased competition, wage increases and stagnant demand caused a reversal in the industry's position with output now at half its 1980 level, low profitability and exports constantly decreasing. Competitiveness has been declining in the 1990s and according to the 1996 export data, the industry can be characterised as uncompetitive.

Factor conditions have not been favourable for the industry in the 1990s. The initial advantage of low wages has been slowly eroded to the point that Greece is now slightly disadvantaged against most other countries, including its low-wage neighbours. The quality of human capital is another area of concern as skilled personnel is hard to find and expensive to train. Raw materials and especially fabrics are almost exclusively bought from foreign firms and the Greek industry has no control over their design or quality. Geographic proximity to Western Europe was one of the industry's initial advantages in basic factors. As, however, competitors emerged among Greece's close neighbours, location is not as favourable to the industry as it was ten years ago. Capital costs have also increased in the 1990s. In terms of advanced factors, a small number of firms are conducting research, mainly on garment design, and a few educational courses are being offered. Nevertheless, the lack of extensive R&D, the scarcity of educational institutions offering courses and the fragmented efforts of other industry-related organisations are disadvantaging the industry and hindering its restructuring efforts.

Demand conditions are not a source of advantage for the Greek industry. Domestic demand had grown in the 1960s and 1970s aiding the industry's expansion. The saturation of the domestic market in the 1980s initially coincided with a surge in exports. However, demand in the 1990s remained stagnant or decreased in certain years and the industry was not able to compensate with any further export increases. Moreover, new fashion-related segments were slow to emerge in Greece as the sophistication of its consumers is not considered high.

Related and supporting industries provide a more mixed picture. Initially the men's outerwear industry was part of a rapidly growing group of apparel industries that pursued exports vigorously. The industry has been among the first to experience losses in competitive position, now shared by many of the other apparel industries and especially the closely related women's outerwear one. The competitive cotton and yarn industries have also had little effect on the industry's competitive advantage as its direct supplier, the fabrics industry, is suffering from low exports and a shrinking number of establishments.

Firms' strategy and structure were initially advantageous for the men's outerwear industry. More recently, especially in the 1990s, the relatively small size, compared to other EU countries, and the low-cost, low-differentiation strategy have not been so effective, as wage costs have increased and the industry is not able to offer a differentiated, high-priced product. There are few firms that have been able to increase their brand awareness and product image while pursuing alliances in Greece and abroad. However, the low levels of automation, the lack of market research, and the absence of extensive firm networks are major disadvantages for the pursuit of a differentiation strategy. Geographic concentration is relatively high, mostly related to the large Athens and Thessaloniki markets. Domestic rivalry is also intense, although it is usually still based on price competition.

The Greek government's role was initially a strong one. Although the industry was not subject to substantial intervention, tariffs and export subsidies were present until well into the 1980s. Protection has decreased to a large extent in the last ten years and the various state and EU assistance schemes have only had a limited impact.

Chance events have also been a source of disadvantage for the industry. The stabilisation programs of the 1980s and 1990s have restricted domestic demand in a critical stage of the industry's development. Decreasing demand in the EU countries, which constituted Greece's major export markets in the early 1990s, has also disadvantaged the Greek industry. The positive developments in the Balkans have not been sufficiently exploited by the Greek industry.

The rapid and substantial decline in competitiveness of the Greek men's outerwear industry is related to a decreasing competitive advantage derived from the diamond determinants. Basic factors are not anymore a source of advantage for the industry, while advanced factors have not developed to a great extent. Demand conditions are also unfavourable, while firms' strategies and structures are not appropriate given the changes in the global market. Government and chance have also affected the industry in a disadvantageous way since the mid-1980s.

One gap in the framework is the presence of some related and supporting industries that are still very competitive, although the direct suppliers to the industry are not and the most closely related industries have experienced competitiveness losses. Domestic rivalry is another major area of concern for the applicability of the diamond framework as it remains intense, although it is mostly focused on price.

7 The Greek Dairy Industry

Introduction

The fifth case study deals with an industry that belongs to the largest and best developed Greek cluster, Food/Beverages. The dairy industry is among the many processed food industries in this cluster that have strengthened their competitive positions in the last decade. With very low exports during the previous decades, the industry was not included in the competitive lists, even for 1985. Then, a sudden and prolonged export surge changed the situation, with Greek dairy exports accounting for more than 0.5% of world exports (double the Greek average) in 1992. In recent years, the high level of exports has been complemented by Foreign Direct Investment in Eastern Europe and the establishment of recognisable Greek brand names in foreign countries.

The dairy industry is present in most countries of the world. Production of milk and milk products is still carried out on farms, most commonly, however, modern production of dairy products takes place at industrial sites, where, under strict guidelines, milk is pasteurised and homogenised and then kept at low temperatures, ready for consumption. Other processes transform raw milk or some of its ingredients into milk cream, milk powder, yoghurt, butter, various types of cheese and several other products. All of them are either consumed directly or used as ingredients in other food products, for example in the sweets and confectionery industries.

Production in industrial units is concentrated essentially in three areas, the European Union, Eastern Europe and North America. A few Asian countries, along with Australia and New Zealand, are the remaining major industrial producers of dairy products (UN, Industrial Commodity Statistics Yearbook). The international trade in dairy products represents only a fraction of total world production. It often consists of surplus production that is channelled to foreign markets, although some countries are systematically producing above their domestic consumption and exporting a substantial part of their output. According to the 1996 data, countries of the European Union account for around 70% of world exports of milk, cream, butter and other dairy products, and more than 80% of cheese exports. Australia and New Zealand account for the bulk of the remaining exports, while Switzerland is also an important exporter of cheese. Europe's share has been declining in the last fifteen years, New Zealand and Australia exhibit a strong and steadily improving export performance, while the USA's share has been fluctuating, being between 1% and 2% for most products in 1996 (UN, International Trade Statistics Yearbook).

The major consumption trends are the world-wide shift towards branded products and the increased consumption of low-fat varieties. Branded products, feverishly promoted by large multinationals and large local firms, are gaining ground, especially in the major markets, over more traditional, unbranded products (Crocombe et al., 1991: 64). This trend is augmented by the introduction of many new product varieties to satisfy particular consumer needs. Among them, the need for healthier eating has prompted a substantial rise in the consumption of low-fat dairy products.

The dairy industry is a major industry of the food sector in many European Union countries. This is evident by the production specialisation ratios of EU members that are calculated as the ratio of dairy production over the country's total manufacturing output, divided by the same ratio for the EU. Ireland, Denmark, Greece and the Netherlands have the highest ratios for 1998 (European Commission and Eurostat, 2000: 123). In terms of production volumes, the largest producing countries are Germany and the UK, which account for about 40% of the EU's production of fresh milk products and drinking milk. In other dairy products, such as cream, milk powder, butter and cheese, it is France and Germany that produce more than 50% of the EU's total, with the exception of concentrated milk, where the Netherlands have the second highest share (Nomisma, 1997).

The main EU producers, Germany, France and the UK, are also responsible for a large part of world exports of milk and milk products. Belgium, and the Netherlands (11% share of world milk and cream exports, 15.9% of world butter exports and 19.8% of world cheese exports in 1996) are also among the major world exporters. Ireland (particularly in butter exports) and Denmark (especially in cheese exports) are the other important EU exporters. Only the Oceanic countries and, to a lesser extent, Switzerland are able to compete with EU producers in export markets (UN, International Trade Statistics Yearbook).

The fragmented nature of the EU industry is slowly changing. Although small firms and co-operatives still account for a large share of the production of dairy products, especially drinking milk and butter, large firms are increasing their market shares across the EU. To some extent, this is the result of a wave of mergers, acquisitions and alliances, where usually small local producers are taken over by larger local firms or by the EU multinationals (ICAP, 1995: 144-146).

The world-wide trend for healthier eating has affected all EU countries. Butter consumption is declining as a result of its 'unhealthy' image, while low-fat cheese sales are growing faster than any other cheese product in the last few years. Overall, demand for dairy products is slowly increasing, while demand for milk is slightly decreasing. The products that are experiencing above average growth rates are yoghurt, fermented and flavoured milk drinks, and soft cheese (Nomisma, 1997: 3.55-3.56).

In the last decades, due to technical improvements in the dairy industry, milk production has been rising, leading to milk production surpluses in many countries, especially in Europe. Consequently, since the early 1970s, the EU and other major milk producers have been operating schemes limiting milk deliveries, through the application of levies, or quotas (OECD, 1983: 51-70). Imports have also been controlled and domestic producers have been guaranteed a steady income, through a variety of measures in Canada, the United States, Japan, Australia, the European Union and most Eastern European countries (OECD, 1997). Nevertheless, international competition is expected to intensify. The results of the Uruguay Round in the GATT negotiations, regarding market access and export subsidies for dairy products, were substantial, in terms of subsidies, tariffs and non-tariff barriers reductions that resulted in a decrease of global subsidised exports (GATT, 1994).

The Greek Dairy Industry

Historical Development

In the mid-19th century, after the establishment of the modern Greek State, farmers' co-operatives and individual merchants financed an expansion of dairy farms' production facilities in many Greek locations. Merchants also distributed milk around Greece and developed export markets for feta cheese, in countries with large Greek communities (for example, Egypt, and later the USA). The first industrial dairy manufacturer in Greece was M. Margaritis, who in 1900 established a butter-producing unit on the island of Corfu. After 1910, on another Greek island, Crete, a co-ordinated effort was made to establish farmers' co-operatives and promote cheese production. The creation in 1916 of a School for Cheese Manufacturing in Ioannina (Epirus), which in 1932 was expanded into the School of Dairy Manufacturing, also contributed to the production of high-quality varieties of dairy products in the 1930s. At the same time production of certain types of cheese increased more than 50% and exports, primarily to Egypt, the USA and South Africa, followed, with high volumes since 1933. During the Second World War, production was substantially reduced and trade completely halted (Zigouris, 1952: 16-45).

In 1934, the first major industrial unit, Evga SA, was incorporated in Athens, while five smaller industrial units were operating in other Greek cities. Evga controlled the market for fresh milk, while small independent producers had a major share of the cheese, butter and ice cream markets. Farmers' co-operatives also started to play a more active role in the dairy industry. In the 1950s, the adoption of 'industrial' fresh milk was rapid, especially in major cities. Total milk production doubled between 1952 and 1962, surpassing the pre-war levels for the first time in 1954. Other products, still mainly manufactured in small 'traditional' establishments, also experienced similar substantial increases in output (Ministry of Commerce, 1963).

The 1960s was a period of change. A number of small producers who had built up a local client base and a reputation for quality decided to expand. A few of them soon established large manufacturing facilities, and among them the most prominent one was Delta, which produced pasteurised milk. Competition intensified in the 1970s as a number of firms entered the industry, and co-operatives increased their output and established their brand-names. Fage was among the most significant entrants, developing from a small shop in Athens before the war and a small-scale yoghurt producer in the 1960s to a major manufacturer in the 1970s (Sideri, 2000: 22). A similar route was followed by Mevgal, in Thessaloniki, in Northern Greece.

In the 1980s, Delta became the leader in fresh milk and some of the milk products in Southern and Central Greece, with Mevgal and Agno (a co-operative of farmers from Northern Greece) controlling the market in Northern Greece. Fage developed the branded, 'industrial' yoghurt market, while in the ice-cream segment Evga, Delta and Lever Hellas (a subsidiary of Unilever) were competing to gain market share. Production rose slowly in the early 1980s, but then in the period 1987-1990 the increases were constant and substantial. Exports became a target of Greek companies in all segments of the industry. Imports also increased as consumers sought greater variety and local raw materials were not sufficient for the rapidly expanding industry (Lioupis, 1991).

Exports and domestic competition were the major areas of change in the early 1990s. Yoghurt exports, that were already high in the late 1980s, increased further, especially by the market leader Fage, that saw its domestic share decline with Delta's entry into the yoghurt segment in 1994. The brand-name Fage is already well-known in the UK and Fage has now targeted other Western European markets (Italy, France, Germany, Austria) along with Australia (ICAP, 1999a: 35). Delta's yoghurt is also being sold abroad, in France, as Danone-Veritable Yoghourt Grec. The same companies (Fage and Delta) competed in the ice-cream market since Fage bought Evga in 1988. The exports, in the early 1990s, came primarily from the third competitor, Lever Hellas, but are now the result mainly of Delta's efforts.

The packaged cheese market, that was very small in previous decades, also expanded in the 1990s and domestic consumption and exports grew accordingly. All cheese exports have doubled in dollar value terms between 1991 and 1995. The introduction of a great number of new product varieties is another characteristic of the 1990s (ICAP, 1995).

Foreign direct investment is a more recent development. Delta has chosen ice-cream, a high value-added product with no particular 'Greek' characteristics, as the appropriate product to be manufactured and sold throughout Eastern Europe. Three factories are currently being operated by Delta in Bulgaria, Romania, and Yugoslavia, while there are plans for a fourth one in the Ukraine. In 1998, for the first time, Delta's ice cream sales in the Balkans surpassed domestic sales, while Delta has a 50% overall market share in the Balkan countries where it operates (Bulgaria, Yugoslavia, Romania and Former Yugoslavian Republic of Macedonia) (Delta, 1999: 16-17). Fage has made the same choice of product, and its co-owner, K. Filippou, has bought Cas-Ice Cream in South Africa.

The Major Firms

Despite the presence of four large producers (Delta, Fage, Mevgal and Agno), which are active in almost all segments of the dairy market in Greece, there are other companies with high market shares in particular products. Farmers' co-operatives are also still operating, while acquisitions and alliances are affecting the industry.

The fresh milk market is essentially controlled by the four major producers. Delta, incorporated in 1968, has been listed on the Athens Stock Exchange since 1990. Nevertheless, the founding Daskalopoulos family still owns a large part of the shares, while the French dairy multinational Danone holds 20% as part of a co-operation agreement.

The other major Greek dairy company, Fage, was initially established in 1926 as a small enterprise, owned by I. Filippou. Its reputation for quality helped it open more shops and then, in 1964, a small manufacturing unit. In 1977 it was incorporated under the form of an SA and started producing in a much larger facility. Since then it has grown enormously, acquiring in 1988 the first major Greek dairy company, Evga. Its co-owners, the founder's grandsons, I. and K. Filippou, also control a number of other, mainly food-related, companies (Sideri, 2000: 22)

The third largest Greek dairy company, and the largest in Northern Greece, is Mevgal. Operating since 1950 it was incorporated as an SA in 1976. The completion, in 1996, of its modernisation programme has enabled it to expand in new products and new geographic markets. Mevgal is now a major producer of fresh milk, yoghurt and cheese (ICAP, 1999b: 62-63).

Agno is the largest co-operative firm in the Greek dairy industry. Established in 1950 and based in Lagadas, near Thessaloniki, it is among the few major dairy companies in Greece that produce their own raw milk.

Despite recent modernisation efforts that have ensured the company's market share in Northern Greece, financial difficulties have been mounting in the last few years. In July 1998, the Agricultural Bank of Greece (Agno's biggest creditor) took over the firm's management, and is now attempting to sell the company or make it part of a larger food-producing firm, controlled by the Bank.

Two more major co-operative firms are Dodoni and Neogal. Dodoni has been operating since 1963 in the Northern province of Epirus, and is a major producer of feta cheese. It exports 22% of its cheese production to a number of European countries, the USA, Australia, Cyprus, and South Africa and accounts for more than 15% of Greek cheese exports (ICAP, 1995: 28; ICAP, 1999b). Neogal, established in Drama (Macedonia) in 1965, is currently controlled by the farmers' co-operatives of the Drama and Kavala prefectures, where it mostly distributes its products.

In terms of other types of milk and milk products, Greece has a relatively high, but steadily declining, consumption of concentrated milk. This is primarily imported, while the only producer in Greece is Nestlé Hellas, that was incorporated in 1973, as a subsidiary of Nestlé. The six companies already mentioned also control the milk cream market, while Fage, Delta and Mevgal are responsible for most of the 'industrial' yoghurt production, and Agno is the major producer of 'traditional' yoghurt.

Evga (owned by Fage), Delta and the rapidly growing Kri-Kri account for a large part of the ice cream production in Greece (Giannakakos, 2000: 78-79). The small and shrinking butter market in Greece is covered by the co-operative firms (including Agno and Dodoni). The major industrial non-co-operative producer is Alpino (ICAP, 1999b: 111-114).

The cheese market is the most fragmented among the segments of the Greek dairy market. Industrial units produce about 60% of total cheese production and among them the major producers are: Dodoni, Mevgal, that pioneered the branded feta sales, Fage, that uses the production of sub-contractors, often partly or wholly controlled by the Fage group, Tyras, a Thessaly cheese-maker and Epirus, a relatively new entrant, established in 1994 (ICAP, 1999b).

The financial situation of the major Greek dairy producers and exporters is presented in Table 7.1. The Greek dairy industry is still in an expansion period. New firms are being established, especially in the markets where there is a high growth potential. Major firms are also expanding rapidly, while maintaining their profitability. Although profit margins are not very high in the industry, there is a constant effort by Greek firms to invest in new product lines and upgrade their production facilities. Investment has been very high since 1989, making the Greek dairy industry among the most capital intensive Greek food industries (Kazakos, 1997: 43).

Table 7.1 Financial results of Greek dairy companies (1999)

Companies	Turnover (million Drachmas)	Net Income (million Drachmas)
Fage	91,051	537
Delta	73,581	1,565
Mevgal	40,263	259
Dodoni	25,290	1,093
Evga	24,492	521
Delta Ice-Cream	21,012	1,504
Tyras	11,897	261
Evrofarma	2,706	401
Kri-Kri	2,488	354
El-gal Riga	1,112	3

Source: ICAP, 2001.

Sources of Competitive Advantage

Factor Conditions

The raw milk used by the industry is primarily of Greek origin. Cow's milk accounts for 40% of total Greek production, sheep's milk for 35% and goat's milk for 25% (ICAP, 1995: 7). The split among the various kinds of milk is not typical of the situation in most countries. About 90% of raw milk produced in the world is cow's milk, and only 3% is sheep's and goat's milk (Crocombe et al., 1991: 61).

   The conditions in most small-size Greek milk farms created a disadvantage for the industry. The lack of specialised personnel and the low level of mechanisation did not allow the animals to produce high yields or superior quality milk. The first signs of improvement were evident with the increases in cow's milk production in the late 1980s, which were due to the increased yields from imported cows (Lioupis, 1991: 53). In the last few years, however, improvements have been substantial. Farmers' co-operatives have traditionally helped farmers by providing loans and technical support. For the 1990s, as my interviews and a recent study (Kazakos, 1997) indicate, the same policy is followed by the other dairy companies as well. The companies have limited the number of supplier farms, for example, Delta has limited the number of its milk suppliers from about 12,000 in the mid-1980s to 1,100 in 1998. However, the major firms are providing these farms with extensive support, in a kind of 'contractual' production of raw material. Delta even offers training programmes, run in a special company-owned farm, that disseminate the company's know-how in fields related to animal feed, reproduction and hygiene of livestock, and even farm management issues (Delta, 1999: 8-9). This has led to the creation of modern farms with very high standards, able to supply milk of the quality required by the industry and in a consistent manner. Smaller firms, mainly some of the cheese manufacturers, are still suffering from the inconsistent quality of the milk produced by their suppliers (Kazakos, 1997: 60).

Other raw materials and especially condensed milk are primarily imported from other European countries. Greece is still not self-sufficient in cow's milk and Greek milk cannot be considered superior to that of other competitor countries. Quality, however, has improved considerably in the 1990s and yields have risen a further 20% (Ministry of Agriculture, 1996). The only clear advantage of the Greek industry is the adequate production of sheep's and goat's milk used in many of the traditional Greek products (like feta cheese), which ensures their superior quality.

The dairy industry is not labour intensive. Most of the personnel is either in sales and marketing or in the operation of complex machinery. The level of skill required is high for both categories. However, none of the major companies experience any problems in hiring qualified employees as wages are considered above average for the manufacturing industry. Moreover, the large companies conduct extensive training seminars using company, government and EU funds. Smaller companies are still operating with limited personnel of lower skill. Nevertheless, as soon as small companies increase their production and expand beyond their local market, they hire qualified managers and skilled technicians. Overall, in the manufacture of dairy products, Greece has the lower personnel costs in the EU and, even when adjusted for labour productivity, wages are still slightly below the EU average (European Commission and Eurostat, 2000: 138).

Capital is not considered a major problem for the industry. Fage, Delta, Mevgal and some of the other large firms have consistently had good financial results and have recently targeted foreign capital markets with bond issues and bank lending. Co-operative firms, the more recent example being Agno, have experienced financial difficulties but have been able to draw funds from various incentive schemes of the Greek government, the Agricultural Bank of Greece and the EU, for modernisation purposes.

The majority of dairy products are transported through the road network. Given the rather poor condition of the roads, the need for constant deliveries in all parts of Greece has been a disadvantage for the industry for many years. Recently, as exports increased towards Balkan and other

Eastern European countries the situation has changed. The experience of large companies in solving problems related to road infrastructure has been valuable in dealing with the less developed road networks of these countries.

Dairy products are very often sold to countries in close proximity to the exporting country. As Greece is not close to the major Western European markets, location was a disadvantage for the industry. In recent years, as the Eastern European markets opened up, geography has been more favourable to the Greek industry, which has taken advantage of it, establishing distribution networks in neighbouring countries. Delta, in addition to its three factories, has 35,000 points of sale in the Balkans and 1,000 more in Russia (Sideri, 1998: 21).

Most of the innovations in the Greek dairy industry have been driven by marketing needs. Extensive market research is conducted by the large companies and marketing departments are introducing new varieties. R&D and engineering departments in these companies are then adapting the production process to suit the manufacturing of the new products. Major improvements in production are less common and most of the production technology is imported.

In terms of educational institutions, the School of Dairy Manufacturing in Ioannina has been operating for decades. There are also relevant undergraduate and postgraduate programs and specialisations in the Agricultural University of Athens (where a specialised Laboratory of Dairy Technology is operating under the auspices of the Department of Food Science and Technology), the Faculty of Agriculture in the School of Geotechnical Sciences of the Aristotle University of Thessaloniki and other Greek educational institutions. Nevertheless, the contacts between Universities and dairy companies are not as widespread or organised as they could be, despite the substantial improvement of the past fifteen years. The Ministry of Agriculture has also supported farmers and industrial producers in technical matters, without however an integrated intervention plan. The Association of Greek Dairy Manufacturers has been relatively active in assisting producers and promoting dairy consumption, even with selective advertising campaigns.

Demand Conditions

Variations in the consumption patterns of dairy products are widespread even among neighbouring countries or countries with similar levels of development. Exporting patterns often follow local consumption preferences. The case of New Zealand is a characteristic example, where per capita consumption of milk and butter is among the highest in the world, while cheese consumption is well below that of other developed countries, matching its export patterns of very high milk and butter exports and relatively low cheese exports (Crocombe et al., 1991: 66; UN, International Trade Statistics Yearbook).

Greek consumption of dairy products has been low compared to other developed countries (Lioupis, 1991: 128). Per capita consumption of fresh milk, milk cream and most other dairy products was among the lowest in the European Union, almost half the EU average (ICAP, 1999a: 208). In certain products, such as cream, Greek per capita consumption was approximately one-fourth of the 1996 EU average (Eurostat, 1998). Butter consumption, was by far the lowest in the EU for 1997 (European Commission and Eurostat, 2000: 123). On the contrary, cheese consumption in the 1990s has been the second highest in the EU (second only to France) and among the highest in the world (ICAP, 1995: 161; Eurostat, 1998; ICAP, 1999b: 194). The 1997 data show Greece leading the EU countries, with a cheese consumption of 24.2 kg/capita (European Commission and Eurostat, 2000: 123). The export patterns of the Greek industry match these consumption preferences. About 80% of Greek dairy exports in recent years have been cheese products, while the remaining 20% consists primarily of yoghurt and ice cream exports (UN, International Trade Statistics Yearbook). In fact, yoghurt and ice cream are the only other dairy products where Greek per capita consumption is not very far from EU averages (Eurostat, 1998; Lioupis, 1991).

Sophistication of Greek consumers was low until the mid-1980s. Besides fresh milk, most other products were unbranded and variety was limited. Then, the introduction of some new products, that were already available for many years in foreign markets, and the wider availability of branded yoghurt and other dairy products reversed the situation. Production of low fat milk surged from less than 1% of fresh milk production in 1985 to more than 20% in 1988. 'Industrial' yoghurt that accounted for slightly more than 50% of Greek yoghurt sales in 1984, increased its share of sales to 75% in 1990 (Lioupis, 1991: 58-63).

In the 1990s as more companies entered all the segments of the dairy market, new products were being continuously introduced. Greek consumers are now able to choose from many different kinds of yoghurt, ice cream and milk desserts, while the market for branded cheese is constantly expanding (ICAP, 1995). Variety is now comparable to that in other developed countries but only in particular segments. Most new products are copies of foreign ones (Kazakos, 1997: 61), although large firms have been able to introduce a few innovative products with a Greek 'character'. In this environment, customers have become more quality-conscious, demanding greater variety and rapidly adopting the new products. Customer sophistication, however, is still not a major advantage for the Greek industry, over its main foreign competitors.

Dairy products have consistently increased their participation in Greek food consumption. In 1980, 14% of private consumption spending on food was spent on dairy products. This proportion rose to 15% in 1984 and then increased even further to 16% between 1985 and 1989 (Lioupis, 1991: 5). In the early 1990s, that proportion remained around 16%, until 1993 when it jumped to 17.5% (ICAP, 1995: 5). In terms of quantities the same trends are evident. Small increases until 1986 (even decreases in some years) were followed by successive large changes between 1988 and 1994. The major increases were in yoghurt, cheese and milk cream consumption, while ice cream and fresh milk demand rose much slower (Lioupis, 1991: 8; ICAP, 1995). Fresh milk, yoghurt, cheese and ice cream consumption continued to rise between 1994 and 1998, while butter and milk cream demand remained steady or declined (ICAP, 1999a: 94-127; ICAP, 1999b: 129-130).

Overall growth of Greek demand in the 1980s and 1990s, and especially rapidly increasing demand for 'industrial' dairy products, has helped the industry expansion and promoted the required innovations in process and product technology. The Ministry of Agriculture's strict regulations, especially on cheese production, where a 'traditional' production process needed to be preserved, has also helped Greek cheese maintain its superior quality. The adoption by Greece of European Council Directive 92/46/EEC of 16 June 1992 that specifies health rules for the production and sale of milk and dairy products has also ensured a strengthening of quality standards in the manufacturing of all dairy products in Greece.

Internationalisation of Greek demand has certainly been an advantage during the industry's development. Greek immigrants abroad were the first source of demand for exports of Greek dairy products and especially Greek cheeses. Then as tourist arrivals increased, both cheese and yoghurt became popular among foreign, and especially European, consumers. Many people were also introduced to these products by the increasing number of Greek restaurants abroad, as soft cheese and 'Greek-style' yoghurt form an essential part of the popular 'Mediterranean diet'.

In the 1990s, after the opening of the Eastern European markets, Greek brands gained a 'high-quality' image, particularly in the Balkan countries. Dairy firms exploited that advantage and exported heavily to these countries, while Delta has already established production facilities there. Exports to Eastern Europe often consist of products that are not 'Greek' in any way, such as ice cream.

Related and Supporting Industries

The Greek dairy industry is part of the most important Greek cluster, Food/Beverages. The increased competitiveness of the Greek dairy industry, coincides with an increase in exports for the whole cluster in the

1990s. New industries have been added to the competitive lists between 1985 and 1992 and most of them have been processed food industries.

Although the dairy industry shares few common technologies with other food industries, it has been using their products throughout its development. Greek fruit has been used for some years in dairy products, as the variety of such products has been increasing since the mid-1980s. Recently other products, such as honey, have been combined with, in this case, yoghurt, to provide new flavours.

In terms of direct suppliers the raw milk producing farms, like most animal-related industries in Greece, were lagging in competitiveness, facing a number of structural problems (KEPE, 1991). However, through the efforts of farmers' co-operatives and large dairy companies a large segment of milk farms have been modernised, producing milk of very high quality.

Other milk-related industries are not developed in Greece. All the dairy machinery is imported, primarily from Germany, while industries related to, for example, the genetic improvement of animals are still in their infancy stage in Greece. Nevertheless, the very competitive Greek packaging industry has been a source of advantage, providing a high quality, affordable product. The variety of such products has helped the Greek dairy industry expand its own product variety.

Firm Strategy, Structure and Rivalry

The two main dairy firms in Greece, Fage and Delta are controlled by two families. Their growth in the last fifteen years has necessitated the expansion of their management team, although they are still headed by members of the respective families. Delta is now listed on the Athens Stock Exchange and part of its shares is owned by the French multinational Danone. The presence of a professional management team combined with the mixed ownership structure has been successful so far, creating little tension and increasing the sources of input to the major decisions.

Fage's ownership is concentrated to the Filippou family. Diversity, however, is provided by the number of acquired or allied companies, that are still managed with some degree of autonomy. Co-operative firms have been less successful in recent years. A number of them have faced financial problems which led them to bankruptcy. Others have resorted to financial assistance from the Agricultural Bank of Greece. However, new start-up companies have emerged in the 1990s, with a rapidly increasing turnover and a high level of profits, that has funded their expansion. Now some of them are turning to the Athens Stock Exchange, with Evrofarma (established in 1991 and listed on the Exchange in June 2000) being the first one.

The strategy of most Greek dairy firms in the 1980s, when their output consisted mainly of low-margin products, was to target costs. Through extensive automation of the production process, they were able to keep costs down, while producing a more standardised product of higher quality (Kazakos, 1997: 67). Most medium and large-sized Greek firms have invested in modernising their facilities (ICAP, 1999a: 3). The more streamlined production process and the emphasis on quality control and packaging allowed them to increase their product variety in the 1990s and establish their brand names, without compromising their low cost position. It was only at this stage, when a low cost, consistent quality product was being produced, that exports were pursued vigorously mainly to developed Western European markets. For that purpose Fage, Delta and other companies secured firm relations with established distribution networks in these countries. Delta also pursued the less developed Eastern European markets creating its own distribution network and a number of production facilities.

Domestic rivalry has been a major driving force for the industry's expansion. First, the establishment of Lever Hellas, immediately increased the level of competition in ice cream. New products of improved quality were the result within only a few years. Then in the early 1990s, the most profound changes took place. In 1993 Fage entered the fresh milk market capturing almost 21% by 1994 (ICAP, 1995: 47). This affected the price, quality and packaging of fresh milk for all of the main competitors. In 1994, partly as a reply to that move, Delta entered the yoghurt market that until then was almost exclusively under the control of Fage. Again, a host of new products, both in the plain yoghurt segment, especially the low-fat varieties, and the yoghurt with fruit and other additions segment, were immediately released by the main competitors, Fage, Delta and Mevgal (ICAP, 1995: 67). The cheese segment is where competition is now increasing. After the initial steps by Mevgal and a smaller company, D. Kolios Ltd., Fage entered the market, mainly using the products of two smaller companies, Tyras SA and Pindos SA. Other small and larger companies, most notably Dodoni and Epirus, which also show a strong export orientation, are now producing packaged cheese. Competition has led to an expanded variety of cheese types and cheese products of excellent quality.

Geographic concentration is increasing in the Greek dairy industry. With the declining performance of most co-operative firms and the increasing share of Fage and Delta, that are both producing in locations near Athens, Attica's share of total production is very high, especially in pasteurised milk (more than 55%), 'industrial' yoghurt (69%) and ice cream (about 75%). Thessaloniki, the second largest city in Greece and its surrounding area, is where Mevgal, Agno and Alpino are located. Butter (54% of total Greek production) and milk cream (about 50%) production is concentrated in the prefecture of Thessaloniki, which also has the second highest share in pasteurised milk (27%) (ICAP, 1999a: 97, 111, 115, 120). Cheese production is not concentrated and takes place in most Greek prefectures, with none having more than a 10% share of total production. Ioannina, Thessaloniki, Larissa and Kilkis are the leading prefectures in cheese production and the only ones close to the 10% mark (ICAP, 1999b: 93-95). The reasons for this lack of concentration are that Fage and Delta, in certain cases, use the cheese production of smaller companies located far from Athens, that some of the other major cheese producers are located in Ioannina (Dodoni, Pindos) and Larissa (Vigla, Olymbos) and that a substantial part of the total production is still carried out in medium-sized, local establishments as the 15 larger Greek cheese manufacturers represent only 40-45% of total industrial production (ICAP, 1999b: 31-52).

The Role of Government

Traditionally, the Greek government has strongly intervened in the dairy industry. A number of products have been under pricing guidelines, while some of the co-operative producers were rescued by the Agricultural Bank of Greece, under the government's guidance. In recent years, these firms were allowed to go bankrupt, while some were sold back to the farmers.

   The efforts to sell and restructure the most indebted co-operative firms, along with the general market liberalisation measures of the late 1980s have decreased the government's involvement. Funding, mainly through EU initiatives and incentive schemes, has increased in recent years, with the emphasis placed on equipment modernisation and acquisition of production technology. The government has, therefore, helped the industry's efforts to expand, both in traditional and new products, while, at the same time, increasing its quality standards.

The Role of Chance

The recent move towards healthier eating has affected positively demand for yoghurt in developed countries. Yoghurt, along with fresh and soft cheese, has been the major area of demand growth in the EU market (Nomisma, 1997: 3.52) The Greek industry has taken advantage of that trend, targeting most Western European markets and, in some cases, establishing its brand-names. Changes in Eastern Europe have also greatly affected the industry. An extensive, underdeveloped market was opened up, with few established brand names. Greek companies were quick to project a 'quality' image and establish extended distribution networks. Sales of many Greek dairy products, produced both in Greece and in other Balkan countries, have been substantial in the 1990s.

Summary

The industrial production of milk and dairy products is about 110 years old. The initial producers, Western Europe and North America, are still controlling a large part of the market, while the role of Australia and New Zealand has increased. Growth of international trade is still limited by government intervention and some products' short shelf-life. Relatively recent moves, and especially the GATT agreements, changed the picture, increasing the opportunities for unsubsidised trade.

The Greek dairy industry has evolved very slowly since the beginning of the century. Although the first major industrial enterprise (Evga) was established in the 1930s, it was only in the 1960s that its dominance was first challenged by small units rapidly expanding. The 1970s was a period of growth for most companies, and in the early 1980s the competitive landscape changed, with a number of efficient competitors in most products. In the mid-1980s production increased along with product variety. This led to an expansion of the industry in the 1990s with exports reaching unprecedented heights. For the first time, production facilities were established in foreign countries, by Delta in the Balkans and Fage in South Africa.

Factor conditions have played a modest role in the industry's development. In terms of raw materials, the availability of sheep's and goat's milk and the recent improvements in the quality of cow's milk, are counter-balanced by the lack of adequate supplies of raw cow's milk and other materials. Personnel and capital are available for the dairy industry at a competitive cost and the level of R&D and employee training are adequate, although not very high. Geography has been beneficial in the 1990s, as have the activities of the industry association and the Ministry of Agriculture. The relevant educational programs and the presence of the specialised School of Dairy Manufacturing have created a satisfactory level of educational infrastructure.

Demand conditions were an impediment in the industry's early stages. The sophistication of customers was very low, since mostly unbranded products were available, and consumption levels were among the lowest for developed countries. In recent years, however, the high consumption of certain products, especially cheese and yoghurt, along with the greater sophistication stemming from the available variety of branded products have changed the role of demand conditions. Internationalisation of demand has also contributed to that positive change.

Related and supporting industries in the wider sense have been advantageous for the industry. The improved performance of the entire Food/Beverages cluster since the mid-1980s has created a positive environment, especially as the dairy industry is now using the products of other related food industries. Raw milk producers have also improved their performance, which was not impressive before the 1980s, while other industries, for example, machinery, are absent. A very strong packaging industry has also been a source of many dairy innovations in Greece.

Firms' strategies, and structures and domestic rivalry have had a positive influence on the Greek industry. The strategy of low cost, automation and export orientation along with the structure of family ownership combined with a professional management team have been key elements in the industry's success. Vigorous domestic rivalry has also been important in stimulating product innovation. Geographic concentration is evident but only in certain products.

Government intervention in the industry was initially high, controlling the market and often distorting competition by supporting failing co-operatives. More recently, the influence of government measures has been lessened and the promotion of various funding initiatives has helped the industry. Chance's role has been positive during the last fifteen years. The 'healthy eating' trend along with the opening of the Eastern European markets has had beneficial implications for Greek companies.

This is an industry where some basic factors were present since its early stages of development. In the last fifteen years these factors have been complemented by advanced factors, improved demand conditions, better related and supporting industries, coherent strategies and a domestic rivalry stronger and intensely personal. This case also vividly illustrates the interactions among Porter's diamond determinants and the self-reinforcing nature of the diamond, as the improvements in some determinants immediately affected other sides of the diamond.

8   Conclusion

This part of the work presents a synthesis of the case study material. It also integrates this material with the observations made in the first chapter, on Porter's *The Competitive Advantage of Nations*, and the second chapter's analysis of the competitive advantage of Greece. The goal is to arrive at certain conclusions on the one hand regarding Porter's work and on the other, the Greek economic environment.

The first section deals with the implications of the five case studies for every element of the diamond framework. Then, the most important points, concerning many aspects of the application of Porter's work in the five case studies, are analysed further. Finally, the last section examines the implications of the state of the Greek industries studied for the wider Greek economy, in the context of its integration with the other EU economies.

Implications of the Case Studies for the Diamond Elements

The five Greek industries (cement, rolled aluminium products, tourism, men's outerwear, and dairy) analysed in detail, revealed a multitude of sources of competitive advantage. A synopsis of those sources, and the mechanisms through which they acted in each individual case, is given at the end of the relevant chapters. The focus of this section, therefore, is on the implications of these individual conclusions for each diamond determinant.

The sources of advantage for each case are summarised in Table 8.1. The table is organised around the diamond elements, so that a general picture can be formed on the impact of every determinant in all the cases studied. This general overview will then be explored in detail.

Factor Conditions

The overall picture of factor conditions seems to conform with Porter's views. Indeed, the cement, rolled aluminium and tourism industries derive substantial advantage from factor conditions, the dairy industry, which has been competitive for a shorter period, presents a more mixed picture, while the uncompetitive men's outerwear industry is disadvantaged by the

Table 8.1   Sources of advantage in the five Greek industries

DIAMOND ELEMENT→ INDUSTRY	Factor Conditions	Demand Conditions	Related and Supporting Industries	Firm Strategy, Structure and Rivalry	The Role of Chance	The Role of Government
CEMENT *(very competitive)*	H[a]	H (*)[b]	H	H	L[c]	M[c]
ROLLED ALUMINIUM PRODUCTS *(competitive)*	H	M	H (*)	M (-)[d]	L	L
TOURISM *(competitive)*	H (*)	M	H	M (-)	L	H
MEN'S OUTERWEAR *(uncompetitive, loss in position)*	L	L	M	L	L	M
DAIRY *(competitive)*	M	M	M	H	H	L

[a] The effect of each diamond element in shaping the industry's competitive advantage has been assessed as 'High' (H), 'Medium' (M), or 'Low' (L).

[b] The asterisk (*) denotes an element where the Greek industry possesses an 'unusual' advantage.

[c] In the government and chance determinants, the symbols H, M, and L demonstrate the overall effect of the determinant in creating the industry's competitive advantage and not the degree of their involvement in the industry's development.

[d] The minus sign (-) indicates an element where there is a wide variation among its different components.

changes in factor conditions during the last fifteen years. This picture, however, is primarily due to basic factor conditions.

Specifically, the cement and aluminium industries draw a lot of advantage from the availability and quality of raw materials, labour and capital, while for the tourism industry basic factors represent an 'unusual' advantage with Greece's combination of geography, climate and unique cultural heritage. The men's outerwear industry, on the other hand, has experienced its most important changes in labour costs and raw material availability, and the dairy industry has emphasised the improvement of the quality of its domestic raw materials and its personnel.

Advanced and specialised factors are much less developed in the Greek industries studied, although, again, a variation exists among them, depending on their competitiveness. This is certainly true in the very competitive cement industry, the relatively competitive dairy industry and the uncompetitive men's outerwear industry. The lack of extensive R&D is the major gap in the rolled aluminium industry, while in the tourism case, certain factors are not yet at the level expected, given the industry's competitiveness.

Part of the problem with Greek factor conditions is due to the state of certain infrastructures (such as the road network). Nevertheless, depending on the nature of the industry and its products, the effects have not been uniform and some industries have been able to circumvent the infrastructure problems, sometimes treating them as selective factor disadvantages. For example, the cement industry has used the poor condition of the road network as an incentive to develop an efficient sea transportation infrastructure which later became an essential part of the industry's export drive.

Overall, factor conditions seem to work according to Porter's expectations. The important role of basic factors is something to be expected, given their central part in most theories of international trade. However, Porter's detailed classification enables a more in-depth analysis of them. Specialised and advanced factors are not developed to the same extent as basic factors. Nevertheless, their status is related to an industry's competitive position. The presence of selective factor disadvantages was also evident in some of the cases. The essential element that enabled an industry to transform a selective factor disadvantage, especially in basic factors, to a sustainable advantage was the condition of the other diamond determinants, as Porter (1990: 85) describes.

Demand Conditions

Demand conditions have played a role in determining the competitive advantage of the Greek industries studied. The small size of the Greek market has been a hindrance to some of the industries studied, primarily the rolled aluminium products industry and, to a lesser extent, the dairy industry. Nevertheless, it seems that the other attributes that Porter emphasises have had a considerable impact on most of the competitive industries.

In the cement case, the per capita consumption (among the highest in the world), along with the phenomenal growth rates and the early saturation of the market, which forced companies to export, have given the industry an 'unusual' advantage. Demand growth and 'mobile buyers' have also been important for the rolled aluminium products industry, while per capita consumption and growth rates have determined the export success in particular segments of the dairy industry.

'Industrial' customers present a more mixed picture. They had a very substantial role in enhancing the competitive advantage of the rolled aluminium products industry, though their sophistication in terms of seeking the latest innovations is questionable. In the cement case, the ready mixed concrete and construction industries are not among the most competitive Greek industries. Nevertheless, their level of sophistication in terms of the specific product can be considered adequate.

In the more consumer-oriented industries, a clearer trend emerges. Sophistication is a key attribute in the industries' competitiveness. While the long-stay, high-spending pattern of Greek tourists has been important for the industry's success, it has not, however, compensated for the lack of emphasis on quality and new or alternative forms of tourism. In the dairy case, customer sophistication is where the changes before and after the late 1980s are more evident. Low customer sophistication has contributed to the decreasing competitiveness of the men's outerwear industry by failing to provide the stimulus for its upgrading from a cost-oriented to a differentiation-based producer.

Overall, it appears that Porter emphasises the correct demand attributes. However, in the rolled aluminium products, cement and tourism industries the role of some of these attributes, such as buyer sophistication, is not entirely clear.

Related and Supporting Industries

The importance of this determinant has been the least contested part of Porter's work. Although part of the influences of this determinant has been captured in factor and demand conditions, the role of interchanges among related and supporting industries has been very strong in the Greek cases.

The rolled aluminium products industry derives an 'unusual' advantage from the presence in Greece of most aluminium-related industries, from bauxite mining and alumina refining to aluminium smelting and most fabricated products industries. The tourism and cement industries have also greatly benefited from the presence of internationally competitive related and supporting industries. In the dairy industry, the recent rises in competitiveness are also a characteristic of many of its related and supporting industries, while the opposite is the case in the declining men's outerwear industry. An aberration in this pattern is the presence, still, of some competitive related industries in the men's outerwear case. These industries, however, are part of a wider cluster that was very competitive until the early 1980s. Since then, all of its industries have experienced substantial declines, especially those more closely linked with the industry studied.

The other aberration from what Porter (1990) expects (at least for a developed country) is the lack of competitive machinery industries and other 'advanced' service industries, like travel automation systems in the case of tourism. Of course, Greece's level of development is lower than that of most of the countries studied in Porter's original work (Porter, 1990). Moreover, most of the relevant machinery industries are global oligopolies, and Greece would naturally not be expected to have a strong presence.

Firm Strategy, Structure and Rivalry

The role of this determinant in creating and sustaining the competitive advantage of Greek firms is mixed. The dairy industry has benefited from intense rivalry between its principal firms and from their appropriate strategies and structures. The cement, tourism and rolled aluminium products have drawn less advantage from this determinant. Specifically, firm strategy and structure has been instrumental in the rolled products industry, and a major impediment to the uncompetitive men's outerwear industry. Certain shortcomings were evident in the strategies and structures of many tourist firms. Domestic rivalry, however, exhibits a different picture. The competitive rolled aluminium products industry is composed of one single firm. In the cement industry an oligopoly (four firms, two main competitors) has been present from its very first steps, in the dairy products there are many producers, although, the two leading companies have combined market shares of more than 50% in some products, and in the uncompetitive men's outerwear industry competition is intense. Individual explanations can be found for each case.

In the dairy industry, the two leading firms are involved in a fierce, and sometimes personal, rivalry, attempting to upstage each other wherever one company holds a dominant position, and using foreign market penetration as a way of gaining what Porter (1990: 119) calls 'bragging rights'. Moreover, new companies are constantly entering the industry, offering innovative products and capturing a substantial proportion of exports. The cement industry is also a case where the two main rivals, and, to a lesser extent, the other two companies, have been involved in intense competition. Moreover, cement is an industry with a high level of concentration in foreign markets as well, with few companies (often one or two) having a controlling share of the local market, even in large and developed countries. The lack of rivalry in the rolled aluminium products and the intense rivalry in the uncompetitive men's outerwear are, however, much harder to explain.

Another problem with this determinant, that has already been pointed out in the evaluation of the determinant in Chapter 1, is the inclusion of two different components in one element. Firm strategy and structure deals entirely with the firm, while domestic rivalry is a characteristic related to the industry. This problem becomes more acute in the rolled aluminium products and tourism industries. The Greek rolled aluminium industry is composed of a monopolist firm that has, nevertheless, greatly benefited from its goals and strategic moves, as well as from its structure. The tourism industry, on the other hand, has not followed appropriate strategies in many instances, while its structure has not adapted to changing circumstances, despite the presence of extensive, and often personal, domestic rivalry. In addition to those two cases, the men's outerwear industry also has firms with inappropriate strategies and structures in an environment of intense rivalry.

Overall, it is certain that Porter's emphasis on firm-level attributes and domestic rivalry is important, especially given his attempts to reconcile industry, firm and country views on competitiveness. The effects, however, of each of the two components on the other, along with the pivotal role that domestic rivalry is assumed to play in the sustainability of competitive advantage merit further discussion.

The Role of Government

The impact of government's actions has been mixed. An undoubtedly positive contribution was made to the tourism industry, where the Greek government, primarily in the industry's initial development during the 1960s and 1970s, has been instrumental for the promotion of the industry's competitive advantage. The rolled aluminium products and dairy industries on the contrary do not owe a lot to the government's interference, that has in times had positive results, while for the men's outerwear industry the initial positive influence appears to have been reduced. Cement is again a special case with government actions in critical times either helping or hindering the industry.

The government has been involved in most sectors of business activity throughout the history of the Greek state, as analysed in Chapter 2. However, this strong role is expected by Porter (1990) in a relatively less developed country. In the tourism industry, the fact that the government's help and direct involvement came in the industry's early stages is also not far from Porter's relevant views.

The Role of Chance

Chance's impact on the competitive advantage of most Greek industries studied appears to have been limited in scope. In two of the cases, tourism and rolled aluminium products, its effect has been small. In the men's outerwear industry it has played a negative role during its recent decline period, while the dairy industry has drawn advantage from positive developments in the last decade. Cement has been the industry where chance has played a much greater role, with events in the early 1970s and 1980s heavily influencing the industry. The combination of very favourable and unfavourable events appears to have had a mildly positive effect on the industry, partly because of the presence of another outside influence to the diamond, government.

The inclusion of chance as an influence to the other four diamond determinants seems to be justified. Its role appears to be indirect in the five Greek cases and its effects are usually related to the responses of the industry, that are usually determined by the condition of the four main determinants.

Overall Implications for the Applicability of Porter's Framework

This section presents the overall evaluation regarding the diamond framework's applicability in the case of Greece. A critical analysis is made both of issues raised in the previous section and of more general points, related to clustering and geographic concentration and the dynamics of competitive advantage.

The issue of domestic rivalry is one that requires further discussion. Porter's (1990) own applications as well as those made by independent researchers (Oz, 1997; 1999), have indicated that a competitive industry can exist in the absence of domestic rivals. Despite that fact, there is no doubt that Porter (1990) considers rivalry an essential element of the diamond, that facilitates the workings of all other elements. The Greek cases, and specifically the four manufacturing industries studied, do not offer unconditional support for this view.

The aberrations in the cement and dairy cases can, however, be attributed to the particular circumstances in these industries, as they were analysed in the previous section. Moreover, the strong rivalry that exists between the dominant firms provides the stimuli for upgrading competitive advantage. The other two aberrations, in the men's outerwear and rolled aluminium products industries, are much harder to explain and indicate an area of concern for the diamond framework.

The intense competition in the uncompetitive men's outerwear industry can be justified by the fact that it is entirely price-driven. It has had, thus, little impact on the upgrading of the quality of the industry's products or on any other of the diamond determinants, and, in fact, Porter characterises price rivalry as destructive, in his latest work (Porter, 1998a: 15). The rolled aluminium case, where a domestic monopoly is present, can also probably be explained using Porter's own assertions. Porter (1990: 121) claims that 'a completely open home market along with extremely global strategies can partially substitute for the lack of domestic rivals in a smaller nation', while in the corresponding footnote (Porter, 1990: 788) he gives the example of an industry (central office telephone switches) with huge economies of scale. Greece certainly fits the description of a small open market for most products, including rolled aluminium. The industry is also scale sensitive, while the dominant Greek firm has an extremely global outlook, with most of its sales efforts directed at foreign markets. It should be noted, however, that Porter considers this a 'second best' solution that cannot confer on the industry the same advantages as intense domestic rivalry.

Rolled aluminium products, along with tourism and men's outerwear, are also the cases where a further aberration in the firm strategy, structure and rivalry determinant is apparent. The influence of firms' structures and strategies in all three of these cases is very different from that of domestic rivalry. The explanations given above for the rivalry in the rolled aluminium products and the men's outerwear, can help settle the issue in those cases. In the tourism case, another justification can be offered, that is, that certain tourist firms, the largest and most dynamic ones, which represent an increasing part of the Greek tourism industry, are changing rapidly their strategies and adapting their structures, thus matching the positive role of the intense domestic rivalry. What is, however, evident in these three cases is the weak links between firm strategy and structure and domestic rivalry. The grouping of domestic rivalry with firm strategy and structure is, therefore, an area that requires further research, especially in terms of the mechanisms that link the two components.

Another grouping, demand conditions, has also not worked entirely the way Porter expects. Most attributes in all cases have exerted their influence in line with Porter's views. Customer sophistication is, however, an attribute that varies among industries. Of course, Porter (1990) mentions in several instances that customer sophistication is among the last attributes to appear when a country progresses along the development path. In the Greek case, however, another explanation may be offered, in conjunction with the country's level of development. As Greece has progressed substantially in the last four decades, changes in customer sophistication have varied among industries. In the dairy industry, improvements have been rapid in the last ten years, while in the rolled aluminium case it has taken more than fifteen. As for the tourism case, it is still an ongoing process after decades of competitive development. An interesting observation connecting these cases is the state of basic factors. The dairy industry, in recent years, has seen improvements in basic factor conditions; it does not, nevertheless, rely on them extensively. The rolled aluminium products industry on the other hand has seen its advantage in basic factors slowly decline and this process has been paralleled with a rise in customer sophistication. Finally, in the tourism case basic factors are still essential to the industry. Therefore it appears that the persistent central role of basic factor advantages is related to a low level of customer sophistication, at least in the competitive industries.

Another interesting fact is that in two of the cases (rolled aluminium products and dairy) increased customer sophistication is partly a result of efforts by domestic firms, rather than other country-specific influences. Firms seek to produce differentiated, innovative, premium products that can provide the necessary revenue to offset any cost disadvantages, from the reduced importance of basic factors (in the aluminium case) or the strong domestic rivalry (in the dairy case), thus 'educating' their buyers. This process, however, is not automatic and is probably related to the condition of the other diamond determinants as is indicated by the men's outerwear industry, where this has failed to happen.

The industries' geographic concentration, is another one of Porter's (1990, 1998a, 1998b) strong findings. In the Greek cases, geographic concentration has been very beneficial to the aluminium-related industries, where interchanges among the firms in these industries were common. However, the apparent concentration in the cement and dairy cases does not appear to have produced a high level of interaction among the firms and is mostly a result of the need to be close to the large markets of Athens (with 35% of the Greek population living in Athens and the surrounding area) and Thessaloniki (the second largest city) in order to minimise transportation costs. In the tourism case, the proximity of basic factors is again the defining characteristic for the firms' location. Therefore, although geographic concentration is a phenomenon present among all the competitive industries studied, the types of advantage derived can vary widely and are sometimes closer to more traditional notions of industry concentration.

The two major contributions of Porter's (1990) book, apart from the diamond framework, have been the emphasis on the industry level and the clustering concept. Regarding the former, Porter's emphasis on the industry instead of the country provides the appropriate perspective for examining competitiveness. A lot of the influences on the competitiveness of the industries studied in Greece would not appear in a more general study of the country. This does not mean that country-level attributes are not important, and Porter's (1990) title (The Competitive Advantage of Nations) indicates that. However, it is ultimately the industry-specific attributes and circumstances that determine an industry's competitiveness. The notion of country competitiveness is not only theoretically weak, but also offers little on the reasons why particular industries rise and fall.

The clustering concept is recognised by most scholars as another of Porter's (1990) main contributions. It has also been the focus of much of his subsequent work (Porter, 1998b). Besides the lack of machinery industries, which is common in all Greek clusters and probably related to the country's level of development as Porter (1990) expects, Greek competitive industries form well-defined clusters. Firms in every cluster have also affected positively the development of related industries. The presence of cross-ownership in the Materials/Metals, Food/Beverages and Housing/Household clusters has been high and it is a result both of acquisitions and of the creation of new firms in related industries ('related diversification'). The only cluster where this trend has been much less pronounced, Textiles/Apparel, is also a cluster whose competitive position has been steadily declining.

In individual cases, interchanges among industries were found to be common in the cement, tourism and, to a lesser extent, dairy industries, while few and decreasing links were characteristic of the uncompetitive men's outerwear industry. The aluminium sector, also reveals close links among its industries. Firms involved in a supplier-buyer relationship are in contact regarding product-related issues, while the association brings together the entire sector. The rolled aluminium products industry has also benefited from the fact that its dominant firm is a member of a group of related companies active in metal processing.

Overall, the diamond framework was proven a valuable tool for the analysis of the competitive advantage of the Greek industries studied. Important influences on the industries' competitiveness were highlighted using the framework and the majority of determinants worked in ways similar to what Porter (1990) expects. Interactions among the 'four-plus-two' diamond determinants have been at the heart of the process of the creation of competitive advantage. The dairy industry, where rivalry changed the nature of home demand or the men's outerwear industry, where inappropriate strategies hurt factor creation mechanisms, are characteristic examples of a phenomenon obvious in all cases. Moreover, the emphasis on the clustering concept, and the geographic concentration of industries provided additional insights on the geographical and sectoral structure of Greek manufacturing and service industries.

Greece's lower level of development, than that of the countries studied by Porter (1990), did affect the conditions of certain advanced and specialised factors, demand attributes, and related and supporting industries in ways, however, similar to those described by Porter (1990). Less related to the level of development are the observations on the relationship between domestic rivalry and firms' strategies and structures, the influences on demand sophistication and the role of geographic concentration. These are the issues that demand further investigation. Additional cases might provide a more conclusive answer.

Implications for the Greek Economy

From the application of Porter's methodology in five particular manufacturing and service industries, certain implications for the Greek economy become apparent, especially for the direction of government policy and company strategies. The presentation, however, of an integrated proposal is undoubtedly beyond the scope of the present study, since it demands the analysis of a larger number of cases, and the use of many additional data and of specialised surveys on particular issues. The goal of this section is therefore to put the case studies in the wider perspective of the Greek economy and to combine them with the analysis of trade data and Greece's economic environment.

Greece's main economic goal in the past decade has been to satisfy the Maastricht criteria for Monetary Union. For this goal, that was achieved in 2000, the government implemented a strict Convergence Programme, with a restrictive monetary policy and low wage increases in the public sector. On the other hand, policies aimed at restructuring the markets and increasing competition in all areas were not promoted with the necessary expediency. Industrial production is on the rise, inflation has been reduced to 2.6% and 3.2% for 1999 and 2000, respectively, while GDP growth has accelerated to 3.4% and 4.1% for 1999 and 2000, respectively (Bank of Greece, 2001: 119-124).

Specific policy measures to improve the competitiveness of Greek industries are needed. Greece can benefit from the increased export opportunities arising from its inclusion in the European Monetary Union, only if many of its industries are internationally competitive. Any measures, however, aimed at the improvement of the international competitiveness of Greek industries must take into account Greece's specific features that often pose important constraints on many Greek industries.

In particular, Greece has no land borders with the other European Union states. Its mountainous terrain, as well as a very large number of islands, create internal barriers and increase infrastructure and transportation costs. Also, more than one-third of the population and the economic activity are concentrated in the region of Attica. For these and other reasons, the country still has significant infrastructure deficiencies mainly in terms of its links with the European Union and the connections between all parts of its territory.

Government Policy

The fiscal stability and the stimulation of economic development must be the two main targets of macroeconomic policy for Greece. Regarding the former, inflation control, low interest rates and decreased public debt are prerequisites for a stable economic environment, while for the latter similar measures to promote economic activity must be taken. Beyond macroeconomic policy and its questionable role according to Porter (1990), there is a series of measures that could potentially contribute to economic development.

A constant strategic priority for Greece has been the investment in various infrastructures such as industrial parks, transportation facilities (roads, airports, railways, harbours), telecommunications and energy networks. Infrastructure networks and nodes should also be the main targets of the public investment programmes, at least in the coming decade. The connection of the Greek infrastructure networks with the ones of the Balkans and Western Europe, will facilitate economic activity and reduce the shortcomings of Greece's peripherality.

The skill level and adaptability of personnel in Greece is another major concern for the industries' competitiveness. The country's educational system is being modernised and integrated, slowly, into the European Union's one. Substantial funds are spent on improving standards in all levels of education, in vocational training and in introducing new specialisations. The grants from the European Social Fund and the various programmes that combat unemployment, have also led to the improvement of the education and training systems of Greece. However, a central problem still remains. It is the need to rebalance supply and future demand for specific skills in certain industries, as skills shortages were apparent in almost all the industries studied. The public sector is also suffering from lack of specialised personnel and from the lack of middle and high level managers with the appropriate training.

Public administration was considered a major impediment in all industries studied because of its complicated processes. The various modernisation programmes have not been implemented with the necessary speed and their scope has been limited. The successful decentralisation of services was not combined with any radical changes in their structures. Further efforts should be made towards eliminating bureaucratic procedures, which create obstacles in business-government relations.

Another major problem in Greece is the low levels of R&D spending (of which 80% is spent by the public sector), the limited production innovations related to local research results and the lack of extensive co-operation between Universities and enterprises. Technology transfer should be promoted by relevant initiatives, while the creation of Technopoles or Science Parks can help in that direction. Firms must be given the incentives to seek new technologies, the 'venture capital' industry, that is still in its infancy stage, must be helped, and educational and other governmental or private institutions should be encouraged to create 'spin-off' companies.

In terms of domestic competition, the abolition of price controls has already created the necessary circumstances for its increase. Nevertheless, the strengthening of the existing Competition Commission of the Ministry of Development is necessary, along with the continuation of the current privatisation programme for public monopolies, especially in energy and telecommunications, with the caveat that these will not be turned into private monopolies.

One of the major tools of the Greek economic policy has been the incentives scheme* for the promotion of economic and regional development. In particular, productive investments are encouraged by cash grants, tax allowances and interest subsidies. Despite the criticisms that this system has received, it has, nevertheless, been effective in increasing the level of investments. Possible modifications to this system could be the reduction of bureaucratic procedures, the improved screening of proposed investments - even at the risk of approving substantially fewer projects - and the increased emphasis on innovative activities. In addition, strict environmental criteria must be set and the whole system can be linked to the various schemes for increasing employees' skills.

The banking system in Greece has not been very effective in financing small and medium sized enterprises, firms in new industries, or high-risk activities and part of the responsibility resides with the government, since a large proportion of the system used to be state-owned. The relatively recent bank privatisation wave and the increased autonomy of state-owned banks have enabled more firms to receive funds at favourable rates. The elimination of public sector deficits, along with a reduction in the taxation levels of banking activities, might contribute further to a reduction in cost of capital for Greek firms.

Greek industries were found to be extensively clustered and, in many cases, this was a central element that contributed to their competitive advantage. Therefore, cluster development, mainly at a sectoral, but also at a spatial, level, must be aided by appropriately co-ordinating banking institutions, research centres, Universities and training centres. New business formation should also be encouraged, while small and medium sized enterprises in industries that are part of, or related to, competitive clusters must be helped.

Company Strategy

The exposure of Greek companies to international competition has been gradual. Although certain industries have been open since the beginning of the 20th century, others were shielded behind walls of tariffs and other measures. Liberalisation of markets is in its last phase in Greece and most industries are now part of the global competition. In this environment, competitive advantage is a combination of national, industry and firm-specific attributes. Firm strategy must then take advantage of national circumstances, which are partly shaped by government, industry associations and other firms. Each firm, however, has its own unique capabilities and each industry its unique characteristics, which affect the strategies of its firms. These variations among industries and firms also make any attempt to provide general recommendations very difficult. Realising these limitations, an effort is made here to highlight certain areas affecting competitiveness in a wider range of industries.

The emphasis on costs, for many Greek industries, has been beneficial. To this end, the presence of additional attributes such as effective marketing, and appropriate logistics and distribution systems was essential. Greater emphasis should now be placed on those two areas, along with attempts to improve product performance and quality. Wage costs are on the rise in Greece and price advantages have disappeared in areas related to basic factors. Efficient marketing, improved product features and rapid distribution are important in order to command the price premiums necessary to balance the cost increases. This strategy should primarily be followed in industries where Greek demand already exhibits favourable trends and customers can appreciate the changes made.

The quality of human resources has been a major concern for Greek industries, with the more competitive ones taking extensive steps for its improvement. Marketing, production processes and information technology skills will be central for sustaining a superior labour force. Extensive European Union support will probably contribute towards this goal.

Management must also evolve, primarily in its attitude towards seeking new ideas, and favouring expansion into foreign markets. Leadership has so far been provided to a great extent by the entrepreneurs who were responsible for the companies' creation or expansion. Other high-level executives, however, need to be involved as well in the setting of company strategy. Managers should also gather information not only on domestic but also on foreign markets. Knowledge of foreign needs, distribution channels and regulations is not only useful for foreign expansion and a more global outlook, but also as an indication of future industry trends.

New ideas might also come from local sources. Co-operation, with the producers of innovation and original research, and strengthening of internal R&D departments can provide firms with an early and in-depth understanding of evolving technologies, products and processes and an opportunity to influence the direction of such research.

The environment of the European Union offers an additional challenge to Greek firms. The opportunity to access foreign markets, especially the more sophisticated ones, must be seized. Mergers, acquisitions and alliances will also become easier, but should be concluded with caution as a proactive step to impending market changes rather than as a reaction to declining prospects. European Union initiatives are also an excellent source of funds and an opportunity to co-operate with foreign partners.

A similar challenge and opportunity is evident if one studies the developments in the 1990s in the neighbouring countries of the Balkans and, moreover, of Eastern Europe. The opening up of a significant potential market, as well as the opportunities for foreign direct investment by Greek firms, are among the forces that will shape the future of many Greek industries. Certain Greek firms have already seen the potential of these new markets and have acted accordingly. An integrated strategy, formulated by all those involved (government, industry associations, individual firms) could act as a catalyst for further positive developments in engaging the Greek firms in a wider Balkan (or even Eastern European) market.

The entry in the EMU in 1/1/2001 and the restructuring of the private and public sectors, which is already under way, will provide the necessary challenges for businesses and government at all levels (national, regional, local) to promote the competitiveness of the internationally oriented industries. These changes will also help sustain the Greek economy in its present high growth path, contributing to the social well-being of Greek citizens.

Appendix

Table A.1 Clusters of internationally competitive Greek industries, 1978

Primary goods	**MATERIALS/METALS** IRON AND STEEL **Ferro-alloys, exc. ferro-manganese*** **Iron, simple steel coils** **Tinned plates, sheets** *Iron, simple steel blooms* *Iron, steel, tubes and pipes* Thin plate, rolled, of iron or simple steel FABRICATED IRON AND STEEL *Iron, steel fencing wire** Iron, steel cables, ropes etc. METAL MANUFACTURES **Steel transport boxes etc.** Metal fencing, gauze etc.** NON-FERROUS METALS **Aluminium and alloys, unwrought** **Aluminium bars, wire etc.** **Aluminium plates, sheets, strip** *Master alloys of copper** *Copper tubes, pipes* Copper plates, sheets and strip OTHER MATERIALS AND WASTE **Clay** **Other crude minerals, exc. clay*** *Refractory bricks etc.* Natural abrasives** Metaliferous non-ferrous waste
Machinery	
Specialty inputs	**Aluminium ores and concentrates** **Alumina (aluminium oxide)** **Zinc ores and concentrates** **Chromium ores and concentrates** **Lead and tin and other base metals ores and concentrates*** *Sulphur*
Services	

Table A.1 (cont.)

Primary goods	FOREST PRODUCTS Wood, simply shaped, and wood based panels*
Machinery	
Specialty inputs	
Services	

Primary goods	PETROLEUM/CHEMICALS PETROLEUM PRODUCTS **Motor, aviation spirit** **Kerosene, including jet-fuel** **Petroleum bitumen and bituminous mixtures*** *Fuel oils, not elsewhere specified* *Lubricants(high petroleum content) etc.* INORGANIC **Metallic oxides of zinc, chromium, iron, lead etc.** Inorganic acids POLYMERS **Polyvinyl chloride in the form of monofil, seamless tubes,** **etc., waste and scrap*** *Polyvinyl chloride plates, strip* Polystyrene, not in primary form* ORGANIC CHEMICALS Halogenated derivatives of hydrocarbons OTHER **Fungicides, disinfectants for retail*** **Anti-knock preparations etc.** Plastic packaging containers, lids Articles of plastic not elsewhere specified, exc. packaging*
Machinery	
Specialty inputs	
Services	

Primary goods	SEMICONDUCTORS/COMPUTERS
Machinery	
Specialty inputs	
Services	

Table A.1 (cont.)

Primary goods	**MULTIPLE BUSINESS** *Meters and counters not elsewhere specified*
Machinery	
Specialty inputs	
Services	

Primary goods	**TRANSPORTATION**
Machinery	
Specialty inputs	
Services	**Shipping#**

Primary goods	**POWER GENERATION AND DISTRIBUTION** *Insulated wire, cable, bars etc.* Inductors and parts electric power machinery** Printed circuits and parts not elsewhere specified*
Machinery	
Specialty inputs	
Services	

Primary goods	**OFFICE**
Machinery	
Specialty inputs	
Services	

Primary goods	**TELECOMMUNICATIONS**
Machinery	
Specialty inputs	
Services	

Primary goods	**DEFENSE**
Machinery	
Specialty inputs	
Services	

Table A.1 (cont.)

Primary goods	**FOOD/BEVERAGES** BASIC FOODS **Flour of wheat or meslin** **Other cereal meals and flours** *Crude animal materials, exc. gut, bladders** Fish, fresh or chilled, exc. fillets Rice in the husk or husked Rice, broken* Spices** FRUITS AND VEGETABLES **Potatoes fresh, exc. sweet** **Other vegetables*** **Oranges, fresh or dried** **Lemons, grapefruit etc.** **Grapes, fresh** **Grapes, dried(raisins)** **Stone fruit, fresh** **Figs and other fruit, fresh or dried*** *Crude vegetable materials, exc. seeds, bulbs etc.** Mandarines, clementines etc., fresh or dried* PROCESSED FOOD **Fruit or vegetable juice, exc. orange*** **Fruit, preserved exc. fruit juices*** **Vegetables, prepared, preserved** *Shell fish, prepared, preserved* Cereal preparations, exc. malt and bakery products** Pastry, cakes etc. Molasses, honey, syrups, caramel* Sugar candy, non-chocolate Coffee roasted and coffee substitutes cont. coffee* EDIBLE OILS **Olive oil** *Other soft fixed vegetable oils** Soya bean oil BEVERAGES **Spirits obtained by distilling wine or grape marc** *Wine of fresh grapes* *Grape must, vermouths, flavoured wines** Non-alcoholic beverages n.e.s. Other alcoholic beverages or compounds*
Machinery	
Specialty inputs	**Durum wheat, unmilled** **Oil-cake and other residues exc. of soya beans*** *Feeding stuff for animals, exc. oil-cake etc.** Seeds for other fixed oils, exc. copra**
Services	

Table A.1 (cont.)

Primary goods	**TEXTILES/APPAREL** FABRICS *Knitted or crocheted natural fabrics** *Tulle, lace, ribbons etc.* *Linens, etc.* *Made-up articles, exc. linens and other furnishings** APPAREL **Men's overcoats, other outer garments, not knitted*** **Women's other outwear, not knitted, of cotton** **Women's other outer garments, of man-made fibres** **Undergarments, of textile fabrics, exc. shirts*** **Other outer garments, accessories*** **Under garments, knitted, of cotton, non-elastic** **Articles of furskin** *Women's suits, exc. of cotton or man-made fibres** Under garments, knitted, other than of cotton* ACCESSORIES *Clothing accessories, knitted* *Artificial fur and articles** FOOTWEAR **Footwear, exc. rubber, leather footwear*** *Leather footwear* OTHER **Hides and skins, raw, exc. bovine*** **Furskins tanned or dressed** Leather, exc. of other bovine cattle* Industrial leather, saddlery, etc.*
Machinery	
Specialty inputs	FIBRES AND YARNS **Cotton yarn, exc. 40-80 km per kg*** **Cotton, carded or combed, inc. linters, waste*** **Yarn, of discontinuous synthetic fibres** **Yarn of regenerated fibres** *Pile and chenile fabrics of man-made fibres* *Raw cotton, exc. linters* *Yarn of synthetic fibres, exc. discontinuous uncombed** *Yarn of wool or animal hair, exc. wool tops**
Services	

Primary Goods	**HEALTH CARE** **Medicaments containing antibiotics**
Machinery	
Specialty inputs	
Services	

Table A.1 (cont.)

Primary goods	**HOUSING/HOUSEHOLD** **Floor coverings, exc. knotted carpets and carpets of man-made materials*** *Domestic refrigerators* *Cutlery* Household equipment of base metal, exc. domestic type heating and cooking apparatus**
Machinery	
Specialty inputs	**Cement** **Building stone, worked** **Lime and unfired mineral building products*** *Stone, sand and gravel*
Services	

Primary goods	**PERSONAL** Combustable products**
Machinery	
Specialty inputs	**Tobacco, unstripped, non-Virginia type*** Essential oils, resinoids
Services	

Primary goods	**ENTERTAINMENT/LEISURE** *Recorded disks, tapes and other recorded media*
Machinery	
Specialty inputs	
Services	**Tourism#**

KEY

Times New Roman	0.26% world export share or higher, but less than 0.52% share
Italics	*0.52% world export share or higher, but less than 1.04% share*
Bold	**1.04% world export share or above**

*	Calculated residuals
**	Added due to significant export value in a segmented industry
#	Added based on in-country research

Source: Author's calculations based on UN, *International Trade Statistics Yearbook*.

Table A.2 Clusters of internationally competitive Greek industries, 1985

	MATERIALS/METALS
Primary goods	IRON AND STEEL **Ferro-alloys, exc. ferro-manganese*** **Iron, other steel bars, hotrolled** **Iron, simple steel hoop, strip** *Tinned plates, sheets* *Iron, simple steel, coils* *Iron, simple steel, wire rod* *Iron, steel, tubes and pipes* *Thin plate, rolled, of iron or simple steel* METAL MANUFACTURES **Steel transport boxes etc.** Metal fencing, gauze etc.** NON-FERROUS METALS **Copper tubes, pipes** **Aluminium bars, wire etc.** **Aluminium foil** *Aluminium plates, sheets, strip* *Aluminium and alloys, unwrought* *Copper plates, sheets and strip* *Aluminium powders, tubes, tube fittings** Silver unwrought Copper, aluminium cables, ropes OTHER MATERIALS AND WASTE **Clay** **Asbestos** **Other crude minerals, exc. clay, asbestos*** **Refractory bricks etc.** *Natural abrasives* *Other refractory construction material** Metaliferous non-ferrous waste
Machinery	
Specialty inputs	**Aluminium ores and concentrates** **Alumina (aluminium oxide)** **Lead and tin and other base metals ores and concentrates*** *Zinc ores and concentrates*
Services	

	SEMICONDUCTORS/COMPUTERS
Primary goods	
Machinery	
Specialty inputs	
Services	

Table A.2 (cont.)

Primary goods	**FOREST PRODUCTS** WOOD **Wood, simply shaped, and wood based panels*** Plywood of wood sheets PAPER Paper and paperboard bulk, corrugated, converted and fibre building board** Paper, etc., containers
Machinery	
Specialty inputs	
Services	

Primary goods	**PETROLEUM/CHEMICALS** PETROLEUM PRODUCTS **Motor, aviation spirit** **Kerosene, including jet-fuel** **Lubricants (high petroleum content), etc.** *Fuel oils, not elsewhere specified* Gas oils## INORGANIC *Inorganic acids* *Other inorganic chemicals** POLYMERS **Polyvinyl chloride in the form of monofil, seamless tubes, etc., waste and scrap*** Polystyrene, not in primary form* ORGANIC CHEMICALS *Halogenated derivatives of hydrocarbons* OTHER **Anti-knock preparations etc.**
Machinery	
Specialty inputs	
Services	

Primary goods	**MULTIPLE BUSINESS** *Meters and counters, not elsewhere specified*
Machinery	
Specialty inputs	
Services	

Primary goods	**TRANSPORTATION** **Trailers for goods, containers***
Machinery	
Specialty inputs	
Services	**Shipping#**

Table A.2 (cont.)

	POWER GENERATION AND DISTRIBUTION
Primary goods	*Insulated wire, cable, bars, etc.*
Machinery	
Specialty inputs	
Services	

	OFFICE
Primary goods	
Machinery	
Specialty inputs	
Services	

	TELECOMMUNICATIONS
Primary goods	
Machinery	
Specialty inputs	
Services	

	DEFENSE
Primary goods	
Machinery	
Specialty inputs	
Services	

	HOUSING/HOUSEHOLD
Primary goods	**Floor coverings, exc. knotted carpets and carpets of man-made materials*** *Household equipment of base metal, exc. domestic type heating and cooking apparatus* *Cutlery*
Machinery	
Specialty inputs	**Cement** **Building stone, worked** *Lime and unfired mineral building products** *Stone, sand and gravel* Articles of cement, artificial stone
Services	

Table A.2 (cont.)

Primary goods	**FOOD/BEVERAGES** BASIC FOODS **Rice in the husk or husked** **Flour of wheat or meslin** **Groats, meal and pellets, of wheat*** *Edible nuts, fresh or dried* *Fish dried, salted, exc. cod* Crude animal materials, exc. gut, bladders* Rice, broken* Spices FRUITS AND VEGETABLES **Potatoes fresh, exc. sweet** **Other vegetables*** **Oranges, fresh or dried** **Lemons, grapefruit etc.** **Grapes, fresh** **Grapes, dried (raisins)** **Stone fruit, fresh** **Figs and other fruit, fresh or dried*** Crude vegetable materials, exc. seeds, bulbs etc.* Apples, fresh PROCESSED FOOD **Shell fish, prepared, preserved** **Fruit, preserved exc. fruit juices*** **Vegetables, prepared, preserved** **Olive oil** **Soya bean oil** *Orange juice* *Fruit or vegetable juice, exc. orange** *Pastry, cakes etc.* *Cereal preparations, exc. malt and bakery products** *Sugar candy, non-chocolate* BEVERAGES **Other alcoholic beverages or compounds*** **Grape must, vermouths, flavoured wines*** *Wine of fresh grapes* Spirits obtained by distilling wine or grape marc
Machinery	
Specialty inputs	**Chemical potassic fertilisers, exc. potassium chloride*** **Nitrogen, phosphorus fertilisers** **Durum wheat, unmilled** *Oil-cake and other residues, exc. of soya beans** *Feeding stuff for animals, exc. oil-cake etc. ** *Cotton, sunflower, rape, colza seeds* Maize (corn), unmilled Seeds for other fixed oils, exc. copra**
Services	

Table A.2 (cont.)

Primary goods	**TEXTILES/APPAREL**
	FABRICS
	Made-up articles, exc. linens and other furnishings*
	Pile etc. cotton fabrics
	Cotton fabrics, woven, finished, exc. pile fabrics*
	Other woven textile fabric*
	Linens, etc.
	Grey woven cotton fabric
	Tulle, lace, ribbons etc. **
	APPAREL
	Men's trousers, of cotton
	Woman's coats and jackets, of man-made fibres
	Woman's coats and jackets, exc. of man-made fibres*
	Women's dresses, exc. of man-made fibres*
	Women's skirts
	Women's blouses, of man-made fibres
	Women's other outwear, not knitted, of cotton
	Jerseys, pull-overs, of synthetic fibres
	Jerseys, pull-overs, of cotton or regenerated fibres*
	Women's dresses, suits, etc., of synthetic fibres
	Women's dresses, suits, etc., exc. of synthetic fibres*
	Other outer garments, accessories*
	Under garments, knitted, of cotton, non-elastic
	Articles of furskin
	Men's trousers, exc. of cotton*
	Men's jackets, blazers etc.
	Men's overcoats, other outer garments, not knitted*
	Women's dresses, of man-made fibres
	Women's blouses, exc. of man-made fibres
	Women's other outer garments of man-made fibres
	Women's suits, exc. of cotton or man-made fibres*
	Undergarments, of textile fabrics, exc. shirts*
	Under garments, knitted, other than of cotton*
	Men's suits
	ACCESSORIES
	Clothing accessories knitted
	Leather clothes, accessories
	FOOTWEAR
	Leather footwear
	OTHER
	Hides and skins, raw, exc. bovine*
	Furskins tanned or dressed
	Leather, exc. of other bovine cattle*
	Industrial leather, saddlery, etc.*
Machinery	

Table A.2 (cont.)

Specialty inputs	**Raw cotton, exc. linters** **Cotton yarn, 40-80 km per kg** **Cotton yarn, exc. 40-80 km per kg*** **Cotton, carded or combed, inc. linters, waste*** **Yarn, textured of continuous polyamide fibres** **Yarn, of discontinuous synthetic fibres** **Yarn of regenerated fibres** *Yarn of wool or animal hair, exc. wool tops** Old textile articles, rags
Services	

	HEALTH CARE
Primary goods	**Medicaments containing antibiotics**
Machinery	
Specialty inputs	
Services	

	PERSONAL
Primary goods	*Other articles of precious metal* Tobacco, manufactured, exc. cigarettes Precious metal jewellery Combustable products**
Machinery	
Specialty inputs	**Tobacco, unstripped, non-Virginia type*** Essential oils, resinoids
Services	

	ENTERTAINMENT/LEISURE
Primary goods	Recorded disks, tapes and other recorded media
Machinery	
Specialty inputs	
Services	**Tourism#**

KEY

Times New Roman	0.24% world export share or higher, but less than 0.48% share
Italics	*0.48% world export share or higher, but less than 0.96% share*
Bold	**0.96% world export share or above**

*	Calculated residuals
**	Added due to significant export value in a segmented industry
#	Added based on in-country research
##	Added due to high export value

Source: Author's calculations based on UN, *International Trade Statistics Yearbook*.

Bibliography

Agapitos, G. (1993), *Developments and Structural Problems of the Greek Economy (1950-1993)*, Athens: To Oikonomiko (in Greek).

Aggelis, G. (2001), 'GNTO a Lever for Tourist Development', *Greek Tourism*, Vol. 39, April, pp. 4-5 (in Greek).

Almantarioti, L. (2000), 'Brand-name and Quality Will Keep the Greek Apparel "Alive", in Express, *Textile and Apparel Industries*, September, Athens: Hellenews (in Greek).

Aluminium de Grèce (1996), *Annual Report 1995*, Athens: Aluminium de Grèce (in Greek).

Aluminium de Grèce (1999), *Annual Report 1998*, Athens: Aluminium de Grèce (in Greek).

Apostolopoulos, Th. (1990), 'A New Strategy for Tourist Development', *Tourismos kai Oikonomia*, No. 144, pp. 228-238 (in Greek).

Archer, B. (1989), 'Trends in International Tourism', in S. F. Witt and L. Moutinho (eds), *Tourism Marketing and Management Handbook*, New York: Prentice Hall, pp. 593-597.

Arthur Andersen (1997), *Yield Management in Small and Medium-Sized Enterprises in the Tourism Industry: General Report*, Luxembourg: Office for Official Publications of the European Communities.

Association of Greek Cement Manufacturers (1994), *Production, Imports and Exports by Country of Destination*, Athens: Association of Greek Cement Manufacturers.

Athanassakopoulos, A. (1997), *Bauxite-Alumina-Aluminium*, Athens: Aluminium de Grèce (in Greek).

Baltzakis, P. and Katsos, G. (1996), 'International Competitiveness of Manufacturing', in B. Droukopoulos (ed.), *Proposals for Structural Policy for Industry and Employment*, Athens: KEPE, pp. 135-144 (in Greek).

Bank of Greece (1978), *The First Fifty Years of the Bank of Greece, 1928-1978*, Athens: Bank of Greece (in Greek).

Bank of Greece (2001), *Monetary Policy 2000-2001*, Athens: Bank of Greece (in Greek).

Bellak, C. and Weiss, A. (1993), 'A Note on the Austrian Diamond', *Management International Review*, Vol. 33 (special issue 2), pp. 109-118.

Bianchi, P. (1982), *Public and Private Control in Mass Product Industry: The Cement Industry Cases*, Studies in Industrial Organisation, Vol. 3, The Hague: Martinus Nijhoff Publishers.

Brown, M. and McKern, B. (1987), *Aluminium, Copper and Steel in Developing Countries*, Paris: OECD.

Bruce, N. (1993), 'The Cost of Capital and Competitive Advantage', in T. J. Courchene and D. D. Purvis (eds), *Productivity, Growth and Canada's International Competitiveness, Proceedings of a Conference Held at Queen's University, 18-19 September, 1992*, Ontario: John Deutsch Institute for the Study of Economic Policy, pp. 77-117.

Bunker, S. and Ciccantell, P. (1994), 'The Evolution of the World Aluminium Industry', in B. Barham, S. Bunker, and D. O'Hearn (eds), *States, Firms and Raw Materials: The World Economy and Ecology of Aluminium*, Madison: The University of Wisconsin Press, pp. 39-62.

Cartwright, W. R. (1993), 'Multiple Linked "Diamonds" and the International Competitiveness of Export-Dependent Industries: The New Zealand Experience', *Management International Review*, Vol. 33 (special issue 2), pp. 55-70.

Cembureau (1997), 'Cement', in European Commission, *Panorama of EU Industry 97*, Vol. 1, Luxembourg: Office for Official Publications of the European Community, pp. 9.33-9.36.

Chapman, M. and Antoniou, Ch. (1998), 'Uncertainty Avoidance in Greece: An Ethnographic Illustration', in P. Buckley, F. Burton and H. Mirza (eds), *The Strategy and Organization of International Business*, London: Macmillan Press, pp. 55-70.

Charontakis, D. (2000), 'The Chatzikyriakeian "Heracles"', *To Bima*, 19 March, p. D16 (in Greek).

Chiotis, G. and Coccossis, H. (1992), 'Tourist Development and Environmental Protection in Greece', in H. Briassoulis and J. Van der Straaten (eds), *Tourism and the Environment*, Dordrecht: Kluwer Academic Publishers, pp. 133-143.

Chrisochou, N. F. (1987), 'Cement Industry Raw Materials', in Greek Association of Chemical Engineers, *The Greek Cement Industry and its Development Prospect, Conference Proceedings, Volos, 14-15 May*, pp. 39-55 (in Greek).

Christodoulou, Ch. (1995), 'Bauxite - Alumina - Aluminium', Speech in the workshop *The Aluminium Sector in Greece*, Athens, 16 March (in Greek).

Christodoulou, Ch. (1996), 'The Greek Aluminium Sector in Europe and the World', Speech in the Exhibition *Aluminium '96*, Athens, 8 November (in Greek).

Chtouris, S. (1995), 'Culture and Tourism: Tourism as a Network Producing Experiences', *Synchrona Themata*, Vol. 55, April-June, pp. 48-56 (in Greek).

Coccossis, H. (1995), 'Tourism and Sustainable Development', *Synchrona Themata*, Vol. 55, April-June, pp. 21-28 (in Greek).

Cooper, W. W. (1992), 'On Porter's Competitive Advantage of Nations', *Omega The International Journal of Management Science*, Vol. 20 (2), pp. 137-138.

Côté, M. (1993), 'Agents of Change and Economic Growth', in T. J. Courchene and D. D. Purvis (eds), *Productivity, Growth and Canada's International Competitiveness, Proceedings of a Conference Held at Queen's University, 18-19 September, 1992*, Ontario: John Deutsch Institute for the Study of Economic Policy, pp. 301-337.

Coutsoumaris, G. (1963), *The Morphology of Greek Industry*, Athens: Centre of Economic Research.

Crocombe, G., Enright, M. and Porter, M. (1991), *Upgrading New Zealand's Competitive Advantage*, Auckland: Oxford University Press.

Daly, D. (1993), 'Porter's Diamond and Exchange Rates', *Management International Review*, Vol. 33 (special issue 2), pp. 119-134.

De Man, A., Van den Bosch, F. and Elfring, T. (1997), 'Porter on National and Regional Competitive Advantage', in F. A. J. Van den Bosch and A. P. De Man (eds), *Perspectives on Strategy: Contributions of Michael E. Porter*, Dordrecht: Kluwer Academic Publishers, pp. 45-59.

Delta (1999), *Annual Report 1998*, Athens: Delta.

Dimakouleas, T. (1996), 'World Ranking of Units: Spectacular Mergers and Acquisitions in World Hoteling', *Tourismos kai Oikonomia*, No. 215, pp. 52-66 (in Greek).

Dobson, P. and Starkey, K. (1992), 'The Competitive Advantage of Nations', *Journal of Management Studies*, Vol. 29 (2), pp. 253-255.

Dokas, A. (2001), 'A Production Raise of 54% is Elval's Goal', *Kathimerini*, 15 February, p. 36 (in Greek).

Doremus, P. N., Keller, W. W., Pauly, L. W. and Reich, S. (1998), *The Myth of the Global Corporation*, Princeton, NJ: Princeton University Press.

Drakatos, K. (1997), *The Great Circle of the Greek Economy (1945-1995)*, Athens: Papazissis (in Greek).

DRI Europe (1997), 'Travel Services', in European Commission, *Panorama of EU Industry 97*, Vol. 2, Luxembourg: Office for Official Publications of the European Community, pp. 22.40-22.46.

Drimoussis, I. and Zissimopoulos, A. (1988), *Vocational Training in the Textiles and Clothing Industries in Greece*, Berlin: CEDEFOP.

Dunning, J. H. (1992), 'The Competitive Advantage of Countries and the Activities of Transnational Corporations', *Transnational Corporations*, Vol. 1 (1), pp. 135-168.

Dunning, J. H. (1993), 'Internationalising Porter's Diamond', *Management International Review*, Vol. 33 (special issue 2), pp. 7-15.

Enright, M. (1990), *Geographical Concentration and Industrial Organisation*, Ph.D. Dissertation, Harvard University.

Epilogi (1998), 'Apparel-Footwear', in Epilogi, *The Greek Economy, 1998*, pp. 285-288 (in Greek).

Epilogi - Statistics (2000), *The Greek Economy in Figures, 2000*, Athens: Epilogi - Ekdoseis Statistics.

ERMCO (1997), 'Ready Mixed Concrete', in European Commission, *Panorama of EU Industry 97*, Vol. 1, Luxembourg: Office for Official Publications of the European Community, pp. 9.43-9.45.

ETVA (1999), *Investment Guide – Appendix*, Athens: ETVA (in Greek).

Eumoiridis (1990), *European Integration and the Textile and Apparel Industries*, 1992: Greek Economy and European Integration Series, Study No. 10, Athens: IOBE (in Greek).

European Commission (1988), *Le "Cout de la non-Europe" des Produits de Construction*, Luxembourg: Office for Official Publications of the European Communities.

European Commission (1993), *The Evolution in Holiday Travel Facilities and in the Flow of Tourism Inside and Outside the European Community, Part I: Main Findings*, Brussels: European Commission.

European Commission (1997), 'Tourism: Overview', in European Commission, *Panorama of EU Industry 1997*, Vol. 2, Luxembourg: Office for Official Publications of the European Communities, pp. 22.1-22.9.

European Commission and Eurostat (2000), *Panorama of European Business, 1999: Data 1988-1998*, Luxembourg: Office for Official Publications of the European Communities.

Eurostat (1998), *Panorama of EU Industry – 1998, Pro Version* (CD-ROM), Luxembourg: Office for Official Publications of the European Communities.

Falirea, L. and Kapsi, N. (1996), 'Domestic Tourism: Aspects and Trends', *Tourismos kai Oikonomia*, No. 206, pp. 14-24 (in Greek).

Fitzpatrick Associates (1993), *All-season Tourism: Analysis of Experience, Suitable Products and Clientele*, Brussels: European Commission.

Fitzpatrick Associates (1997), 'Restaurants', in European Commission, *Panorama of EU Industry 97*, Vol. 2, Luxembourg: Office for Official Publications of the European Community, pp. 22.10-22.16.

Foster, D. (1985), *Travel and Tourist Management*, London: Macmillan.

Fotinopoulou, K. and Manolopoulos, N. (1991), *Technical Training Requirements of Middle Management in the Greek Textile and Clothing Industries*, Berlin: CEDEFOP.

GATT (1987), *Background Study on Aluminium and Aluminium Products*, Geneva: GATT.

GATT (1994), *Summary of the Results of the Uruguay Round in the Dairy Sector*, Geneva: GATT.

Geelhoed, L. (1997), 'The Netherlands: More than Flower Power', in F. A. J. Van den Bosch and A. P. De Man (eds), *Perspectives on Strategy: Contributions of Michael E. Porter*, Dordrecht: Kluwer Academic Publishers, pp. 61-66.

Ghekas, D. (1985), *The Greek Aluminium Fabrication Industry in 1983*, Athens: IOBE (in Greek).

Giannakakos, G. (2000), 'What the Ice Cream Producers are Planning for Greece and Abroad', *Isotimia*, 3-4 June, pp. 78-79 (in Greek).

Giannaros, I. (1997), 'Products from Non-Metallic Minerals', in V. Patsouratis and P. Rossolymos (eds), *Panorama of Economic Activity, Vol. 1: Manufacturing*, Athens: Commercial and Industrial Chamber of Athens, pp. 549-590 (in Greek).

Giannitsis, T. (1983), *The Greek Industry: Development and Crisis*, Athens: Gutenberg (in Greek).

Giannitsis, T. (1988a), *Accession to EEC and Effects on Industry and Trade*, Athens: Foundation for Mediterranean Studies (in Greek).

Giannitsis, T. (1988b), 'External Exchanges and Greece's Position in the International Labour Specialisation in the Prospect of the Year 2000', in H. Katsoulis, T. Giannitsis and P. Kazakos (eds), *Greece Towards the Year 2000, Politics, Society, Economy and External Relations*, Athens: Papazissis, pp. 310-334 (in Greek).

Giannitsis, T. and Vaitsos, K. (1987), *Technological Transformation and Economic Development*, Athens: Gutenberg (in Greek).

Glytsos, N. (1995), 'Human Capital', in A. Kintis (ed.), *The Greek Economy in the Eve of the 21st Century*, Athens: Ionian Bank, pp. 275-332 (in Greek).

GNTO (1996), *The Progress of Tourism in Greece: 1981-1996*, Athens: GNTO - National Technical University of Athens (in Greek).

GNTO (1999), *Operational Programme Tourism-Culture (Provisional): Subprogramme Tourism, for the Third Community Support Framework 2000-2006*, Athens: Ministry of Development (in Greek).

Grant, R. M. (1991), 'Porter's "Competitive Advantage of Nations": An Assessment', *Strategic Management Journal*, Vol. 12 (7), pp. 535-548.

Gray, H. (1991), 'International Competitiveness: A Review Article', *The International Trade Journal*, Vol. 5, pp. 503-517.

Greek Mining Enterprises Association (2000), *Activity Report 1999*, Athens: Greek Mining Enterprises Association (in Greek).

Greenaway, D. (1993), 'The Competitive Advantage of Nations', *Kyklos*, Vol. 46 (1), pp. 145-146.

Halyps (1999), *Annual Report 1998*, Aspropyrgos: Halyps (in Greek).

Harris, R. G. and Watson, W. G. (1993), 'Three Visions of Competitiveness: Porter, Reich and Thurow on Economic Growth and Policy', in T. J. Courchene and D. D. Purvis (eds), *Productivity, Growth and Canada's International Competitiveness, Proceedings of a Conference Held at Queen's University, 18-19 September, 1992*, Ontario: John Deutsch Institute for the Study of Economic Policy, pp. 233-280.

Hassid, I. (1994), *Adjustments and Competitiveness in Greek Industry*, Special Studies, Study No. 23, Athens: IOBE (in Greek).

Hassid, I. and Katsos, G. (1992), *European Integration and Greek Industry*, 1992: Greek Economy and European Integration Series, Study No. 17, Athens: IOBE (in Greek).

Hodgetts, R. M. (1993), 'Porter's Diamond Framework in a Mexican Context', *Management International Review*, Vol. 33 (special issue 2), pp. 41-54.

Hoffman, K. and Rush, H. (1988), *Micro-Electronics and Clothing: The Impact of Technical Change on a Global Industry*, New York: Praeger.

Holloway, J. (1998), *The Business of Tourism*, Fifth Edition, Harlow: Longman.

ICAP (1994), *Ready-made Men's Formal Outerwear*, Athens: ICAP (in Greek).

ICAP (1995), *Dairy Products*, Athens: ICAP (in Greek).

ICAP (1996), *Rolled and Extruded Aluminium Products*, Athens: ICAP (in Greek).

ICAP (1997a), *Fabrics*, Athens: ICAP (in Greek).

ICAP (1997b), *Elval Company Report*, Athens: ICAP (in Greek).

ICAP (1998), *Products of Extruded and Rolled Aluminium*, Athens: ICAP (in Greek).

ICAP (1999a), *Dairy Products*, Athens: ICAP (in Greek).

ICAP (1999b), *Cheese Products*, Athens: ICAP (in Greek).

ICAP (1999c), *Travel Agencies*, Athens: ICAP (in Greek).

ICAP (1999d), *Hotel Enterprises (Lux, A', B')*, Part A, Athens: ICAP (in Greek).

ICAP (1999e), *Men's Formal Outerwear*, Athens: ICAP (in Greek).

ICAP (1999f), *Construction Materials*, Athens: ICAP (in Greek).

ICAP (1999g), *Concrete*, Athens: ICAP (in Greek).

ICAP (2000), *Rolling and Extrusion of Aluminium*, Athens: ICAP (in Greek).

ICAP (2001), *Greek Financial Directory*, Athens: ICAP.

IEA (1996), *Energy Prices and Taxes*, Paris: OECD.

ILO (1994), *The Effects of Technological Changes in the Clothing Industry*, Geneva: ILO.

Ioakeimidis, P. K. (1996), 'European Union: Selection of Basic Bibliography 1981-1996', *Oikonomikos Tachydromos*, 19 December, pp. 154-160 (in Greek).

IOBE (1982), *Sectoral Report: Cement Industry*, Athens: IOBE (in Greek).

IOBE (1983), *Sectoral Report: Packaging Products from Aluminium*, Athens: IOBE (in Greek).

IOBE (1993), *Metallic Packaging*, Athens: IOBE (in Greek).

Isard, W. (1960), *Methods of Regional Analysis: an Introduction to Regional Science*, Cambridge, MA: The M.I.T. Press.

Isotimia (1997), 'Men's Formal Outerwear: Stagnation and Reduced Investment Interest', *Isotimia*, 20-21 December, p. 59 (in Greek).

Jacobs, D. and De Jong, M. W. (1992), 'Industrial Clusters and the Competitiveness of the Netherlands', *De Economist*, Vol. 140 (2), pp. 233-252.

Jasinowski, J. J. (1990), 'Although Michael Porter ...', in L. A. McCauley (ed.), Letters to the Editor, *Harvard Business Review*, May-June, Vol. 90 (3), pp. 196-198.

Jelinek, M. (1992), 'The Competitive Advantage of Nations', *Administrative Science Quarterly*, Vol. 37 (3), pp. 507-510.

Kalloniatis, K. (1995), *The Sector of Ready-made Garments*, Athens: IOBE (in Greek).

Kalloniatis, K. (1996a), 'Accelerated Recovery of the Cement Producing Industry', *Epilogi*, October, pp. 51-58 (in Greek).

Kalloniatis, K. (1996b), 'Positive - Under Circumstances - are the Prospects of the Aluminium Sector', *Epilogi*, December, pp. 88-95 (in Greek).

Kanellopoulos, K., Kousoulakos, I. and Rapanos, V. (1995), *Underground Economy and Tax Evasion: Measurements and Financial Consequences*, Athens: KEPE (in Greek).

Karagiannopoulou, D. (1998), 'Shrinking and Competition are Threatening the Greek Yarn Industry', *Isotimia*, 12-13 December, p. 39 (in Greek).

Karra, S. (1985), *The Cement Industry (Complement to the Basic Report 1982)*, Athens: IOBE (in Greek).

Karsaba, D. (1997), *The Cement Industry*, Athens: IOBE (in Greek).

Kathimerini (2001), 'Population Increases by (only) 6.6%', *Kathimerini*, 27 March, p. 7 (in Greek).

Katochianou, D. (1995), 'Economic and Spatial Development of Tourism in Greece: a First Look', *Synchrona Themata*, Vol. 55, April-June, pp. 62-71 (in Greek).

Kazabakas, X. (1997), 'Apparel', in V. Patsouratis and P. Rossolymos (eds), *Panorama of Economic Activity, Vol. 1: Manufacturing*, Athens: Commercial and Industrial Chamber of Athens, pp. 205-255 (in Greek).

Kazakos, I. (1997), 'Food', in V. Patsouratis and P. Rossolymos (eds), *Panorama of Economic Activity, Vol. 1: Manufacturing*, Athens: Commercial and Industrial Chamber of Athens, pp. 33-67 (in Greek).

KEPE (1991), *Animal Production*, Report 20 for the Plan 1988-1992, Athens: KEPE (in Greek).

Kintis, A. (1995), 'Manufacturing Industry: Performance, Crisis, Prospects (?)', in A. Kintis. (ed.), *2004: The Greek Economy on the Eve of the 21st Century*, Athens: Ionian Bank, pp. 527-588 (in Greek).

Kofos, E. (1977), 'A Period of Contemplation (1869-1875)', in Ekdotiki Athinon, *The History of the Greek Nation*, Vol. IC, Athens: Ekdotiki Athinon, pp. 305-317 (in Greek).

Konsola, D. (1993), 'Cultural Tourism and Regional Development', in D. Konsola (ed.), *Culture, Environment and Regional Development*, Athens: Regional Development Institute, pp. 19-43.

Konsola, D. (1995), *The International Protection of the World Cultural Heritage*, Athens: Papazissis (in Greek).

Konsolas, I. and Oz, O. (1996), 'The Evolution in the Competitive Structures of Turkish and Greek Industries', in L. G. Brusati (ed.), *Business, Government and Society, Proceedings of the Second AIDEA Giovani International Conference*, Milan, June 6-8, Milan: CUEM.

Konsolas, N. (1992), 'EEC Regional Policy and Integrated Mediterranean Programs', in M. Tykkylainen (ed.), *Development Issues and Strategies in the New Europe*, Aldershot: Avebury, pp. 41-52.

Konsolas, N. (1998), 'The Development Perspective of the "Kapodistrias" Programme', in Epilogi, *The Greek Economy, 1998*, pp. 222-226 (in Greek).

Konsolas, N. and Zacharatos, G. (1992), 'Regionalisation of Tourism Activity in Greece: Problems and Policies', in H. Briassoulis and J. Van der Straaten (eds), *Tourism and the Environment*, Dordrecht: Kluwer Academic Publishers, pp. 57-65.

Kottis, G. (1981), *Selected Economic Issues*, Athens: Papazissis (in Greek).

Koumelis, Th. and Karantzavelou, V. (2000), 'Ferry Companies – Where Are They Heading?', *Epilogi*, May, pp. 82-84 (in Greek).

Kouzelis, A. (2000), *Evaluation of the Effectiveness of Investment Incentives: The Greek Experience*, Study No. 9, Athens: RIT (in Greek).

Krugman, P. and Obstfield, M. (1997), *International Economics: Theory and Policy*, Fourth Edition, Reading, MA: Addison-Wesley.

Lagos, D. (1990), 'The Structural Problems of Greek Tourism', *Tourismos kai Oikonomia*, No. 136, pp. 168-178 (in Greek).

Lagos, D. (1996), *The Economic Consequences of Tourism on Regional Development*, Ph.D. Dissertation, Panteion University of Social and Political Sciences (in Greek).

Lagos, D. (1998), 'Tourism as a Means of Promoting Regional Development', *Topos Review of Urban and Regional Studies*, No. 14, pp. 47-65 (in Greek).

Lavery, P. (1989), 'European Destination Marketing', in S. F. Witt and L. Moutinho (eds), *Tourism Marketing and Management Handbook*, New York: Prentice Hall, pp. 141-146.

Leamer, E. E. (1984), *Sources of International Comparative Advantage: Theory and Evidence*, Cambridge, MA: The MIT Press.

Leontidou, L. (1991), 'Greece: Prospects and Contradictions of Tourism in the 1980s', in A. M. Williams and G. Shaw (eds), *Tourism & Economic Development: Western European Experiences*, Second Edition, New York: Belhaven Press, pp. 84-106.

Lioupis, G. (1991), *The Greek Milk Industry*, Athens: IOBE (in Greek).

Lolos, S. and Papagiannakis, L. (1993), *Greek Industry in the European Community*, Athens: Academy of Athens (in Greek).

Lyberaki, A. (1992), 'Crisis and Restructuring in the Greek Apparel Industry: Some New Trends Regarding the Size and Location of Enterprises', in Regional Development Institute, *Epistimoniki Epetirida 3*, Athens: Regional Development Institute, pp. 273-291 (in Greek).

Magaziner, I. C. (1990), 'Michael Porter's message ...', in L. A. McCauley (ed.), Letters to the Editor, *Harvard Business Review*, May-June, Vol. 90 (3), pp. 189-192.

Makrydimitris, A. (1996), 'Public Administration', *Oikonomikos Tachydromos*, 19 December, pp. 124-130 (in Greek).
Malecki, E. (1997), *Technology and Economic Development: the Dynamics of Local, Regional and National Competitiveness*, Second Edition, Harlow: Longman.
Maucher, H. (1990), 'The Competitive Advantage of Nations ...', in L. A. McCauley (ed.), Letters to the Editor, *Harvard Business Review*, May-June, Vol. 90 (3), pp. 188-189.
Ministry of Agriculture (1996), *Development of Milk Production*, Athens: Ministry of Agriculture (in Greek).
Ministry of Commerce (1963), *Study on Greek Cheese*, Athens: Ministry of Commerce (in Greek).
Ministry of Co-ordination (1976), *National Accounts of Greece, 1948-1975*, Athens: Ministry of Co-ordination (in Greek).
Ministry of Foreign Affairs (1980), *Greece in the European Community*, Athens: Ministry of Foreign Affairs (in Greek).
Ministry of National Economy (1998), *The Greek Economy 1960-1997: Long-term Macroeconomic Statistical Series*, Athens: Ministry of National Economy (in Greek).
Mitsos, A. (1989), *Greek Industry in the International Market*, Athens: Themelio (in Greek).
Mylonas, A. (1996), 'Tourism: Trends and Prospects', in A. Kintis (ed.), *The Greek Economy in the Eve of the 21st Century*, Athens: Ionian Bank, pp. 719-773 (in Greek).
Mylonas, A. (1997), *Tourism: Policy, Developments, Prospects and Contribution to the Economy*, Athens: KEPE (in Greek).
Narula, R. (1993), 'Technology, International Business and Porter's "Diamond": Synthesizing a Dynamic Competitive Development Model', *Management International Review*, Vol. 33 (special issue 2), pp. 85-107.
Negreponti-Delivani, M. (1986), *The Problematic Greek Industry and Some Solutions...*, Second Edition, Thessaloniki: Paratiritis (in Greek).
Nicholson, P. (1993), 'Comment on Harris and Watson: Three Visions of Competitiveness', in T. J. Courchene and D. D. Purvis (eds), *Productivity, Growth and Canada's International Competitiveness, Proceedings of a Conference Held at Queen's University, 18-19 September, 1992*, Ontario: John Deutsch Institute for the Study of Economic Policy, pp. 281-296.
Nomisma (1997), 'Dairy Products', in European Commission, *Panorama of EU Industry 97*, Vol. 1, Luxembourg: Office for Official Publications of the European Community, pp. 3.52-3.60.
O' Donnellan, N. (1994), 'The Presence of Porter's Sectoral Clustering in Irish Manufacturing', *The Economic and Social Review*, Vol. 25 (3), pp. 221-232.
OECD (1983), *Positive Adjustment Policies in the Dairy Sector*, Paris: OECD.

OECD (1997), *The Market of Dairy Products and Dairy Policies in the OECD and Observer Countries: Developments Since 1st August 1995*, OECD Working Papers, Vol. V, No. 4, Paris: OECD.

OETH (1995), 'Clothing', in European Commission, *Panorama of EU Industry 95/96*, Vol. 1, Luxembourg: Office for Official Publications of the European Community, pp. 14.15-14.21.

OETH (1997), 'Clothing', in European Commission, *Panorama of EU Industry 97*, Vol. 1, Luxembourg: Office for Official Publications of the European Community, pp. 4.17- 4.23.

Ohmae, K. (1990), *The Borderless World*, London: Harper Collins Publishers.

Oikonomikos Tachydromos (1996), 'The Painful War and Occupation Period', *Oikonomikos Tachydromos*, 19 December, pp. 58-60 (in Greek).

Oikonomou, N. (1977), 'Greek Society and Economy in the First Decade of the 20th Century', in Ekdotiki Athinon, *The History of the Greek Nation*, Vol. ID, Athens: Ekdotiki Athinon, pp. 192-197 (in Greek).

Oz, O. (1997), *The Competitive Advantage of Nations: The Case of Turkey*, Ph.D. Dissertation, The London School of Economics and Political Science.

Oz, O. (1999), *The Competitive Advantage of Nations: The Case of Turkey*, Aldershot: Ashgate.

Papanikos, G. Th. (2000), *Greek Small and Medium Sized Hotel Enterprises*, Study No. 10, Athens: RIT (in Greek).

Pappas, S. (1997), 'Tourist Enterprises', in V. Patsouratis and P. Rossolymos (eds), *Panorama of Economic Activity, Vol. 2: Commerce and Services*, Athens: Commercial and Industrial Chamber of Athens, pp. 71-111 (in Greek).

Patsouratis, V. (1985), *The Industry of Ready-made Garments*, Athens: IOBE (in Greek).

Patsouratis, V. and Rossolymos, P. (eds) (1997), *Panorama of Economic Activity, Vol. 1: Manufacturing, Vol. 2: Commerce and Services*, Athens: Commercial and Industrial Chamber of Athens (in Greek).

Pavlopoulos, P. (1987), *The Underground Economy in Greece*, Athens: IOBE (in Greek).

Penttinen, R. (1994), *Summary of the Critique on Porter's Diamond Model*, Discussion Papers No. 462, Helsinki: The Research Institute of the Finnish Economy.

Petropoulos, I. and Koumarianou, A. (1977), 'Period of King Othon 1833-1862', in Ekdotiki Athinon, *The History of the Greek Nation*, Vol. IC, Athens: Ekdotiki Athinon, pp. 8-105 (in Greek).

Pheng, L. and Bee, T. (1993), *The Global Cement Industry*, Singapore: Singapore University Press.

Pindyck, R. and Rubinfeld, D. (1991), *Econometric Models and Economic Forecasts*, New York: McGraw-Hill.

Pitelis, Ch. et al. (1997), *Report on Competitiveness and Industrial Strategy in Greece*, Athens: Ministry of Development (in Greek).

200   *The Competitive Advantage of Greece*

Porter, M. E. (1990), *The Competitive Advantage of Nations*, New York: Free Press.

Porter, M. (1992), 'A Note on Culture and Competitive Advantage: Response to Van den Bosch and Van Prooijen', *European Management Journal*, Vol. 10 (2), p. 178.

Porter, M. E. (1998a), 'Introduction', in M. E. Porter, *On Competition*, Boston: Harvard Business Review Press, pp. 1-17.

Porter, M. E. (1998b), 'Clusters and Competition: New Agendas for Companies, Governments, and Institutions', in M. E. Porter, *On Competition*, Boston: Harvard Business Review Press, pp. 197-287.

Porter, M. E. and Monitor Company (1991), *Canada at the Cross-roads: The Reality of a New Competitive Environment*, Ottawa: Business Council on National Issues.

Prodromidis, K. (1976), *Foreign Trade of Greece: A Quantitative Analysis at a Sectoral Level*, Athens: KEPE.

RIT (1997), *Greek Economy and Tourism*, Issue No. 3, May (in Greek).

RIT (2000), *Greek Economy and Tourism*, Issue No. 10, November (in Greek).

Rugman, A. M. (1991), 'Diamond in the Rough', *Business Quarterly*, Vol. 55 (3), pp. 61-64.

Rugman, A. M. and D'Cruz, J. R. (1993), 'The "Double-Diamond" Model of International Competitiveness: The Canadian Experience', *Management International Review*, Vol. 33 (special issue 2), pp. 17-39.

Rugman, A. M. and Verbeke, A. (1993), 'Foreign Subsidiaries and Multinational Strategic Management: An Extension and Correction of Porter's Single Diamond Framework', *Management International Review*, Vol. 33 (special issue 2), pp. 71-84.

Sefertzi, E. (1998), 'Crisis, Restructuring and Innovative Development in the Textile and Apparel Industry', in E. Sefertzi (ed.), *Innovation*, Athens: Gutenberg (in Greek).

Sideri, M. (1998), 'DELTA Becomes More Powerful in SE Europe', *Kathimerini*, 4 September, p. 21 (in Greek).

Sideri, M. (2000), 'Two Brothers Gaze at the Top', *Kathimerini*, 11 May, p. 22 (in Greek).

Sideri, M. (2001), 'Dairy Products: Increased Activity among the Powerful Enterprises of the Industry', *Epilogi*, April, pp. 78-80 (in Greek).

Singleton, J. (1997), *The World Textile Industry*, London: Routledge.

Sinha, S. (1990), *Mini-cement: A Review of Indian Experience*, London: Intermediate Technology Publications.

Smit, R. (1997), 'Rotterdam Seen Through Porter-coloured Glasses', in F. A. J. Van den Bosch and A. P. De Man (eds), *Perspectives on Strategy: Contributions of Michael E. Porter*, Dordrecht: Kluwer Academic Publishers, pp. 67-79.

Smith, S. C. (1993), 'The Competitive Advantage of Nations', *Journal of Development Economics*, Vol. 40 (2), pp. 399-404.

Solvell, O., Zander, I. and Porter, M. (1992), *Advantage: Sweden*, Second Edition, London: The Macmillan Press.

Stefanidis, D. (1952), *Introduction to the Applied Social Economics*, Vol. B, Athens (in Greek).

Stopford, J. and Strange, S. (1991), *Rival States, Rival Firms: Competition for World Market Shares*, Cambridge: Cambridge University Press.

Thurow, L. (1990), 'Competing Nations: Survival of the Fittest', *Sloan Management Review*, Vol. 32 (1), pp. 95-97.

Titan (1992a), *80 Years Titan*, Athens: Titan (in Greek).

Titan (1992b), *Production*, Athens: Titan (in Greek).

Titan (1996), *Social Report 1995*, Athens: Titan (in Greek).

Titan (2000), *Annual Report 1999*, Athens: Titan (in Greek).

Tortopidis, A. (2001), 'The Greek Industry in the Last Decade: Prospects for the Following Years', in Epilogi-All Media, *Taseis, The Greek Economy, 2001*, February, pp. 324-349 (in Greek).

Tsamopoulos, M. (2000), 'In a Race of Acquisitions and Investments', *Epilogi Isologismon 2000*, pp. 33-37 (in Greek).

Tsekrekos, V. (1998), 'The Promotion of Bauxite is in Greece's Favour', *Oikonomikos Tachydromos*, 8 October, pp. 92-93 (in Greek).

Tsitouras, A. (1998), *The Seasonality of Tourism in Greece and the Competitor Countries*, Study No. 4, Athens: RIT (in Greek).

UN, *Industrial Commodity Statistics Yearbook*, New York: UN, various years.

UN, *International Trade Statistics Yearbook*, New York: UN, various years.

Vamvoukas, G. (1991), 'State Deficits: Causes, Side-effects, Proposals for Economic Policy', in N. Tatsos (ed.), *Public Finances in Greece*, Athens: To Oikonomiko, pp. 411- 440 (in Greek).

Van den Bosch, F. and De Man, A. (1994), 'Government's Impact on the Business Environment and Strategic Management', *Journal of General Management*, Vol. 19 (3), pp. 50-59.

Van den Bosch, F. A. J. and Van Prooijen, A. A. (1992), 'The Competitive Advantage of European Nations: The Impact of National Culture - a Missing Element in Porter's Analysis?', *European Management Journal*, Vol. 10 (2), pp. 173-177.

Varvaressos, S. (1998), *Tourism: Concepts, Figures, Structures, the Greek Reality*, Athens: Propompos (in Greek).

Vavouras, I. and Karavitis, N. (1997), 'The Problem of the Underground Economy in Greece: Extent, Impact, Policy Measures', in A. A. Kintis (ed.), *The Present and Future of the Greek Economy*, Vol. B, Athens: Gutenberg, pp. 125-136 (in Greek).

Vernon, R. (1966), 'International Investment and International Trade in the Product Cycle', *Quarterly Journal of Economics*, Vol. 80 (2), pp. 190-207.

Viochalco (1997), *Information Bulletin on the Group's Mergers*, Athens: Viochalco (in Greek).

Weber, A. (1929), *Theory of the Location of Industries*, (translated by Carl J. Friedrich), Chicago: The University of Chicago Press.

Wexler, I. (1983), *The Marshall Plan Revisited*, Westport: Greenwood Press.

World Tourism Organisation (2000), *World Tourism Results Revised Upwards*, Press Release, 11 May, Madrid: WTO.

World Tourism Organisation (2001), *Millennium Tourist Boom in 2000*, News Release, 31 January, Madrid: WTO.

Yin, R. (1994), *Case Study Research: Design and Methods*, Second Edition, London: Sage Publications.

Zacharatos, G. (2000), *Package Tour: Production and Sale of Tourist Travel*, Athens: Propompos (in Greek).

Zigouris, N. (1952), *The Milk Industry*, Second Edition, Athens: Ministry of Agriculture (in Greek).

For Product Safety Concerns and Information please contact
our EU representative GPSR@taylorandfrancis.com Taylor & Francis
Verlag GmbH, Kaufingerstraße 24, 80331 München, Germany

T - #0113 - 160425 - C0 - 219/146/12 - PB - 9781138723177 - Gloss Lamination